Praise for *On Borrowed Words*

"A droll intellectual journey through books, countries, and languages in search of an elusive home in the shifting waters of literature and memory."   —Ariel Dorfman

"The sensitivity and worldly perspective which Ilan Stavans has previously brought to works of literature, he now applies to his own experiences, with stunning effect. This is the rare memoir that manages to be both emotionally and intellectually honest, both nakedly exposed and adorned with literary pleasures."
          —Phillip Lopate

"In the multicultural rainbow that is contemporary America, no one may be more representative of the state of the union than Ilan Stavans."   —*Newsday*

"In *On Borrowed Words* the author examines the roles that four languages play in his life, allowing us a vibrant look at his world, or, more specifically, his worlds." —*The Boston Globe*

"Moving from Mexico to Spain, Israel to America, he shed en route fidelities to the languages of his personal diaspora—Spanish, Yiddish, Hebrew, Latino—before arriving at an English that melds all these into a heartfelt dialect of infectious intellect; a culturally polyglot English tongue for which he's shown, in this present volume, a fluency verging on brilliance."
          —*San Francisco Chronicle*

"This beautifully written memoir is the tale of a search—for a homeland, for a language and for a calling."
          —*Publishers Weekly* (starred)

"A fiction writer, essayist, and scholar, Stavans aspires toward something grand with his autobiography, something that transcends the pop-culture fascination with memoirs. The beauty of such a pursuit is a celebration of thought."
          —*Lingua Franca*

Ilan Stavans is the author of *The Hispanic Condition*, *The Riddle of Cantinflas*, and *The One-Handed Pianist and Other Stories*, as well as the editor of *The Oxford Book of Jewish Stories* and a dictionary of Spanglish. He is the recipient of a Guggenheim Fellowship and the Latino Literature Prize, among other honors. Stavans is Lewis Sebring Professor of Latin American and Latino Cultures at Amherst College.

ILAN STAVANS

On Borrowed Words

{ A MEMOIR OF LANGUAGE }

PENGUIN BOOKS

PENGUIN BOOKS

Published by the Penguin Group

Penguin Putnam Inc., 375 Hudson Street, New York, New York 10014, U.S.A.
Penguin Books Ltd, 80 Strand, London WC2R 0RL, England
Penguin Books Australia Ltd, 250 Camberwell Road,
Camberwell, Victoria 3124, Australia
Penguin Books Canada Ltd, 10 Alcorn Avenue,
Toronto, Ontario, Canada M4V 3B2
Penguin Books India (P) Ltd, 11 Community Centre,
Panchsheel Park, New Delhi – 110 017, India
Penguin Books (N.Z.) Ltd, Cnr Rosedale and Airborne Roads,
Albany, Auckland, New Zealand
Penguin Books (South Africa) (Pty) Ltd, 24 Sturdee Avenue,
Rosebank, Johannesburg 2196, South Africa

Penguin Books Ltd, Registered Offices: Harmondsworth, Middlesex, England

First published in the United States of America by Viking Penguin,
a member of Penguin Putnam Inc. 2001
Published in Penguin Books 2002

7 9 10 8 6

This book was made possible thanks to a generous grant
from the John Simon Guggenheim Foundation

"Night Storm" by Shlomo ibn Gabirol and "My Heart Is in the East" by Yehuda Halevi,
from the *Penguin Book of Hebrew Verse*, edited and translated by T. Carmi (Penguin
Books, 1981). Copyright © 1981 by T. Carmi. Used by permission of the publisher.

"Zog Nit Keyn Mol!: Hymn of the Partisans," from *Mir Trogn a Gezang: Favorite Yiddish
Songs*, compiled and edited by Eleanor Gordon Mlotek (Adama Books, 1986).
Copyright © 1972 by the Education Department of the Workmen's Circle,
45 East 33 Street, New York, NY 10016. Used by permission.

"Adon Olam," from the *Complete Artscroll Siddur*. Translation and anthologized
commentary by Rabbi Nasson Scherman, coedited by Rabbi Meir Zlotowitz
(Mesorah Publications, Ltd., 1984).

Some portions of this volume first appeared, in somewhat different form,
in *Transition*, *Agni*, the *Literary Review*, and *Pakn Treger*.

THE LIBRARY OF CONGRESS HAS CATALOGED THE HARDCOVER EDITION AS FOLLOWS:
Stavans, Ilan.
On borrowed words : a memoir of language / Ilan Stavans.
p. cm.
ISBN 0-670-87763-8 (hc.)
ISBN 0 14 20.0094 9 (pbk.)
1. Stavans, Ilan. 2. Mexican-American authors—Biography.
3. Authors, American—20th century—Biography. I. Title.
PQ7079.2.S78 Z47 2001
868'.6409—dc21
[B]   00-068586

Printed in the United States of America
Set in Janson Text / Designed by Sara E. Stemen

Contents

No man sins for someone else.

—TALMUD, BABA METZIAH

{ 1 }

México Lindo

In order to enjoy life, we should not enjoy it too much.

—VLADIMIR NABOKOV

I AM PACKING my library. I reach for the books, browse calmly through their pages, dust off the jackets, and proceed to store them in empty cartons. I will number these boxes from one to sixty. When the books come out again, I will arrange them in an altogether different order. Their overall setting will be different, too. There is a certain sweetness to the whole enterprise in which I am involved, for I realize how much my library and I have changed together this past decade. We began modestly and now we hardly recognize each other. Are all these volumes really mine? What do they say about me? And what can I, their collector, say about them?

Suddenly, I don't know why but I recall an object from my childhood: *la pistola*—a small, antiquated pistol, .22-caliber. Books . . . No, they hardly played a part in my childhood. I was an outdoor kid, hiking, collecting butterflies. Books symbolized passivity, a reluctance to act, to be part of the universe. I only began to fall for them in my late adolescence, when I realized how exciting the life of the imagination could be—as exciting, for sure, as any real adventure under the open sky. My library was nonexistent when I was seventeen or eighteen. Every volume my parents bought for me was relegated to a shelf I could hardly reach in my bedroom. Ah, but the pistol, *la pistola* . . . Throughout my childhood I was obsessed by it. Why did my father keep it hidden in a safe-deposit box inside his closet? He would open this box on very rare occasions—to take a pair of earrings out, to deposit a gold necklace my mother inherited from my grandmother Bobbe Miriam, to make sure his pile of dollars was intact. While the door was open, I would glance at the pistol furtively, fearfully, from the corner of my eye, imagining all sorts of possible connections. Why on earth was it in *my* home? What was its real purpose? Who gave it to my father and why? Whenever I asked him, he would say, "I just like to keep it around. No particular reason, nothing to think about, really." But no reason to him was reason enough for a child like me to worry, and so I speculated about it. As a young man, his own father, Zeyde Srulek, I told myself, had used it during a pogrom in Eastern Europe. Or it was the remnant of an obscure, violent period in my father's life he had gone out of his way to conceal from me? That it was simply a defense weapon in case of burglary crossed my mind several times, of course, but I dismissed this explanation as too simple and unconvincing.

I had recurrent dreams in which *la pistola* appeared: in the most haunting one, which I had around the age of ten, my father and I were members of an anthropological expedition to Chiapas. After crossing the high, primeval Lacandonian jungle, we came upon a system of caves in the mountains. Here, an Indian tribe had survived from time immemorial. My father talked to a priest, who invited us to a religious ceremony. We were taken to an immense central grotto with a pointed Gothic roof. A set of ancient rites unfolded before us, until the dream reached its climax. Fixed on the wall of the cave was a wooden bust in the shape of an immense head of a divinity; the head opened and closed its mouth; the priest told my father the head wanted me as a sacrifice; my father took the pistol out of a backpack, but instead of firing it, he put it right on the floor and smiled. Then he looked at me. "Don't worry, *mi amor*," he said. "The pistol will satisfy their god's appetite." "How do you know?" I screamed at him, awfully scared. But before he had a chance to answer, the dream ended.

Mexico, I still tell myself, is, has always been, an arsenal of the most deadly firearms, a massive ammunition depot capable of exploding any minute. Weapons are ubiquitous even when they are absent. In the photographs by Manuel Álvarez Bravo, María Izquierdo, and Tina Modotti, for instance, pistols are hardly around, but their presence is invariably felt. Their images are about outrage, injustice, suffering. Is the country about anything else? A particular image, one from home, comes to mind. In 1967, when I was six years old, my father acted in an inflammatory play: *Viet Rock*, directed by Rafael López Miarnau, which, aside from its denunciation of U.S. imperialism in Southeast Asia, contained profane and antipatriotic language. In the middle of a performance, a group of ruffians belonging to MURO, a right-wing faction affiliated with the Catholic Church, jumped onstage during a Sunday-afternoon performance, chains and sticks in hand, and began beating the actors; before the police could stop it, the attackers vanished into the dark. (Would the police have actually stopped them if they could, I wonder?) People were rushed to the hospital with concussions and skull fractures. But other images are equally upsetting: the currency of blood in the films by Emilio "El Indio" Fernández, for instance; or the tacit violence in Malcolm Lowry's *Under the Volcano;* and the unexplained death of Wilfrid Ewart, the British author of the novel *Way of Revelation*, by a stray bullet in a downtown hotel. Graham Greene saw turmoil everywhere in Mexico—in the eyes of a drunken priest, in the anger of the anticlericalism of the 1920s. Death—*la muerte:* it is always around the corner in Mexico, and pistols are its conduit, *el mecanismo.* The one my father had at home is perfectly visible in my mind as I sit alone, late at night, in my apartment on New York's Upper West Side, ready to leave the city.

TO LEAVE AND return. This has been a decade of enlightenment. I had come to New York with only a handful of books. It was here, I thought, I would either become a writer or vanish into oblivion. At twenty-four, just before my departure from Mexico, I had made a secret pact with myself: if a day after my thirty-third birthday, the age of Jesus Christ on his crucifixion, I had not published a major book, I would acquire *una pistola* just like my father's and shoot myself in my right temple. Boom, boom, kaboom!!! Literature is a passion that ought not be wasted, I repeated in my heart. The journey, I foresaw, would be twice as difficult, for somewhere along the line I had made the conscious decision to find my voice in a language and habitat not my own. The wandering Jew—how rewarding a pursuit it has been is made clear by how much the books I am packing mean to me.

Moving out of the city doesn't mean defeat. On the contrary, it is a sign of success. There are already too many books. They need room to breathe. The floor might not be strong enough to sustain their weight. I first arrived with one suitcase and a dozen books, mostly in Spanish. Selecting them had made me feel like a doomed sailor forced to rescue only a handful of items from a shipwreck. They were the books I couldn't do without, the ones I would unequivocally return to time and time again on sleepless nights. They were talismans, a way of survival. They included two collections by Borges, *The Aleph* and *Other Inquisitions*. Having them at my side was reassuring. Not only had they convinced me of the relevance of literature, but, most important, they had a mythical quality to them. Years ago I had memorized numerous passages from these collections, and each time I recited them, I realized the world made more sense: it seemed brighter, more intelligible.

Like me, these two volumes were survivors. When I began to write, Borges had been a decisive influence. His pure, precise, almost mathematical style; his intelligent plots; his abhorrence of *verborrea*—the overflow of words without end or reason, still a common malady in Spanish literature today. He, more than anyone before (including the *modernista* poet from Nicaragua, Rubén Darío), had taught a lesson: literature ought to be a conduit for ideas. But his lesson was hard to absorb, if only because Hispanic civilization is so unconcerned with ideas, so irritable about debate, so unconcerned with systematic inquiries. Life is too rough, too unfinished to be wasted on philosophical disquisition. It is not by chance, of course, that Borges was an Argentine. It couldn't have been otherwise, for Argentina perceives itself—or, rather, it *used to* perceive itself—as a European enclave in the Southern Hemisphere. Buenos Aires, its citizens would tell you in the 1940s, is the capital of the world, with Paris as a provincial second best.

As soon as I discovered Borges, I realized, much as others have, that I had to own him. I acquired every edition I could put my hands on, not only in Spanish but in their French, British, Italian, German, and Hebrew translations, as well as copies of the Argentine monthly *Sur*, where his best work was originally featured, and interviews in journals. My collection began to grow as I embarked on my own first experiences with literature: tight descriptions, brief stories, passionless literary essays. Rather quickly the influence he exerted on me became obvious. In consolation, I would paraphrase for myself the famous line from "Decalogue of the Perfect Storyteller"—in Spanish its title is infinitely better: *"Decálogo del perfecto cuentista"*—by Horacio Quiroga, a celebrated if tragic turn-of-the-century Uruguayan author: to be born, a young writer should *imitate* his beloved masters as much as possible. The maxim, I realize today, is not without dangerous implications; it has encouraged derivativeness and perhaps even plagiarism in Latin American letters. But I was blind to such views. My only hope as a litterateur was not to be like Borges, but to *be* Borges. How absurd that sounds now!

Influence turned into anxiety, and anxiety into discomfort. Would I ever have my own voice? One desperate afternoon, incapable of drafting a single line I could call my own, I brought down all the Borges titles I owned, piled them in the garage, poured gasoline over them, and set them on fire. It was a form of revenge, a sacramental act of desperation: the struggle to be born, to own a place of my own, to be like no one else—or, at least, unlike Borges. The flames shot up at first, and eventually, slowly, died down. I saw the volumes, between fifty and seventy in total, turn bright, then brown, then become ash. I smiled, thinking, in embarrassment, of Hitler's Germany, Pinochet's Chile, and Mao's China. I thought of Elias Canetti's *Auto da Fé* and Ray Bradbury's *Fahrenheit 451*. I thought of the scores of prayer books, Talmuds, and other rabbinical literature burnt by the Holy Inquisition in Spain and the New World, in places not far from my home. And I also invoked Borges's own essay, "The Wall and the Books," about Shih Huang Ti, the first emperor of China, a contemporary of Hannibal, whose reign was marked by the construction of the Wall of China, and also by a campaign to burn all history books. Shih Huang Ti saw himself as a new beginning. History needed to start over.

I am ashamed today. I began to write more freely soon after, but did I need to destroy the volumes physically? Wouldn't a mere symbolic burning have achieved the same thing? I know it couldn't, for I tried repeatedly, and symbolism was only that, a sheer abstraction. I simply wished, as my own oeuvre has grown, to have my original Borges volumes with me. I could place them in my library, proof of the progress I have made. But they are gone. The only survivors were two tiny volumes, *The Aleph* and *Other Inquisitions*, in inexpensive Emecé paperback editions, which I had misplaced and discovered after the burning.

ALONG WITH THEM I took novels by writers I lionized: Kafka, Joseph Conrad, Gabriel García Márquez, Joyce, Nabokov, and Mario Vargas Llosa. I have *Don Quixote*, of course; in Yiddish, I have *Tevye* and Isaac Bashevis Singer's *Satan in Goray*; and in Hebrew, I have Shmuel Yosef Agnon's *The Bridal Canopy*. Their literature was for me a religion. I had come to New York to be a newspaper correspondent and also to study at the Jewish Theological Seminary, located at Broadway and 122nd Street. This institution would become a door for me to medieval philosophy and mysticism as well as to nineteenth-century Yiddish. The fact that it was in New York made it the perfect place. My experience growing up in Mexico had instilled a sense of marginality in me; a move to the city George Steiner described as "the capital of the twentieth century" was a way to overcome that handicap. When I got a letter from the seminary granting me tuition, room, and board, I was overwhelmed. True, I knew next to nothing about the seminary or about New York. Worse, my English was ridiculous, if it was anything at all. I had the skills of a two-year-old: I could babble, hoping to be understood. But so what? I felt like an immigrant dreaming of a new life. I could not wait to experience New York's roughness, its acerbic rhythms. That, I told myself, was in and of itself the best university I could ever hope for.

The room I first lived in, a block away from the seminary, was no larger than seven square feet. It had a kitchen nearby, and a shared bathroom only a few steps away. Fortunately, it wasn't dark; it did not have a spectacular view, but its mid-size windows allowed me to experience the change of seasons, although the noise from traffic jams below my window was at times offensive. I never complained about how small my room was; most New Yorkers, after all, live in similarly constricted spaces, dismayed by the cacophony of street life. What else was the city about but intensity, neurosis, and speed—attributes I actually found quite stimulating?

Shortly after my arrival I bought myself a cheap wooden bookshelf at a nearby lumberyard. I needed to have my books out in the open, right in front of me. I unpacked them and stared at the haphazard order I had given them. Were they really as invaluable as I had thought a few days earlier, when I left Mexico? Would I reread them with the regularity I had envisioned?

The only thing I wanted to do every day was to be out and about, walking the city, *reading* it, navigating its neighborhoods, deciphering its countless mysteries. I was reminded of my youthful allergy toward books: Why waste time if the universe is so rich in experience? From the first moment I stepped out into New York, it appeared to me like a huge book, a novel-in-progress perhaps, filled with anecdotes, with a multilingual poetry impossible to repress. What an astonishing place it was! I had seen other American cities and felt disappointed in them. My parents took me on a trip to the Southwest when I was in my mid-teens. We entered the United States through Laredo and from there reached San Antonio, Houston, and Dallas. Eventually, our vacation took us to New Mexico and Colorado, and it ended in California, where we visited Disneylandia. (The kitschiness invoked by the word rings louder in Spanish.) I entered these cities with a deep desire to find out how different they were from the noisy, monotonous metropolis of my childhood, Ciudad de México. And indeed they were. No previous knowledge could have prepared me for their ugliness: they were throbbing places, no doubt, but banal and pretentious and without a single hint of mystery. Though Mexico's capital might well have been less livable, it had a charm, an ethos none of these urban centers knew anything about. It was the ethos of ambiguity, of not making up its mind between endorsing the Indian past and the European present, of a colonial history filled with oppressive Christian symbols, that made it so suffocating to me. In my adolescence I used to travel with my father to the Zócalo, wandering around its streets while he took care of his errands: so overcrowded, so inhuman! But fascinating, too. My primary target was the city's heart, giving weight to the whole metropolis: the Catedral de la Vírgen de Guadalupe, opposite the President's Palace. Madrid, which I visited extensively in the early 1980s, in many ways a mirror of modern Mexico, is *catedral-less*, making the place almost weightless. In contrast, the American cities I visited during that same time had a heart but no sense of history, as if a disoriented god had created them while in a depressed mood. The few historic sites I found in San Antonio, most notably the Alamo, seemed to be tourist attractions: they appeared to have been built with an eye on commerce, not by architects but by businessmen.

In fact, from whatever viewpoint I approached them, these places presented themselves as amusement parks. People moved around with a sense of satisfaction, of professed happiness. Everything was for sale but nothing had enough value to be irreplaceable. I would turn the TV on and immediately a station would begin begging for public money to subsist; I would walk through a downtown square and a gospel preacher would promote a fashionable chamber of heaven, which for a few dollars I could acquire right away; or I would take a bus, and a captivating photo of a nearby zoo would invite me to experience fear and the feeling of adventure. The constant stimulation made these cities move at an incredible speed—but the people seemed like robots, obsessed with reaching a destination that would make them more fulfilled. In Mexico, by comparison, the population allows itself an afternoon siesta to catch its breath, to reconnect with itself, to become human again. But in these cities the absence of movement was equated with death, so nobody stopped to reconsider. In the American city, I came to believe, everyone and everything was on the run and made out of plastic; it was illusory in the way T. S. Eliot described it in *The Waste Land:* "Unreal City . . . I had not thought death had undone so many." In retrospect, Disneyland struck me as the archetype of them all: artificial but without false pretension.

It took me four or five years more to make it to New York, but once this happened it was clear I had made it to *the real thing*. This, surely, is the source of sources, a city of fraternal strangers, of cultural sophistication and high civilization, the city of Walt Whitman and Federico García Lorca and Henry Roth, where tongues intermingle to such a degree that a new language seems to be born every other second, where everyone pretends to be a bit more than what he really is, where all nationalities and backgrounds coexist by seeing each other face to face without an alibi. Mixture, impurity, promiscuity, heat. In New York every fake item becomes original. The mercantile frenzy in other American cities is, by contrast, but an innuendo: fortunes are done and undone here at the speed of light, and reputations, too; life is elusive, transitory; people are always exhausted, but they keep themselves going by sheer magic, because today might be the last day of life and one needs to seize it without remorse. Pretensions are so overblown, so beyond imagination, the concept of pretension itself needs to be redefined. In New York, to be pretentious is, simply, to be.

Most important, nothing is sacred and everything is humorous. The whole city is a pagan temple that worships leisure and easy redemption. Among the first verbal memories I have of the place is an irreverent sign promoting the different religions of the world:

TAOISM: Shit happens.

HINDUISM: This shit happened before.

CONFUCIANISM: Confucius says, "Shit happens."

BUDDHISM: If shit happens, it isn't really shit.

ZEN: What is the sound of shit happening?

ISLAM: If shit happens, it is the Will of Allah.

JEHOVAH'S WITNESSES: Knock, Knock: "Shit happens."

ATHEISM: There is no shit.

AGNOSTICISM: I don't know whether shit happens.

PROTESTANTISM: Shit won't happen if I work harder.

CATHOLICISM: If shit happens, I deserve it.

JUDAISM: Why does shit always happen to us?

Is there a better advertisement for the eclecticism of the city than this? In the eight years I lived there, I must have walked almost every alley of it. Each block had its own style, its own atmosphere. So much variety, so much electricity. Did I ever come across the same face twice? Of course, quite often. It took me no time to realize the degree to which New Yorkers are concerned with their own identity. Their bodies are their most cherished assets: they live to show their bodies off, to polish them; their cloth, their gestures are a message: "Look at me," they shriek, "I've managed to become myself, to be distinct, unique, unlike you." But this obsession is but a mirage, is it not? Or perhaps it is a fear of blending in without restrictions and losing one's identity, for New Yorkers aren't all alike: each of them walks differently, dresses differently, eats and dreams differently—and, especially, thinks differently.

What has attracted me the most since the beginning are the complex ways in which the city communicates. This is a milieu where chaos and order are in constant conflict, and the battle emerges most clearly in the way people talk, always invading each other's space, overlapping words, or failing to finish a sentence, as if life is too short and one needs to move quickly to the next stage. When I crossed from one section of the city to another, I would realize the extent to which its citizens live in parallel, disconnected universes. Polyglotism is a common characteristic: New Yorkers know three, four different languages, each useful to transmit a different meaning and to communicate with a different type of person. Each of these tongues strive for their own space.

And then there's graffiti and the never-ending war against it. In the Mexico of my adolescence, graffiti almost always had political connotations. It was about inequity, about the struggle for a better future: *¡Viva el Ché!*, *¡Muerte a los diputados asesinos!*, *¡Huelga contra Pinochet!* The connections between politics and the Church are unavoidable, as right-wing groups respond with messages about *"Cristo Rey"* written by "Opus Dei" and dating back to the reaction to the so-called Christian War—La Cristada—of the 1920s. Swastikas and anti-Semitic slurs often appear, too. And the standard love note *"Juan Diego ama a Rosita"* is as omnipresent as spring rain. Add, also, the anarchic graffiti attached to rock bands imported south of the Rio Grande in the 1980s, which manifested itself on city walls, even on the pavement, the morning after a cataclysmic concert. By and large, however, the general approach has remained the same, and not only there but in cities throughout Latin America. (I recall a discordant, more sapient one I once saw in my own neighborhood, composed in poor Italian: *"Mange bene, cague forte, e non temere a la morte."*) In New York, on the other hand, the graffiti's meanings, also ideological, have more to do with youthful rebellion, with gangs and turfs. I arrived in the city when a new model of subway car, looking like aluminum-foil tents, had been introduced, to which graffiti would not stick—or at least that was the assumption. The loss, as far as I'm concerned, was tremendous. Yes, anarchy was pushed to the background, segregated once again in ghettos; cleanliness returned, giving civilization the tranquillity it strives for. But this only forced youngsters to find other, less public, more introverted venues to express their angst—an angst, I'm convinced, less manageable when not out in the open. The old subway cars were works of art, weren't they? Still, graffiti didn't disappear; it simply relocated, as it always will, for it is as much a part of the New York landscape as is an advertisement. It happens simply to prove that order cannot exist without chaos looming in the background, threatening to collapse the whole urban structure. Sure, graffiti is portrayed as obnoxious and unpleasant by government bureaucrats. But they fail to see its unparalleled harmony and uncompromising message: that, as much as we strive to eradicate anarchy, it will always live within us.

AS I PACK my books, I think of how very much I've changed, and the transformation has been thanks to New York. I remember the moment I arrived from Mexico. Is that Ilan Stavans still to be found somewhere? The books I brought with me then I had acquired in Mexico, the Middle East, Europe, Cuba, and on occasional trips to the United States. How did I arrange them on the newly acquired shelf? How should one, however disorganized one's nature, shape one's own personal library? The issue has puzzled me for years, and I know now I shall die without having solved it. Should one follow the standard approach by subject and nationality, as libraries worldwide do? Or should one accommodate books alphabetically by author? Either way is hazardous: making room for newly acquired titles is always a challenge. And so should one simply let books fall into their own place and space without any preconceived notion? This is the way I always shelve my books, perhaps by default, since the pitfalls are easily recognizable: I, and no one else, know where each book is, unless I forget, and then, of course, it is days, even weeks, and sometimes months before I find it again. Walter Benjamin was right when he claimed that a real library is always impenetrable and at the same time unique. My success in America would come when I would once again have a plentiful library, personal in the complete sense of the word—i.e., built on caprice.

I had anxiously waited for the moment when I would

occupy a space I would call my own, to make myself at home. But now I'm leaving it behind. I'm leaving New York City. My library has grown, and so have I. Honestly, I hardly ever opened my Spanish translation of Joyce's *Ulysses:* too artificial, I hear myself uttering. I eventually exchanged it for its original, as I did with Conrad and Nabokov, and confess to have had the sense, at least at first, that these volumes were but improved versions of a lost item. For what makes a text authentic—the bona-fide source of sources—in our age of instant translations, where books are rendered into other tongues not from the original but from a translation, and even from a retranslation of a translation? These ruminations make me come alive in New York City, *el ombligo del mundo*, the heart of the heart of the matter, to paraphrase in a single line Graham Greene and William H. Gass; for in it I was among books—or, better, I lived inside a Book of Books. The word is what the place is made of: newsstands are veritable feasts of letters and images; the amount of books on sale and recycled is astonishing. Everyone reads— bums, secretaries, subway conductors, nannies—a far cry from my illiterate Mexico, where the written word has always felt like an imposition, a foreign import. Furthermore, New York is a city that is omnipresent in literature, so much so that if a catastrophe ever occurred one would be able to re-create its sidewalks, dance clubs, and subway stations, its love affairs and robberies, even the shadow projected by a restless fly on a rain-soaked umbrella, through what its inhabitants write about it.

Literature—my passion, my obsession—slowly made its way into my library. And I allowed myself to be hypnotized by the outpour, even if I wasn't quite in control of

Shakespeare's tongue: Paul Auster's overintellectualized mysteries, Nicholson Baker's minimalist rendezvous, Abraham Cahan's odyssey of the shtetl Jew transformed into an urban dweller, Edith Wharton's evocation of the Belle Époque. . . . *Orbis et urbis.* One day I would read a story by Isaac Bashevis Singer about a cafeteria, and a few days later I would wander around the neighborhood looking around to contrast the real place with the imaginative version. Literature was my compass: I visited bars near Columbia at the suggestion of Allen Ginsberg and Jack Kerouac; I wandered around the Lower East Side (called by Nuyoricans "La Loisiada"), tracing David Schearl's path in *Call It Sleep;* I looked for the Harlem *rumberos* Oscar Hijuelos sang to in *The Mambo Kings Play Songs of Love;* I visited Wall Street and saw a Bartleby in the face of homeless sheltered under a stairway or behind a revolving door. Jewish and black writers particularly fascinated me. In James Baldwin I found a haunting essayist turning a somber Harlem into a field of lyrical possibilities; in Cynthia Ozick, a religious dilettante, a mannerist making sense of the pagan rituals that surrounded her; and Irving Howe, in whose essays the mix of literature and politics make for a most stunning read. Saul Bellow and Ralph Ellison, Philip Roth and Toni Morrison, all of them alien to New York City, were embraced by it. Even the seminary, in my eyes, was an intellectual nest: the distasteful Norman Podhoretz had passed through its halls, and so had his archenemy, Michael Lerner. My beloved Latin Americans—with the exception of Borges—became secondary. Why? I ask. My answer is unequivocal: their concerns, suddenly, became remote and unappealing; I began to see them as another aspect of world letters and not, as I had in my early twenties, as the unsurpassed masters whose fiction spoke louder than anything else.

I STOP FOR a respite. The sofa nearby has been a favorite reading spot. I take some volumes with me, sit down, and browse around. Soon I realized that *ninguno*, not a single one, of the books I took with me years ago from Mexico is— *sorpresa, sorpresa*—about Mexico itself. Do I really need them now? Is it time to let them go?

I left Ciudad de México in 1985, eight years ago. Have I missed it? Perhaps at the very beginning, when my father flew with me to New York, made sure I had everything necessary in my little room, and said goodbye a block away from his hotel at Lexington and 53rd Street. But the city never truly spoke to me. Yes, I loved its Basílica, its baroque downtown buildings, but what else? And why didn't I love it? Why didn't I make myself miss it? Perhaps because I had been born and raised in it, and it is difficult to appreciate our surroundings until we suddenly lose them. But there is a more complex explanation: I felt throughout my childhood that Mexican Jews never made themselves part of the environment. Their affection for it was—and still is, I'm afraid— ambivalent at best. At no time have I felt its electricity enrich me; on the contrary, I often feel exhausted after just a brief period, overwhelmed by its *ensimismamiento*, its chaotic assemblage of stimulation. When my father said goodbye to me, it was him, it was my family, that I began to miss, not the city where they lived. I cried, for I loved him dearly and I would not see him again for months, perhaps a year. To attenuate the pain, I quickly entered a cinema. What did I see?

Ettore Scola's *Le Bal*, an Italian film about a dance hall that had not a word in it, not a single one. Silence surrounded me, and it was fitting. Deep inside his heart—though he would deny it—my father, I know, was convinced I would not succeed on my own in New York's jungle; nostalgia would ultimately bring me back home. Decades before, he himself had attempted a similar move, but had returned home after nine months.

He was wrong. I turned Manhattan into my true home. No matter where I live, no matter where I travel, the only place I feel I truly belong is New York. Why? The answer is: its literature. I can invoke, with accuracy, the Manhattan site in which I first read a book; or, better, where a book first grabbed me. My memory of 116th Street and Broadway is attached to Felipe Alfau's *Locos: A Comedy of Gestures*, for it was there, waiting almost an hour for a friend to arrive, where I fell under the spell of its Hispanicized English prose; 82nd Street and Broadway, my destination on Sunday afternoons, belongs to Truman Capote's *In Cold Blood*; Houston Street, near the offices of *El Diario/La Prensa*, a subway stop I frequented while writing my newspaper column in Spanish in the late 1980s, corresponds, to a large extent, with Don Delillo's *The Names*; and whenever I return to 47th Street and Madison, I think of Nicholson Baker's *The Mezzanine*. I also remember reading Schopenhauer near the Dakota, Faulkner in Riverside Park, Franz Rosenzweig's *The Star of Redemption* in Coney Island, and Maimonides' *Guide for the Perplexed* at Kennedy Airport.

Nostalgia—my father has a disposition toward it, but I don't. I am not the least sentimental toward the Mexico of my past. Immigrants turn their place of origin into a frozen tableau. I have done so, too, to some extent; but I feel no need to return. I missed my parents and, to a lesser extent, my brother and sister. But I did not suffer. Close to my departure, family, friends, and relatives organized a farewell party for me, and I pretended to be overwhelmed by sadness. *Fingí dolor.* To act otherwise would have been rude. A cake was baked, letters filled with intense reminiscences were drafted, tears were spilled, smiles were displayed, photographs were taken. Honestly, though, I couldn't wait to reach my new home, to unpack my books in solitude. So why, of all images of my past, has the pistol stuck with me? I couldn't, for the life of me, come up with an explanation. My emigration was carefully planned. I was not a *bracero*, a wetback running away from poverty, whose swim across the Rio Grande was the chance of a better future, filled with that magical American word "opportunity." My admiration for the wetbacks is enormous. Could I have undergone a similar adventure? I doubt it. I was a spoiled middle-class, educated child. I always had a shower, a bowl of soup, handsome clothes to wear. My move was motivated by freedom: I wanted to live in a land of free speech, where words and arguments mattered; a place where my Jewishness was valued; I wanted to have inexhaustible, labyrinthine libraries around me, where I could get lost.

MÉXICO LINDO. WHAT makes me Mexican? White-skinned, blond, brown-eyed, with a name like Ilan, which in Hebrew means "palm tree," and a surname like Stavans. What makes me a Mexican? And what, after all these years, attaches me to the land where I was born and raised? I have no easy answers, of course. Ours is an age of miscegenation and dislocation. To be born and raised in the same place is no longer the norm.

I never learned to love Mexico. Instead, *adoro* the Spanish language. It is far easier for me to think of my birth as having occurred in the tongue of Quevedo, Cervantes, Borges, and Octavio Paz than to perceive myself as *un mexicano hecho y derecho*. I like to repeat Yehuda Halevi's famous stanza: "My heart is in the East and I am at the Edge of the West. Then how can I taste what I eat, how can I enjoy it? How can I fulfill my vows and pledges while Zion is in the domain of Edom, and I am in the bounds of Arabia?" Where my heart could *not* be found was in Mexico. This is sheer ambivalence, of the type Jews have turned into a profession in the diaspora. In Mexico I was, am, and will always be a welcome guest in a rented house, one I can never fully own.

This ambivalence, it goes without saying, was in the water when I grew up, and it resulted in a sort of contempt I would feel toward Mexican Jews. Why didn't they ever truly assimilate? Why keep a sense of being perpetual visitors? Many of my Yiddish school friends were wealthy. They kept houses across the border—in Miami, San Diego, Houston— and apartments in Tel Aviv and Haifa and, on occasion, in Paris, too. These places were talked about openly not as vacation spots but as hideouts. Since Mexico's economy is always unstable, since its government is eternally disconnected to the overall population, escape was álways in the Jewish mind. What if . . . ? *¿Y qué si ocurriera lo impensable?* All of us, including my family, invariably kept bank accounts in U.S. dollars abroad, for one never knows. Particularly in a place where anti-Semitism has been promulgated subtly by the government and the Church.

Still, unlike Argentina, Mexico never had a full-fledged

pogrom. Which doesn't mean it never saw a Jew killed out of hatred. Literature portraying Jewish people as avaricious moneylenders is omnipresent. Negative stereotypes of Jews—the deep pocket, the sharp nose—air unchallenged on TV and radio. Ever since the 1940s, the infamous *Protocols of the Elders of Zion* has been a runaway best-seller, sold in inexpensive editions on newsstands. And Adolf Hitler remains an all-time hero among the disenchanted, his cleansing campaign to eradicate the Jews from the globe a worthy one. During the Yom Kippur War, I remember clearly how we prayed in Beth-El, a synagogue in the Polanco neighborhood, while police cars waited outside the building, protecting it. Between prayers, I would wander outside and look at the officers, whose eyes were fixed on me and the other Jewish congregants. What were we doing? they seemed to be saying. What were those tiny hats on our heads? What is a synagogue, anyway? Then, inside the temple, we would hear rumors of bombs exploding in nearby synagogues—in the Kehila in Colonia Condesa, in Adat Israel in Colonia Alamos, in Alianza Monte Sinaí in Colonia Roma—all, fortunately, unfounded.

Occasionally, a Jewish girl from Tecamachalco is kidnapped, raped, and killed. Such news receives a low profile, and the Jewish community helps by establishing that the motive was unclear, that it had to do with class and not religion. The community most vulnerable to attacks, particularly to harassment and kidnappings, is in Guadalajara, where the Sephardic boyfriend of a cousin of mine was killed by an extreme right-wing faction, his lifeless body found tortured. Little has been done, at least when it came to isolated incidents. A more orchestrated response was, indeed, in store: Bitakhon, whose name was the Hebrew word for "security." This response, obviously, was the brainchild of a generation closer to Zionism than to the Yiddish civilization of Eastern Europe, rooted in a Bundist ideology: self-defense, rather than self-determination, is its primary objective. It took the form of a secret brigade which, in the darkness of night, would emerge to erase anti-Semitic graffiti and, on a few occasions, to harass a Jew-hater.

I myself was a member. It occurred more or less at the same time I was enlisted in the Mexican military, a routine activity every male adolescent had to undergo in order to get a *cartilla*, which cleared the way to a passport. The experience was utterly ridiculous. We used to joke that, in our day and age, it would take the U.S. a mere hour and a half to occupy Mexico, the time needed for high-speed jets to fly from air bases in Texas to the Isthmus of Tehuantepec and the border with Guatemala. The dismal reputation of the army had harked back to the French and American invasions in the nineteenth centuries and, to my generation at least, culminated in the nation's shameful—though heroic—participation in the Second World War, when Mexico, full of pride and ready to show its support for the Allies, sent an aircraft carrier, the famous *Escuadrón 201*, to fight on European soil, but the plane crashed before arrival. (Pedro Infante, a late-1940s Mexican film idol—my mother's James Dean—played the lead role in an eponymous film based on the incident.) My involvement lasted a total of twelve months. At the time the military had organized a lottery, and those with the winning numbers were exempted from service. I was not among the lucky ones and had to be encamped twice a week, on Thursdays and Saturdays, somewhere in the northern suburb of Satelite, my hair crew cut, my dark-green uniform and camouflage fatigues turning me into the cadet I had never imagined myself to be. I was taught to use various weapons—old-fashioned pistols, rusted rifles, empty hand grenades, nothing capable of doing any real damage against menacing enemies—to do endless physical exercise, and to stand under the hot sun awaiting nonsensical orders from a lieutenant. Fortunately, the lieutenant often took the day off, so we simply had to pass attendance and then leave. How much did I learn from it? Nothing, really. It was a nuisance and I simply enjoyed it as another aspect of my anachronistic Mexican-Jewish upbringing. I remember being asked the hypothetical question by my friends who were luckier in the lottery draw, whose exemption from the army had made them terribly happy: if suddenly Mexico and Israel went to war, on which side would I fight? My cowardly answer was plain and simple: "I really wasn't cut out to be a soldier. So on neither one, since I'm a pacifist."

Well, at least I thought so, but my recruitment by Bitakhon, which took place during my last year of high school, I took more seriously. It was 1978 and I was seventeen years old. One afternoon, after class, I was approached by a mysterious young man whom I had seen wandering around in the corridors, though I knew neither his name nor his political affiliation. He gave me the impression of having graduated not too long ago, but had been hired by the school to return not as a student but as a worker of some sort. At any rate, he pushed me aside and asked if I was willing to talk to him about matters of importance to *nosotros, los judíos mexicanos*. We slowly walked together to a soccer field at the back of the school and, with nobody around, he explained the difficult times that engulfed Mexico's Jewish community. "We have to defend ourselves," he said. "How much longer will we allow anti-Semites to say what they want in the open? When a bomb is ticking, sooner or later it will explode. Israel cannot do anything for us other than promote *aliyah*. But how many are ready to move to a kibbutz? Are you, for instance? So we are forced to organize, and I have been sent here to ask you to become one of us."

"Of *us*?" I asked, puzzled.

"You might have noticed, Ilan, that sometimes a schoolmate of yours arrives in class with a black eye. Or perhaps a bruised knee."

I had noticed, indeed, and when I asked, had received the most unlikely response. I had even suspected some bizarre involvement in paramilitary activities, but had convinced myself this was absurd. My interlocutor then explained the secret activities of the brigade: it met at midnight, sometimes later, at the gym of the Centro Deportivo Israelita, known by its initials, CDI; it practiced exercises in self-defense, taught its members to use weapons—*pistolas*, etc.—and carried out dangerous missions during the night. Members returned to their homes at dawn, ready for school.

"Why does it need to be secret?" I queried. "Why not engage in an open political debate? Why not force the leaders of the Jewish community to be more active in national politics? Why not denounce anti-Semitism in the media? Why do the whole damn thing surreptitiously?"

His answer was sharp: Mexico has an endemic allergy toward open debate. The Jewish community, since its beginning, has kept itself on the margins. Those are the parameters within which we must act.

I became a member, along with scores of my friends, not out of desire but out of duty. The evening sessions were exhausting, but also invigorating. For the first time in my life I felt I was not a target, even though my skills as a street fighter were far from enviable. In fact, I always suspected I had been recruited not to be a cadet but to help in the brigade's intelligence activities. The high-ranking leaders of Bitakhon always showed up behind a white screen, but the identity of our immediate superiors, men and women a bit older than I, was not a secret. I am convinced the Mossad, Israel's secret service, gave advice. In judo- and T'ai-chi–like exercises, my mobility was limited; I would barely lift one leg when a kick from my opponent would land in my stomach. Several times I returned home with a black eye and a sore thigh. My pride as a defender was more a matter of self-delusion than a convincing display. In fact, I knew that behind my back my friends often made nasty comments about my performance. "He would be killed in a second," I heard one utter. The whole experience reminded me of Isaac Babel's envy of the Cossacks in *Red Cavalry:* in his eyes, they represent muscular strength, whereas the Jew is a pitiful, crushable creature. The dichotomy, obviously, was incorrect, for around me were vigorous Mexican Jews, male and female, more than capable of overwhelming me. Clearly, I was my own problem: I'm quite clumsy and have no talent for fighting.

And yet my superiors sent me out into the streets. During my tenure, we bruised some hooligans that were about to leave a restaurant, and fought a gang on an empty street. I had left by the time the activities of the brigade intensified, in 1982, when President José López Portillo nationalized the bank industry. It was a broad move designed to awaken a

sense of nationalism at a time when people were highly suspicious of political corruption and skeptical about the nation's future. Classes were canceled, and the whole family sat
that September afternoon watching the president deliver his
speech on TV. "I shall defend the peso like a dog," he said.
(The nickname stuck: thereafter López Portillo was known
as El Perro.) This was not the first time such a broad patri-
otic move had been made in Mexico. In the 1930s, populist
President Lázaro Cárdenas, in an open attack against British
and American petroleum companies, announced the nation-
alization of the oil industry. But the events in the 1980s
struck an anti-Jewish note when López Portillo's Cabinet
threatened to publicize a list of *sacadólares*, the names of rich
people whose fat dollars were deposited in foreign bank accounts. It was widely rumored, of course, that many prominent Jews were on the list. Every morning, hate graffiti
would appear on Avenida Insurgentes, Viaducto, and Avenida
Reforma, especially near Jewish neighborhoods. But it
would disappear in the blink of an eye.

NEITHER THE MEXICAN army nor Bitakhon alleviated my
ambivalence toward Mexico. Quite the opposite. I increasingly felt at the periphery, a citizen without full privileges.
"Real Mexicans" were more genuine than I, and I concluded
that it was my Jewishness that had made me unique. Actually, hard as I sought, I could not, for the life of me, pin down
lo mexicano in me, although I knew it existed somehow, a Platonic attribute in most of what surrounded me. Later on, in
New York, it would be easy to find it in the engravings of
José Guadalupe Posada, in a bowl of *pozole*, in half a dozen

tacos al pastor with onions, perhaps even in the murals of Diego Rivera and José Clemente Orozco, even though I've always been aware, no doubt as a result of my hybrid identity, of the gap between the artist and reality. But not while in Mexico. In an inspiring essay, "The Argentine Writer and Tradition," Borges addressed the issue of the native. His argument, which I've used time and again, was a raison d'être. I memorized its lucid paragraphs, such as this:

> Some days past I have found a curious confirmation of the fact that what is truly native can and often does dispense with local color; I found this confirmation in Gibbon's *Decline and Fall of the Roman Empire*. Gibbon observes that in the Arabian book par excellence, in the *Koran*, there are no camels; I believe if there were any doubts as to the authenticity of the *Koran*, this absence of camels would be sufficient to prove it is an Arabian work. It was written by Mohammed, and Mohammed, as an Arab, had no reason to know that camels were especially Arabian; for him they were part of reality, he had no reason to emphasize them; on the other hand, the first thing a falsifier, a tourist, an Arab nationalist would do is have a surfeit of camels, caravans of camels, one every page; but Mohammed, as an Arab, was unconcerned; he knew he could be an Arab without camels.

And so, as I think back on my Mexican experience, I see books by Nabokov and Kafka, and foreign films. Why not Mexican? What was my reaction to the movies by Pedro Infante and Jorge Negrete I saw in my adolescence? And what about those by Cantinflas and "La India" María? I saw plenty of them, but the environment that nurtured me considered them *rascuache*—i.e., unworthy vis-à-vis their European counterparts. Hardly anything produced in Mexico was perceived as high-caliber, such was the *malinchismo*, the inferiority complex, among the people all around me. Only when I crossed the border did I realize how significant Cantinflas's popular movie, *Ahí está el detalle*, was and also how much meaning could be found in *Nosotros los pobres*, with Pedro Infante. You could actually explain the country's *Weltanschauung*, its history, and its present through these movies. In fact, it was through foreign eyes that I learned to *read* Mexico: the impact of the 1910–11 revolution of Pancho Villa and Emiliano Zapata through John Reed; the role of Catholicism through Buñuel; the effects of magic and the dreamlike universe through André Breton. Italo Calvino, in a story he wrote in 1982 after a trip to Mexico, entitled "Under the Jaguar Sun," describes a kind of uneasiness he experienced while indulging his senses in a fiesta of colors and tastes. That is what Mexico was for him, but only after I read the story did I become fully conscious of them.

When Mexico seems most emblematic, even contradictory, to me, I find myself singing the famous *canción* popularized by the mariachi Jorge Negrete, about nostalgia, about the type of longing Mexico inspires:

México lindo y querido,	*Mexico lovely and beloved,*
si muero lejos de tí,	*if I should die apart,*
que digan que estoy dormido,	*then let them say that I'm asleep*
y que me traigan aquí.	*so they can bring me back.*

And I laugh—to myself, quietly. While in Mexico, I used to sing *"México Lindo"* to ridicule my lack of patriotism, my *un-Mexicanness*. But far away, in busy New York, the *canción* has acquired a different flavor: It is about my inner contradictions, about trying to define myself as Mexican and not finding a fully satisfying explanation. It is about the desire to explain why I don't fit in.

These matters, as most others that pertain to identity, might be inconsequential but for one thing—I often wonder, like the immigrant that I am, where shall I be buried? The issue creates much angst in me. I am married and have two children, all American. Though I remain loyal to Spanish and to a lesser extent to Yiddish, I have switched to English. Which of these languages is truly my own? I no longer know. Nor do I feel that Mexico is where I belong. Should I be buried in New York, then? But New York, in spite of its appeal, is too impersonal. What kind of lasting place does a Jew have in it? By leaving *home*, I not only left behind my friends and immediate family, and the theater of my early memories; I also abandoned the earth under me, the ground on which my forefathers thrived and where they are buried. Is that where I will always belong? I tell myself not to kid around: who cares where one is buried? After all, death is the end of consciousness. I won't be around to know, will I? A Jewish burial, however, is not for the dead but for the living.

Indeed, I am so concerned with my death that I often dream about my own funeral. I see the casket in which I have been placed, my corpse naked and properly washed for the obsequies. The chief rabbi reads Psalm 13, my son Joshua recites the Kaddish. . . . Am I controlling the living from the tomb? Yes, but don't the dead always do that? More worrisome to me is the question, *where* will this illusory burial take place?

These are preposterous thoughts. Death is the ultimate

equalizer. Nothing of us remains, except memory. And memory—our memory, once we depart—doesn't belong to us anymore but to tradition.

ON A WINDY morning a few days before my plane took off from Mexico to New York, my father asked me to accompany him to the Jewish cemetery. *"Vamos a despedirnos,"* he told me, to say goodbye. He wanted me to be near the tombs of his father, Zeyde Srulek, and his father-in-law, Zeyde Jaime, for the last time, at least for the last time while I was still a native Mexican. "You have to put a stone on each." Of course, he and I knew I would be able to come back later on, during a vacation trip; but this time was different. *"Ya no te tendrán cerca*, you shall be far from them. . . ."

The crowded graveyard, on Avenida Constituyentes, is in the northern part of the Ciudad de México, not far from Polanco and Tecamachalco, the bourgeois neighborhoods of the so-called *ghetto judío*, where most Mexican Jews live today. This Jewish cemetery is less than eighty years old. It isn't the oldest in the country—the ones in Tampico and Jalapa are older—but it is by far the most important. It has a twenty-four-hour guard, a non-Jew whose watchful eye and gardening skills are handsomely remunerated by the children of the deceased. The *casa de limpia*, the site where the ritual cleaning of the dead is performed, is the first feature welcoming the visitor. Bobbe Miriam, my maternal grandmother, bought a plot for herself so she could be at the side of her husband, Zeyde Jaime. And these plots are only a few steps away from where Zeyde Srulek was laid to rest.

Family tombs. The cemetery on Avenida Constituyentes

also contains the graves of more distant relatives, particularly my maternal great-grandfather, Calmen, known as the *tzaddik*, a deeply revered but authoritarian Hasid from Warsaw devoted to the teachings of the Ba'al Shem Tov, who died at the age of fifty-nine of a heart attack and after whom I am named in Hebrew. (My legal name is Ilan Calmen Stavchansky Slomianski.) His tomb, in the form of a monument, is in the central corridor in the old section of the graveyard, evidence of his revered status within the Jewish community. (The only item I inherited from him is a sepia photograph in which he stands with other community leaders in the Ashkenazic synagogue in Nidje Israel.) Nearby is the sepulcher of his wife, Pese Eisenberg, a devoted housewife responsible for keeping the family afloat while her husband nourished his faith and hardly supported the family as a peddler of sacred books and other religious paraphernalia. Of her I know only that she died a slow, agonizing death after being paralyzed by an embolism; she remained in a wheelchair for many long, insufferable years, incapable of speaking—almost the same fate Bobbe Miriam would suffer prior to her death in 1991. This absence of speech always struck me as symbolic. As a grandmotherly figure, she had been a primary force, a point of gravity, designing the path her children should take. Her voice had been the main source of control, but in the end the voice disappeared and she became but a ghost.

Beyond these unknown but precious ancestors, the Mexican soil is meaningless to me—utterly inconsequential. Death doesn't know any borders. Previous generations are buried in their shtetls in Russia, near Warsaw, in Brazil, in Jerusalem, Paris, New York, and Illinois. The ashes of innumerable others are spread in Auschwitz and Birkenau. In

Una scienza nuova, the Italian philosopher Giambattista Vico admonishes that the cemetery is the basis of civilization, marking the transition between nomadic life and permanent settlements. Has Mexico become my soil? Why should my body be claimed by it? Of all my relatives, the ones who suffered the most horrifying end are my forebears in Yashinovska, a Polish shtetl hidden behind thick woods near the province of Białystok in which almost everybody was engaged in leather processing, where Jaime, my mother's father, was born. Jaime and his older brother Isaac dreamed of sailing to America, but in 1928 the immigration quota was closed, and so they sailed to Jalapa, a port in the state of Veracruz, on the Gulf of Mexico. Their older siblings, Sender and Bofschel, stayed behind with their parents. Jaime found out that his mother, Feige, had died of diabetes during the Second World War when a photograph of her tomb in the cemetery of Yashinovska was mailed to him. My wife and I, during our honeymoon, traveled to Poland and the former Czechoslovakia in an attempt to trace our genealogical roots. But much as I wanted to, circumstances made it impossible to visit the graveyard. It would have been a moving tribute, for apparently only Feige has a tomb in the Old World. The fate of her husband and two older children is tragic. The geographical location of Yashinovska kept the town hidden from the Germans and, miraculously, made it possible for them to survive the war. They listened with uncontainable enthusiasm to the radio announcing the end of violent aggression. But shortly afterward, a Nazi troop entered the town and massacred everyone. Relatives from Israel told Jaime that his father's corpse had last been seen in his leather workshop, not far from those of Sender and Bofschel. And so they were left accounted for, forgotten—perhaps happily so, for wouldn't it have been worse to be buried in a land where you had been unwelcome since the beginning?

Cancer, diabetes, heart failure—these diseases constitute the hourglass of all males in the family, and I will probably die of one. Men rarely get past the age of sixty-three: they suffer a fulminating heart attack, often so powerful that their bodies are found several meters away from where they were last seen alive. The cemetery includes *matzeives*, the tombstones for Calmen's wife, Pese, as well as for one of their six children, Tío Morris, a mythical hero of sorts about whom we, members of the younger generation, know just enough to idealize him. As it happened, my mother accompanied us as we wandered around the cemetery for more than an hour that sunny and brisk afternoon. The place has grown so much in size that a whole hill was acquired with community money, and so one walks through an internal gate that separates the old tombs from the new. I remember asking her about Tío Morris, her uncle, a handsome fellow, whom she adored ("my secret adolescent love"), who died from a heart attack after a quick trip to Chicago to visit relatives. He was a popular bachelor, part of the extended family that had settled in the United States prior to the Second World War. In fact, Tío Morris enlisted in the army and served in Central Europe. This injected a degree of adventure into his life that he would nurture until his death. Together with a brother, he made a handsome living trading expensive leather and furs, specializing in mink. He had the life-style of a gigolo, charming others with his elegant looks and generosity, investing his money in fanciful tastes, and, more than anything, refusing to marry and settle down. He would make it an annual event to drive down from Illinois to Mexico in his luxurious purple Studebaker. His trips established a level of communication between the English- and the Spanish-speaking sides of the family that could go beyond an epistolary dialogue. Tío Morris would arrive in mid-December and leave approximately a month later. He would spend Hanukkah and New Year's with his Mexican relatives, first at Colonia Portales, where my mother's family lived, then to their home in Colonia Alamos, arriving with a trunk filled with an assortment of presents for the young and old. And my mother was his favorite: he would bring her much-cherished sweets and goodies from America and take her out to a nearby soda fountain, where she would have an ice cream and he his favorite drink, an iced Coca-Cola. Apparently, he had been on active duty when my mother was born, in 1941, and did not find out about her birth until he arrived in Mexico in the late 1940s. His surprise at seeing a bewitching young girl ignited his interest, and an unbreakable bond between them was established.

My mother was not alone in adoring him: Bobbe Miriam and other senior family members would attempt to find him a match. They dreamed of having him resettle in Mexico. Zeyde Jaime was also in the leather trade, so Tío Morris could easily find a lucrative job and a niche among the community. But the mere suggestion was preposterous, if only because the westbound immigration flux that began in Poland could never go from north to south. Why would he exchange his stable, democratic status in Chicago for the fancifulness of the tropics? I never met Tío Morris, of course—he died some eight years before I was born—but the stories about him portray someone passionately enamored with the exotic and outlandish aspects of Mexico. In his eyes, this was a land of quests. In his native Illinois, adventure was limited to evening outings.

He was forty-seven on his last visit. By all accounts, he did not drive anymore. The family drove a couple of hours to pick him up at the airport. Tío Morris suffered from a heart condition and looked terribly pale. Doctors in Chicago had warned him about the altitude in Ciudad de México, almost two thousand feet above sea level. But he couldn't postpone his annual visit. It was 1953, and as soon as he landed, he fell ill. A cousin of his was a resident doctor and took him under her supervision. But he refused to relax. He had promised my mother he would take her to see the port of Acapulco, on the Pacific, for the first time, and the night before his death he called her to make final arrangements. The doctors had given him permission. He would pick her up early the next morning. But his heart detonated while he was in bed, sometime after midnight, and his body was thrown down onto the floor.

Death: it is always on the way. How long will Tío Morris be remembered? And by whom? He left no children. His tomb sits alone in the Jewish cemetery. Had he died in Chicago, his place in the family memory would be secure, but in Mexico he was only a guest, a fanciful visitor appearing and disappearing as if by magic. Even if younger members of the Illinois family have heard of him, he is too distant, too abstract a ghost for them. And among my own relatives south of the Rio Grande, few have even heard his name. But ever since my mother began telling and retelling his story to me, he became a symbol of sorts, a reminder of the failed north-south connection, an American that succumbed to the temptations of the exotic.

Kafka says: "There is only one cardinal sin: impatience. Because of impatience we were driven out of Paradise, because of impatience we cannot return." But at no time while walking around the cemetery did I ever wonder if I myself would be buried there—of this, I am sure. Where else could I be buried? Besides, I was in my mid-twenties; why should I think of it? This was also my soil, the earth that fed and bred me. I am a third-generation Mexican Jew, and though I was ready to take off, to look for a better life elsewhere, though I could relentlessly question my status as a Mexican, it did not cross my mind that I should be buried anywhere else but in this place. The site, clearly, was overcrowded, and the community elders had no intention whatsoever of following the pattern of the old Jewish cemetery in Prague by establishing layer upon layer of stones. No, Mexico has always been perceived by its immigrants as the ultimate frontier, a limitless geography, both in terms of size and possibilities. In the early 1920s, immigrants might have lived in small rooms, but, unlike the Lower East Side, for instance, space was never in short supply. So, when the last cemetery lot is filled, extra land will be acquired, either tangential to the established site, or in another location. But unless a catastrophe—G–d forbid—takes place, or an attempt to break the cycle of social conventions succeeds, those of my generation will find their resting place not far from the tombs of my relatives.

The wind was blowing my hair. I found some pebbles and placed them on top of the tombs of my grandparents. My father was not at my side. He had taken a walk on his own, so I had time to reflect. I told myself, "What a triumph it was for a Jew of that generation to die a natural death."

The pistol—my father's pistol . . . As I sat on my sofa in

my Upper West Side apartment, I recalled the moment at the Jewish cemetery when the gun became symbolic of my entire Mexican upbringing. It was at that precise moment, when I found myself alone near Zeyde Srulek's tomb. Why on earth would the pistol acquire such transcendental meaning when my childhood and adolescence were spent in relative peace with my environment? Nor, for that matter, had I seen a pistol in my eight years in Manhattan. The debate on radio and TV on gun control, the atrocities perpetrated by demented loners in McDonald's in Dallas and Maine, the endless, often drug-related chain of deaths in Harlem, the Mafia "acts" in Little Italy, the killing of tourists at the U.S. Open Tennis, the usual subway criminal desperate for money. Like everyone else, I heard much about pistols in schools, about their abundance in the inner city. While sitting on the train, I would look at those around me suspiciously, fearing for my life. But aside from an irrelevant encounter with a lunatic on Broadway who, on my way to teach at Columbia, suddenly kicked me in the chest at an early hour of the morning, I was never exposed, fortunately, to firearms. Never . . . In Mexico, on the other hand, I had played with weapons much more frequently. I had seen them in neighbors' houses, for sale in stores. More significant even, as a Jew I had heard discussion about their use in acts of self-defense against anti-Semites. On a few occasions, I had been the target of nasty comments by Gentile street acquaintances. And I had seen numerous swastikas on walls, particularly near the campus of the Universidad Nacional Autónoma de México, UNAM, the nation's largest public university, just a few blocks away from my home. My father's pistol was to be used against *our* attackers, I finally concluded—anti-Semites ready to eject us from Mexican soil.

I FINALLY ASKED my father about the pistol on a gusty morning after he returned from work. He laughed at first. *"¡Lo que tú elucubras, hijo mío!"* he stated. Finally, he submitted to an interrogation, through which I saw how much my view of Mexico had been artificial, misconstrued even, before I left the country altogether. He told me he got it when one of his clients at Forrajera Nacional, S.A., failed to pay him a long-standing debt. He kept it hidden in the safe-deposit box in our house in Copilco (also known as Copilco el Alto) for fear someone would misuse it. "Besides, a pistol should not be around children, should it?" Our modern three-story house was located in the southeastern part of the capital, a gentrified, quiet, middle-class neighborhood. A block away was an unmanicured public garden, and a quarter-mile in the opposite direction was an abandoned factory.

Copilco el Alto was an island of sorts. To the south and southeast was Copilco el Bajo, a shantytown, a *villamiseria* where *campesinos* from faraway provinces, commonly known as *paracaidistas*, in English "parachuters," would build their improvised tin-and-rubber shelters, getting water from fire hydrants and making improvised electrical connections to get their television antennas activated. These poor villages, I thought, were always on the brink of violence, particularly at times when the masses were most agitated by police brutality and government corruption. They could take up arms any minute and attack us, the foreigners, *los judíos*, could they not? On the other hand, I couldn't for the life of me envision my father raising the pistol against anyone, not even in self-defense, so benign, charitable, and warmhearted is he.

"You were wise," I told my father. "The weapon has always given me a sense of security."

Again, he laughed.

"*¿Contra ladrones?*" he replied. Our house was robbed once, the week after we sold it. During our tenure, no break-in ever occurred.

"Against thieves, sure, but also against anti-Semites."

"Ilan, I never had the courage to buy any bullets."

I'VE FINISHED PACKING. The boxes are sealed. The handful of books I originally brought with me from Mexico have their own box, and I've played with the idea of deliberately leaving it behind in this apartment, once the movers are out and there's nobody to notice. What use do I have for them? Yes, they are my past, I repeat, a testimony of the person I was eight years ago. Do I throw away old photographs? Besides, isn't that the purpose of a library, to be built by layers, like an onion, the oldest books at its core, and the periphery made of fresh acquisitions? But what good is Vargas Llosa's *Conversation in the Cathedral* to me now in Spanish? Or García Marquez's *Leafstorm*? Mexican public libraries are a triumph of natural chaos: they are disorganized, unreliable. Just the opposite of Massachusetts, where I'm heading to: libraries there are pantheons of wisdom. I can get a copy of any Spanish book in a matter of days, if not faster, can I not?

Truth is, Vargas Llosa I have stopped reading altogether. He belongs to a period of the early 1980s when I thought art and politics were twin siblings; I no longer think that way. García Marquez remains of interest, especially *One Hundred Years of Solitude*, his masterpiece, the type of novel that justifies a single life twice over. But I have had the heretical impression that the Colombian has written little of consequence ever since, with the exception, perhaps, of *Love in the Time of Cholera*, a minor gem. His politics bore me, and so does his repetitiveness. *Don Quixote*, on the other hand, has grown deeper in my eyes as I grow older. It has no substitute, even though Cervantes, as I scrutinize him time and again, emerges as a fabulous storyteller but a lousy stylist. Anyway, he and Borges, whom I retrieved from the ashes, are both a compass and a set of totems. Or shall I say talismans? I have them at my side every time I start writing, hoping their genius will spill over. Not long ago I began reading the pages of Borges I had memorized in their English translation. Their beauty left me breathless. Although drafted in Spanish, they seem to have been imagined in Shakespeare's tongue. This, to me, is proof of their transcendence, for English, I now tell myself, is the language of *true* literature. Transcendence: Borges felt closest to Emerson, Whitman, Melville, and Hawthorne, all New Englanders, their homeland but a few miles away from where I've chosen to move to—my new home.

Who would I be without Cervantes and Borges? Knowledge is not achieved but accumulated. We never get to know things completely, we only get a grasp of what they are at a certain moment. The things that are most meaningful to us are the ones that change with time. The ones that change *with* us. *Don Quixote*, *The Aleph*, and *Other Inquisitions* I have not even packed in boxes. Instead, I have placed them in my personal hand luggage. I want to drive them myself to their new location, place them at center stage in my new library. Libraries, much like life itself, are a work in eternal mutation. The coming decade will surely push the titles I now hold dearest to another corner. Will Cervantes and Borges also move to a dark corner, or even be left forgotten, in my next move?

For the time being, though, I feel at peace. Speed will soon give away to quietude. The cartons I've packed include a harvest of books written by myself. And I am taking New York—and all the cities it encompasses, all my past—along with me.

{ 2 }

The Rise and Fall
of Yiddish

In Yiddish the boundary between comedy and tragedy, and between fact and fiction, is always a thin and wavering line.

—IRVING HOWE

Bela Stavchansky, a small, imposing old lady known among her grandchildren as Bobbe Bela—and, in the jargon of Mexico's Ashkenazic Jews, as *La Bobe*—utters delicious Yiddish sentences to herself in the dark. She is not alone in her one-bedroom apartment. María—aka Mari—her temperamental maid, is around. But the two are always fighting: in polite Spanish, Bobbe Bela asks for something—a glass of hot tea with a sugar cube, a Tylenol, her daily dose of vitamins; Mari, in a terrible mood, won't answer. So Bela switches languages. This is a recurrent strategy: when in distress, return to your homeland, your first tongue. Bela talks to herself and, thus, to the ghosts of her past. Or else she calls her beloved second child, my father, Abremele or Abraham.

Generally, it is an answering machine she gets on the other end. "*H-o-l-a, h-a-b-l-a B-e-l-a. . . . Abremele, quiero hablar contigo. Háblame.*" Is her voice on tape already? Must she press a particular number? Will her Abremele listen to her? These machines are magic. How do they work? Do they have a genie inside? She might simply wait until somebody answers the phone, for she surely prefers a living person. Why should she talk to a machine? She needs company, a voice to listen to. So she calls again, hours later. "*Abremele chulo,*" she says, carefully avoiding Mari's name so as not to announce her intentions, "*vos ken men ton mit di goye? Zi redt mir nisht.*" The maid is driving her crazy, she says. She does not answer her queries and is always in a bad temper. And then again, an hour later. And again. Soon Abremele will listen patiently to her complaints, first on tape, then live through the miracle of phones from Bela's apartment in Colonia Polanco. He can't avoid them. He is used to them. "You've had her for almost twenty years, Mami," he replies. "Will you finally fire her? Who will help you? You're alone. Your three children are too busy. . . . Do you want to move to the *heischel*?" he wonders, referring to the Jewish Home for the Elderly in Cuernavaca, Morelos, also known as *moishe zkeinim*, some fifty-five miles south of Mexico's capital. "I will take you whenever you want."

Bela isn't ready. She is eighty-four but looks at least a decade younger. Her buoyancy is her most admirable quality: wrinkled as a prune, but with a drive as spirited as an Olympic champion. No, life is not finished yet. There is still more, much more—to see, to read, and to appreciate. Her eyes are tired all right, and her bones are heavy. She has lost her hearing, so Abremele must shout on the phone for her to understand—"What? I don't understand"—and he tries again, but she doesn't register. *"Zog es mir in Yiddish?"*—"Switch to Yiddish?"—she suggests, for Yiddish is *der mame-loshen*, the language of stomach and soul. It is also the language of the dead. And if the dead can understand it, why shouldn't she? My father complies, only to realize what he has known all along: Bela is really not interested in conversation; dialogue is too exhausting an enterprise for her, too demanding. Three, four fixed ideas are all she has in her mind, and nothing in the world, not even a major catastrophe, will change them. Mari is not her problem. It's her restlessness, the isolation that comes with old age. *"Ya he pasado de la tercera a la cuarta edad. No sirvo. . . . Estoy descompuesta,"* she tells him: "I'm useless, I'm damaged, I have reached a point of no return." She isn't, obviously. She might be losing it, but she is as vigorous as a horse: every day she walks a few blocks to the supermarket, in the afternoons she plays poker with friends, on Friday nights she attends services at a nearby synagogue, and on weekends she visits her children and grandchildren.

"Abremele, *zug mir, main liebe kind: ¿Y qué con Ilán?* Has he written back?"

"What do you mean, 'What is with Ilan'? *Está ocupado.* He is busy, Mamá, just like all of us. He has a family to attend, and . . ."

Not always have I been a jewel in Bela's crown. For years I wasn't good enough. What kind of money does a writer earn? Isn't it like acting? Can he support a family? Look at your father. Didn't he have problems raising his family? Your cousins in Israel and Philadelphia, ah, they do have solid professions, don't they? Nevertheless, since my essays have begun appearing in national newspapers, since my name circulates among her friends—*Dain liebe einikel, Bela!*—I'm the grandchild she thinks about.

"Did he get my package? You haven't told me . . ." she wonders.

"Of course I did," he replied impatiently.

More than a month ago, she sent to my New York address a package that included some correspondence and a tightly wrapped bound notebook. *MI DIARIO*, she titled it, my diary, though it has no daily entries to speak of. She also calls it, in broken Spanish, *un chico relato*, a brief tale. It has a total of thirty-seven pages, all typed in capital letters. My mother did the secretarial work: Bela would give her a pile of handwritten pages; my mother transcribed them meticulously and sent them back; then Bela revised the typed version once, twice, until fully satisfied. She began writing it around 1980 and finished thirteen years later.

"So—has he read it?" Bela is anxious to hear my reaction, for I am, as of late, the literary genius in the family, and whatever I say goes.

"He has, Mamita, he has, believe me. I'm sure he'll write you directly. Soon."

And I do, of course, in a matter of days. I cannot cherish her diary enough, so important is it for me. I have reread it three, four, five times, trying to find meaning between the lines. The style is unintentionally loose, chaotic, repetitive, ungrammatical; it pays no attention to accents and punctuation. Nevertheless, it is invaluable in its warmth, conviction, and clarity of vision. Bela is overwhelmed by nostalgia, uncritical of her past. How could she not be? What else could one expect from a self-made woman whose schooling didn't reach beyond second grade?

Why did she write her *diario*? So as not to waste her

memory, I tell myself at first. So as to turn her life into an asset for future generations. What if all of a sudden she became an amnesiac? Or is this a gimmick to manipulate the family's collective memory? The more I think of it, the better I realize that "why did she write it?" is the wrong kind of question. Don't all of us want to leave a mark, set the record straight before time runs out? Don't we all dream of changing the world at least a bit by solidifying our place in it? History (with a capital "H") doesn't claim her as a hero. She grew up, escaped Poland shortly before Hitler invaded, settled in Mexico, prospered, had children and grandchildren. . . . Nothing intrepid about it, except for the feeling, so deep in her heart, that we are what our words say we are, and *tsvzein* is different from the Polish *byc*, the Hebrew *leiyot*, and the Spanish *ser*.

Bobbe Bela dedicates her diary not only to me but to my wife and one-year-old son as well: *"Dedico mi [diario] [o un chico relato] de mi juventud a mis queridos nietos, Ilán, Alison y Josh, como recuerdo de Bobe Bela."* She dedicates it in Spanish, though. I wonder why. And not only is the dedication in Spanish but also the entire narrative. This, in fact, is the most urgent question I have, the one I would love to discuss with Bela. Why not in Yiddish, her mother tongue, the tongue in which instinctively she sobs and screams? I know the answer, of course: she wants to be read, understood, appreciated; she is eager to reach not only me but my wife and, sometime in the future, my children as well. I don't for a second doubt the truthfulness of her *diario*. But her words have been modified—or shall I say, betrayed—have they not? And yet I won't raise the issue in my letter. First, because, as susceptible as she is, my remarks will surely be misunderstood. She might suspect that implicit in my query is a censure of her written Spanish, although that is the last thing I would dare to imply. Her Spanish is pidgin all right—broken, un-grammatical—but it is hers all the same: it has style, it has pathos, it has power. It is the tongue of an immigrant—embryonic, wobbly, in constant mutation. It came to her at age nineteen, when, alone, scared to death, she crossed the Atlantic and settled in Mexico. She appropriated the language so that I, thirty years later, could make it my own. So I don't dare to question her. Who am I to dispute her choice of language? A guardian of *der mame-loshen*?

Háblale, Ilan. . . . *Órale*. She wants to know what you think!

And what do I think? I treasure the text, for sure. I have read segments of her *diario* to Joshua. As I wander through its descriptions, I seize, with amazement, the scope of her existential journey, for Bela is a natural polyglot: besides Yiddish, she was fluent in Polish and Russian, and with time she learned a broken English and a bit of Hebrew as well—six languages, including Spanish. She was born in 1909, in Nowe Brodno, now a suburb of Warsaw. When she emigrated to Mexico in 1929, she made a conscious decision never to use Polish and Russian again. Astonishing, I tell myself: most people have trouble even pronouncing a second tongue, but Bela was verbally so rich that she could afford to give up two languages. "Rich," obviously, is the wrong adjective, for her rejection of Polish and Russian didn't come as a result of a surplus of words. Instead, it was a matter of survival, a brusque but healthy attitude she forced herself to take so as to achieve the only available peace of mind she could dream of: she was a youngster, ready to begin her new life; her past needed to be overcome, even erased, if survival was to be achieved. Not only a new country and a new culture but a language was on the horizon when she left Nowe Brodno.

Poverty was not a curse but a state of mind. "When you don't know what you're missing," she once told me in broken Spanish, "you aren't really missing it, are you?" Bela's maiden name, Altschuler, means in German "old-synagogue attendee." Perhaps the family originated in Provence in the thirteenth century and later on moved to Prague, and from there to Galicia, in the Austro-Hungarian Empire. They were lower-middle-class. Her father, Yankev Yosef, owned a garment store with a pretentious English name: Sklep Manufactory. A two-story building with wooden floors, it also functioned as the family's home. I visualize its pallid colors, not unlike the settings of an Andrzej Wajda film. Every time a customer entered through the front door, a bell would announce his arrival. A little window allowed Bela's mother to see from the kitchen who it was. On the first floor was the kitchen, separated from the store by a door through which entering customers could be seen and heard, as a small bell announced anyone stepping in. At the kitchen's center was a charcoal oven. Dovidl, Bela's younger brother, whom I would later on hear about as Tío David, would sleep next to the oven, for there was never enough room upstairs for two adults and six children. A back room behind the store functioned as a bunker: preserves, blankets, and extra clothes were stored in case an anti-Semitic attack occurred, and I also conjecture a sharp ax often used to cut wood. (A pistol might have been of use, of course, but Polish Jews were not allowed to possess weapons.) In the rear of the building was a kitchen, with a small furnace and a bed for one of the seven children. Bela and her sister Reisl slept on the second floor.

Fear, *el miedo*, is the unifying message throughout Bela's *diario*. In the first part alone the words *el antisemitismo* appear a total of seventeen times, more than any other proper noun.

Nowe Brodno was infested with it. I picture the town through Bela's childish eyes, artificially, realizing it is but a figment of my imagination, a hazy marketplace of noise and odor, silhouettes shuffling around, Orthodox Jews confabulating in a corner, automobiles gaining attention, horses carrying milk and butter. Nowe Brodno was divided in half by Białolenska Street, a commercial road, wide, newly asphalted by the Polish authorities, on which Sklep Manufactory was located. The street reminds me of Isaac Babel's Odessa in "Story of My Dovecot," a haunting tale I've reread a thousand times if only to evoke a past I'm convinced I had a share in, a story where *el miedo* is described in such a subtle, indirect way that the reader is left thinking after the last line is over whether life for the Jews on the banks of the Black Sea and in Central Europe in general was ever about anything else.

The Altschulers were urban dwellers. The women, it seems, were much more cosmopolitan and enlightened than their male counterparts. They took care of business while their husbands prayed at the synagogue. I'm tempted to describe them, anachronistically, as *maskilim*, a term that traditionally applied to the enlightened male Jewish establishment from the eighteenth century onward. Perhaps not full-fledged intellectuals, but attentive listeners to the voices of the mind. Whereas the men believed the universe is filled with angels and demons, the women were hard-nosed and utilitarian. They looked down at the shtetl, as most others in Nowe Brodno did, approaching it as too parochial, too confined to a medieval superstition that the Haskalah, as the Jewish "age of reason" is called in Hebrew, had painstakingly struggled to overcome.

I confess to feeling insecure. Am I portraying them as more educated than they really were? Was superstition not an essential element in their husbands' daily life? When, as a child, I would visit Bela at her previous apartment, in Colonia Hipódromo, I would hear more than I could ever digest about fanatical beliefs. On a dinner table, the salt shaker should not be passed from hand to hand, for the devil thus spreads his influence—as he does when Jews whistle, so *nunca chifles*. If a sibling is ever lying flat on the ground, do not jump over him, for *la muerte lo condenará*—the Angel of Death might quickly follow. . . . I am still perplexed at how Bela, like other women of her generation, conveyed these superstitions to me. Was there not a hint of irony in their tone? Or were they convinced that evil forces, *Yetzer ha-rah*, could suddenly overwhelm us all? Is this too literal an approach—females as practical, males as somewhat fanatical? In the Mexico of my childhood, Jewish men were out making money to support the family, and women stayed at home. But this was only a superficial division, for women had the upper hand when it came to family business. Even after a discussion occurred, *di yiddishe mame* ruled, never through easy-to-understand sound bites but through forceful persuasion that left no room for doubt.

Gender issues might not have been aired, but morality was, and in a way that turned it into the sine-qua-non topic of conversation: Does the individual bring on his own downfall, or is everything predestined? Are we free to battle the forces of darkness? Are they a test the Almighty lays out for us? The Altschulers were not a conflicted crew: society was moving forward toward a less mystical, more scientific future; religion played a role in their daily routine, but it was clear, from the children's various interests, that ideology could soon replace it as the next generation's idol worship. Nowe Brodno, I read in Bela's *diario*, was some forty miles away from Warsaw. To get there, one took a train to cross Prague, a small district, and then crossed the Vistula River. The trip could take hours, but the closeness of the capital, with all its financial and cultural attractions, made life in provincial Nowe Brodno bearable. This proximity to the center of Polish culture allowed for a sense of superiority, a kind of distinction nurtured by the modernity that surrounded them. And it marked Bela's views: in spite of the tricks destiny held in store for her, she would strive to educate herself, to elevate her soul, to be above others, particularly above the Gentile peasantry, whose illiteracy she perceived as a prison.

On Friday night, when the cleanup was over, a white tablecloth was spread on the table by Reisl and Bela. It was *shabbes*. The candlesticks would be placed at the center, surrounded by *challa*s, the traditional bread rolls. Bela's mother was short, obese, and blue-eyed. She knew arithmetic, which made her a *chuchem*, a wise woman. She took care of the store's finances and often traveled with her son Gil to Warsaw to buy merchandise. In Warsaw she also bathed in the *mikveh*. Bela's father, on the other hand, was a Hasid belonging to a mystical sect tied to the emanating glory of the Ba'al Shem Tov. He prayed twice a day and spent long hours reading the Talmud. But he was a family creature, just like my own father: he woke up early every morning to prepare tea for his wife, which he took to her bed; next he cooked breakfast for the entire family; in the afternoon he fixed tea with *chicoria*. A loyal husband, it seems, and a trusted father.

THE ALTSCHULERS DIDN'T last long in Nowe Brodno. A pogrom convinced Shloyme, one of Bela's siblings, to move, and he took the family to nearby Pułtusk, apparently a more protected and peaceful town, where an older brother had established himself with his wife and newborn baby. But the general sense of insecurity—*el miedo*, yet again—soon reached Pułtusk as well, and both Bela and her older brother Gil were victims of physical attacks. By then Bela was an ardent Zionist and often spent her free hours disseminating propaganda at public meetings. Once, a gang of young Poles had caught up with her after school. They pushed her aside, ridiculed her in public, rudely pulled her long pigtails, and screamed at her: "Pig Jew. Why don't you move to Palestine, where you and your putrid friends belong, and help in the cleansing of Poland?" This scene is conveyed in Bela's *diario* with enormous pathos but without embellishment, in a matter-of-fact fashion. The words "Pig Jew"—*puerco judío*—seem written in fire.

I can see why Bobbe Bela would become a Zionist. She has never really talked to me about her adolescent ideologies, and her narrative is silent on this issue. Abraham, my father, has told me her Zionist dreams were short-lived. "I don't believe she ever truly considered moving to Palestine, like some of her friends did," he says. It wasn't only a matter of emigration, though. For her, Palestine was not, I believe, a Jewish state in the future, but an alternative in the present: an escape, a safe haven. Many years later, in the late 1970s, her oldest grandchild would emigrate to Israel. With time she would go visit him. But Israel, in her eyes, was too rough, too ironbound. Could she ever have moved there for good? She is, she always was, a diasporist—a guest, a renter of someone else's property. Still, she paints herself as a restless, committed feminist whose family poverty made it impossible for her to enter institutions of higher learning and thus become a leader of her own people. An accurate picture? Impossible to know. Other women, of not-so-dissimilar backgrounds, did excel: Emma Goldman, Golda Meier, Dvora Baron. Bela's father hired a *lerer*, a Yiddish teacher, whose responsibility it was to instruct the children in religious and secular subjects. But she was ambitious, she wanted more—to the point, as she puts it, of ingratitude. In one scene, Bela has a terrible fight with her parents, which she soon after regrets, for not allowing her to study in a respected Warsaw school. In another, she suggests a number of possible plots for novels she could have written, had she received the proper education. Memoirs are subjective, manipulative, driven by our desire to improve our prospects in human memory, and, as rudimentary as it is, Bela's is no exception. Her flattering self-portrait is in sharp contrast with the domineering, exploitative, conservative lady she has always been, at least within family circles.

True, her literary interests are obvious. She is, and has been since I can remember, a voracious reader, if not a versatile debater. An avid borrower of library books from the CDI, the Jewish sports and entertainment center in Mexico's capital, she is known to the librarians simply as *"Señora Stavchansky."* They see her regularly and are even prepared to send her titles home on request, should she be unfit to make the journey from Colonia Polanco to the northern edge of the city. She reads everything, in Yiddish, Spanish, and, with difficulty, English: from the weekly *Der Shtime* to Chaim Potok's novels, from Sholem Asch to Saul Bellow, even though, as she confessed to me once, *Humboldt's Gift* made absolutely no sense to her. I once gave her a Spanish translation of *My Life as a Man*, by Philip Roth, as a birthday present. She hated its open sexuality, its condescending tone. "Too dirty," she pronounced as she returned it to me. She was not an enthusiastic fan of Bashevis Singer, but in her eyes he was a champion of the Yiddish language in a post-Holocaust era, and thus needed to be read, even in translation, if only to pay homage to a culture that is no more. In private, though, she believed him too erotic as well. (She didn't know, nor did I tell her, that Singer was publishing stories in *Playboy* at the time.) Bashevis's older brother, Israel Joshua, was more akin to her spirit. She adored *The Brothers Ashkenazi*, which she read in Yiddish, as well as *The Family Carnovsky*, a novel we were made to read in junior high. When, in 1978, Isaac Bashevis Singer was awarded the Nobel Prize in Literature, Bela was thunderstruck by excitement, as if she herself had been the recipient of the Stockholm honor. She immediately called me: "What joy, Ilancito!" she said.

Deep inside, she is sentimental and even melodramatic, and her descendants are well aware of it. The most beloved present she ever received was a seventy-five-minute video—kitsch in its most tangible incarnation—made by her three children, Tió Isaac, my father, and Tía Elenita, on the occasion of her eightieth birthday. A sequence of stills, first in black and white and then in color, juxtaposed with real-life sequences of Bela having breakfast, Bela at the beauty salon, Bela in the park, Bela smiling to—and for—her grandchildren, is accompanied by chewing-gum music. I wasn't present when she received it, at a sumptuous fiesta, but heard all about it: Bela wept inconsolably, her life parading before her toward the happiest of endings. Her love of melodrama was revealed in her one and only icon: Danielle Steele. She has read every single one of Steele's sagas of love and money. For a time, she would try to persuade me to read at least one. What Bela liked about them was their emphasis on feelings and the conflicted passions they described; and the fact that

the sex scenes were never too explicit. So infatuated was sh
with Danielle Steele that, much as her father, a G–d-fearing
Hasid at the turn of the century, sought the helpful advice of
erudite rabbis in time of trouble, so did the vulnerable Bela
turn to Steele. When Galia, her youngest granddaughter,
suddenly ran away with a Gentile—a *shaygets*, in Bela's
Yiddish terminology—she wrote a long, tortured letter to
Steele asking for guidance. She asked me if this would be
proper. She was eager to know if novelists of her stature occasionally responded to their fan mail. And she asked if I
could provide her with Steele's address. To me, the whole
situation was painfully comic. I was torn: I loved Bela with
all my might, but I felt she was doing herself a disservice by
seeking help from so cheap a writer. Still, all she asked for
was an address, not my advice. Did my sense of intellectual
superiority need to intrude? Who was I to stop her? Had not
Bela succeeded in rebuilding her life from scratch? In the
end, I gave her the address of Danielle Steele's publisher in
New York and told her not to expect too much: authors of
her stature responded to their mail, but not directly; they did
it through a secretary, who probably had three or four standard letters sent out to millions all over the globe. In the
end, I was wrong, of course. Not only did Danielle Steele
write back to Bela, she actually composed a long and de-
tailed letter about Galia's escapade. She asked Bela to be patient and, more important, to allow the young of today to
seek their own path without intrusion. Steele obviously took
my grandmother's pain quite seriously, and with her reply
made Bela the happiest woman on earth.

She also worshipped, and wished she had corresponded
with, Sholem Aleichem—Pan Sholem Aleichem—about

whom I heard her talk at considerable length while growing up. No doubt my own passion for *Tevye the Dairyman* was a result of her influence. Several times in 1974, Bobbe Bela took me to see *Violinista en el tejado*, the Spanish adaptation of *Fiddler on the Roof*. The lead actor was the legendary Manolo Fábregas, a megastar on the Mexican stage and the child of refugees of the Spanish Civil War. The melodies of the syrupy show still cling in my mind: "*Si yo fuera rico, yaddah, yaddaaaah daddah daddah daaaah* . . ." Bobbe Bela obviously thought we would all get a strong dose of *Yiddishkeit* by listening to an imposing Gentile actor portray Sholem Aleichem's character in a way that recalled Anthony Quinn in *Zorba the Greek*. I wasn't as attuned to the delicacies of translation as I would later become, but even then it struck me as fanciful that a completely Gentile cast would talk about dybbuks and shlimazls. Could a goy teach *Yiddishkeit*?

Bobbe Bela often reminisced about public readings that the author of her favorite characters—Tevye himself, as well as Motl Peyse, Menachem Mendel, and Shayne Shayndl—delivered to cheering crowds in Warsaw and all through Galicia. In Nowe Brodno, these gatherings were a catalyst of sorts for the Jewish community, illuminating moral values in a rapidly changing time. Sholem Aleichem, in a way, was a rabbi, a spiritual leader: in an age of secularism, wherein hordes of Jews abandoned tradition, he, more than any other Yiddish fabulist (Isaac Leib Peretz, Sholem Asch, Itzik Manger), articulated the dilemmas of ideology and faith with the kind of humor people found utterly irresistible. He died in 1916, around the time when Bela turned ten years of age, and was buried in Brooklyn. The last years of his life had been marked by dislocation, first in Denmark, then in the United States. She was sorry not to have attended a reading, for, as her *diario* silently acknowledges, she nourished the dream of one day becoming a writer herself: a prestigious one, capable of hypnotizing big audiences with enchanting tales of love and treason. Truth is, she had neither the imagination nor the verbal dexterity to accomplish this goal. I cannot recall a single occasion on which she told me a story. Nor can I remember her having a disposition toward the "plot lines of our convoluted world," as Charles Dickens once put it. Her dream, I think, was the result of a distinguished career as reader: Bela, after all, would devour full books in a matter of days, although she hardly reflected on them with others; it was, clearly, her way of escape, of inhabiting a reality far better than the one fate had bestowed on her. And if she only had the talent and opportunity to shape that imaginary reality, to make it her own, she would be a far happier person.

For Bela in essence was sour and unforgiving. The strategy of abandoning Polish and Russian in order to begin a new life is, at first sight, a survivor's triumph. But it also denotes an uncompromising approach to the past: pain and unpleasantness ought to be ignored, eliminated from memory, nullified. This approach permeated her whole existence. My father would often complain of not having the chance to discuss anything remotely painful with his mother. When he was a boy, she had several miscarriages—or, most probably, they were abortions. He and Tío Isaac would be given money and sent out to the movies in a nearby theater. They knew, of course, their mother was undergoing some sort of operation—in my mind, I picture buckets of blood—but when they returned home, not a word would be uttered about it. Silence reigned. Can I blame Bela for censoring her past? Isn't immigration, by definition, a search for a different self? History, in her view, was a cruel monster ready to obliterate everything in its path. Of Bela's five siblings, three perished under the Nazis. Their individual stories are heartbreaking. I invoke them frequently, puzzled at how human affairs are ruled by accidents. What else, if not randomness, explains her survival?

Herschel, her oldest brother, managed to emigrate to Rio de Janeiro with his young wife, Javche, and their little children. Brazil had opened its doors to the Jews; Herschel saw prosperity ahead and even prophesied that the entire Altschuler family would soon be transported to the New World. It was not meant to be. Javche died tragically while giving birth to their third son. Herschel returned to Warsaw with the children, and they were all killed in Auschwitz. Bela's mother died shortly before Herschel's return and is buried in Pułtusk, but almost everyone else ended in the gas chambers. Three of Bela's siblings—Gil, Moishe, and Dovidl—emigrated to the New World at various times: the first in the early 1920s to Tampico, a busy coastal town on the Gulf of Mexico; the second to Paris around the same time, where he miraculously survived the Holocaust hidden on a farm and became a partisan; and Dovidl remained near his parents and Bela until she was already resettled in Mexico. From Tampico, Gil sent letters back to Pułtusk—in Yiddish, all of them lost—promising to send money to bring his parents, Bela, and Dovidl. But saving enough money for the travel expenses, and gathering all the necessary legal documents, proved to be a most difficult task. She waited for long months as the bureaucracy moved at turtle speed. Finally, at the age of twenty-one, she was ready. Luck was on her side: *"Me saqué la lotería,"* she once told me in Spanish. It was mid-1930, and the outbursts of anti-Semitism were becoming more common. The prospects of freedom and a solid education, especially for women, were almost nonexistent. Also, Poland embraced laws drafting Jewish cadets into the army, many of whom were subjected to the cruelest of regimes and were not seen alive again. I remember Bobbe Bela telling me once, for example, how a male friend of hers had cut off some fingers on his right hand so as to avoid the draft. "Better an invalid than a conscript for the czar, *¿no es cierto?*" I asked her if the czar was Poland's ruler. "No, he ruled Russia, but it was all the same."

This portion of Bobbe Bela's past feels like a horror tale by H. P. Lovecraft. I see it as if through a veil, with a bizarre sense of having suddenly been invited into a medieval landscape, filled with witches and wolves. Is this a deliberate feeling she wants to provoke? Dates are confusing, historical figures appear in anachronistic settings, people's lives are reduced to a single harrowing incident, and rumors prevail. As an adolescent, I remember her talking about the accusation that Jews killed Gentile children and used their blood to bake matzoh. And about the incessant question, did Jews kill Jesus Christ? This feeling of bewilderment, of course I realize, pertains not only to her universe; I experienced it during my Yiddish schooling, in scores of books and movies. The Jewish past in the Old World, the message was, oscillates between laughter and fear: on one side is Sholem Aleichem's enchanting universe of miserable yet gentle, compassionate souls, all tied together by tradition; on the other is a terrifying atmosphere where Jews are worms.

When Bela's papers arrived, her mother packed a single suitcase with all her belongings—"They constitute your only dowry," she said—and, in deep sorrow, the girl said goodbye. "*Zai gezunt.* . . . *Shreibm undz a bribele, Bela main tayerer.*" Did she know it was the last time she would see her parents? She claims she did, but her parents nurtured the dream of following her. The trip lasted a total of thirty-five days. Her *diario* lists October 29, 1930, as the date she left Warsaw's railway station. Her siblings and their in-laws came to wish her happiness. Her father, his hands on Bela's head, said the Hebrew blessing: "*Baruch Atah Adonai, Eloheynu Melej A-Holam.* . . ." The train took her to Berlin—where she spent time with an old boyfriend, of whom, I believe, she still keeps a yellowish photograph taken on the Alexanderplatz—then to Amsterdam. Her brother Gil had sent her a ticket for the *Sparndam*, on the Holland-America Line. Hitler would be elected German chancellor three years later.

As it turned out, she severed the only connections to her past. With Gil she continued to have relations, but Gil didn't like Bela's husband, Srulek. He thought of him as a failure, a businessman with neither vision nor guts. And Bela, in his view, was oversensitive. So it was mostly in connection with finances that Gil's name was invoked. Bela's other two siblings in the New World fared better, but only slightly. Her brother Moishe had married a French woman. One of his children, Tío Marcel, joined the resistance and eventually moved to Israel, where he was enlisted in Tzahal, Israel's army, during the War of Independence. But once the Jewish State was established, in 1948, Israel lost its appeal; he moved into Bela's home in Ciudad de México, where his relationship with her was tense and quickly deteriorated. He regularly complained she treated him unfairly, like a servant, sending him to do errands like buying challah at Señor Burakoff's store. Soon he moved to Guadalajara, a prosperous metropolis. Tío Marcel married a Sephardic Jewess, brought his father over from Paris, and became a shoemaker and eventually a very prosperous entrepreneur. Ironically, for decades the family in Mexico's capital—Bela's three children and their progeny—knew next to nothing about him and his descendants in Guadalajara. The reason, it seems, is a fight Bela had with Moishe, most surely about money. Perhaps he wanted to borrow some from my grandfather Srulek, Bela's husband, when Srulek was dying of stomach cancer. Moishe wanted to buy a house in Guadalajara, but the Stavchanskys had no money. Medical expenses were high, and Zeyde Srulek's ruinous business deals had engulfed the family in debt. Moishe was offended and never spoke to Bela again—ever. She dealt with this by erasing his name from the family's memory. I, for one, don't remember her ever uttering it, even though my father occasionally made an elusive reference to his Tío Moishe.

How was it possible, to this day I ask, for Bela to ignore the remnants of her past? I found out about the Guadalajara connection the day Marcel's oldest daughter, Sandra—aka Sany—arrived unexpectedly in the late 1970s, announcing an end to the feud. "Enough," she said in a rather confident tone. "The quarrel is so old, nobody even seems to remember what the feud is about." And she challenged my father and others to recall what had sparked the anger between her grandfather and Bela. Nobody could; and if they did, it was time to forget, for a new generation had been raised, and the sins of the parents are not to be inherited by their children. In time, everyone came around. Only Bela herself remained silent, trapped for years in her bitterness, even after my parents and uncles happily visited Guadalajara to spend precious time with their rediscovered relatives.

To me Moishe's story is hard to fathom, but the one about David Altschuler is a testament to Bela's astonishing instinct to survive and also of her fierce destructiveness. My father, my brother, and I all see it, each in his own way, as a symbol of the kind of tragedy always looming ahead of us. Dovidl was the youngest of Bela's siblings, the most fragile and inventive. His was a bohemian, sensitive spirit. He immigrated around 1938 to Mexico's capital—also helped by Gil, but he landed in Bela's house. My father was five years old. It is mostly through him that I've learned the details of the story. My father turned Tío David into an idol. He sided with him when Bela harassed him. Was he really a talent? It is impossible for me to know; beyond the myths my father constructed, Dovidl's odyssey is buried in secrecy. Bela doesn't talk about him. Nor does my own uncle Tío Isaac. And there is no one else alive to be asked.

Tío David dreamed of becoming an artist (a painter, perhaps a writer), of devoting his days to the appreciation of the beauties of nature, but his hopes were ruined by Bela's conservatism. He would spend the entire morning at home, wandering from one room to another in pajamas, with a teacup held in his hand, reflecting on the immortality of the soul, awaiting artistic inspiration. His hours were devoted to avid reading: first in Yiddish, then—slowly—in Spanish. Perhaps he hoped to become the writer I would become half a century later. Or he might have pondered the opportunities that lay ahead of him in the Americas, wondering, as I often do, if success is not a product of sheer and absolute chance, for talent is crucial but surely secondary as one shapes a career by throwing the net as wide as possible and hoping an abundance of fish will fall into it. But Tío David was not given a fair chance. His sister Bela, at first a friend, rapidly became an enemy—in a matter of weeks. She disliked him thoroughly, and apparently so did Gil, probably under her influence. A hoodlum, they said, a *bueno-paranada*. They believed their younger sibling was too vulnerable. He could easily fall into the wrong circles. So they decided that Tío David would move to a form of internal exile in Tampico, far from the immediate family, where Gil had a furniture store. Gil would name David its general manager. In Tampico, if he wanted, he could pursue his artistic and literary passions.

Their fears became a reality. At the store, Tío David got involved with one of the workers—a Gentile, of course—whose name, I believe, was Nelly. I have never known any details about her. Nelly in Mexico's Spanish is a shortened version of Nélida. But I prefer to call her Nelly, for the name rings truer to the legend. She obviously saw in him—he was, by then, "David," no longer the alien "Dovidl"—as a sensitive soul and a promising Jewish husband. Who was Nelly? Where did she come from? Was she able to provide the love Tío David did not receive from his immediate family? At any rate, soon Nelly was pregnant. The Altschulers in the nation's capital could not tolerate that, of course. His involvement with a shiksa merited excommunication. He was a *desgraciado*, a scoundrel, exiled once again from the Altschulers, this time to the newly formed State of Israel, where Bela and Tío Gil sent him, *huyendo*, throwing him away so as not to have to deal with him anymore. If he could not be saved from himself, at least the family could be spared the embarrassment.

"Ysröel," as Bobbe Bela always pronounced it: the Promised Land, sure, but also a safe haven for philanderers and bankrupt businessmen of the diaspora. Tío David and my father loved each other dearly. The elder was unconventional, irreverent, rebellious, and my father emulated these qualities as much as he could. And as an ancestor who shared my father's insurgent élan vital, and as Bela's antithesis, he was a hero of mine and my brother's as well. In Israel, David was even more unhappy. *Un malparido*, a born loser. Did Nelly give birth to a child? Yes, it was *un secreto a voces*, a widely known secret, for everyone was aware that Tío David had added a bastard child to the family constellation, even though no one wanted to openly recognize the baby. Not surprisingly, Nelly had such anger for the Altschulers that her relationship with David quickly broke apart, and the child, a little boy, never saw his father. *Más vale olvido que pena*, better to forget than to suffer. As for the whereabouts of Tío David in Israel, they remained a mystery: Was he in Haifa or Tel Aviv? Did he have an address? News was sparse. At some point, he got involved with another woman, a Romanian Jew, but somehow this liaison also received the disapproval of Tío David's siblings in Mexico and collapsed. By the time my father, on his honeymoon in 1960, met him one last time, he was psychologically unstable, a ruined soul incapable of remembering anything. Not much later, he was institutionalized in a psychiatric asylum, paid for by the Mexican family. That, as far as I have been able to gather, is the end of his story, for when and how he died nobody knows. To be left to oblivion—is there a worse ignominy?

The story has an unpalatable coda, one with an even more calamitous conclusion. I thought, for a while, of adding it in parentheses, but doing so would diminish its echoes and affront, yet again, Tío David's blessed memory. More than two decades later, very soon after I had emigrated to New York, a beloved family friend, the journalist Golde Cuckier, died with her three children—the youngest, Ilan, still a toddler, had been named after me—in a preventable Aeroméxico plane crash en route to Manzanillo. A day or so after the accident, overwhelmed by sadness and spending half of my days reciting the Kaddish in synagogue, I read in the *New York Times* the list of passengers. Not only were Golde and her children in the plane, but so was David's son, along with his wife and children. Was it an act of divine will, to eliminate all traces of Dovidl's steps on this earth? I often ask myself this question, knowing, of course, that I'll get no answer.

ABOARD THE TRANS-ATLANTIC boat *Sparndam*, Bela found few other Yiddish speakers, but when she landed in Tampico, the verbal, social, and natural landscapes changed dramatically. Mexico: How did she end up in such an alien, exotic, "uncivilized" locale? How were these ports of entry chosen? What made Herschel, Bela's older brother, travel to Rio de Janeiro? And what made their sibling Gil choose the ancient land of the Aztecs? How on earth did they know about these unlikely places in the misnamed Nuevo Mundo? At that time shtetl dwellers and other Eastern European Jews were emigrating to North and South America, especially to New York and, to a lesser extent, the Argentine Pampas, thanks in large degree to the encouragement of philanthropist Baron Maurice de Hirsch. But other nations of the Americas were also actively seeking immigrants at the turn of the century. In Buenos Aires, since the mid-nineteenth century a debate on the backwardness of the countryside had established that the only way to "civilize" the nation was by developing cosmopolitan urban centers as much as possible. Immigrants were perceived as agents of progress and capitalism, and, in spite of a strong feeling of anti-Semitism sponsored by the Catholic Church, the doors were opened to the Jews. They settled in small communes in central Argentina, such as Moisésville and Rajíl. By the second generation, though, most of them had moved to Buenos Aires and other major cities. Brazil, too, had opened the doors to Eastern European Jews. By 1915, Argentina had around twenty-six thousand, Brazil approximately eighteen thousand. In the Southern Hemisphere, these were the largest magnets for Yiddish-speaking immigrants, followed, in descending order, by Mexico, Cuba, Colombia, and Peru.

It is next to impossible—*un acertijo*, a puzzle—to track down why Bela ended up in Mexico. Or so it seems to me. Was it because it was close to the United States, and a different destination at a time when Yiddish-language Eastern European dailies were wondering, in loud editorials, how many immigrants America could really digest? Or was it a comment by a forgotten friend, a chance encounter, or a small newspaper advertisement, perhaps, in a corner of the section devoted to opportunities abroad? What is unquestionable was that the U.S. immigration quota was restricting entry for Jewish immigrants, and an alternative needed to be found. This quota, in fact, made Bela and her descendants Mexican, did it not? At the heart of her rebirth across the Atlantic was a negation: Thou shall not be American. Whatever it was, I cannot avoid describing it as *ain tzufal, un accidente:* the enigma of arrival as an accident of fate. In her memoir, Bela's arrival in Tampico is described in astonishing detail. As the vessel approached the port, she saw from afar the many shanties, *las chozas y casuchas*. The town was rustic and primitive, nothing like Warsaw in sophistication. She disembarked from the *Sparndam* and was exposed, for the first time, to a different type of muzhik: the mestizo. Repeatedly, I have tried to visualize these first few minutes— the shock, the disquieting confusion. It appears, at least at first sight, as if Bela's past, tense and miserable, was replaced by a destiny equally tense and miserable.

She would often invoke the wise Ecclesiastes: *nada hay nuevo bajo el sol*, there is nothing new under the sun. Often she thought of returning to Nowe Brodno and her parents and friends. How could she not? The chaos, the anxiety came to her in the syncopated rhythms of Spanish, a language that at first overwhelmed Bela. It was too guttural. But it was hers: to survive, she would need to master it, to make it her own. One day, she would need to feel as if Polish was nothing but a loose thread in her past, a memory. She would think: What is "nostalgia" in Polish? And she would not be able to come up with the right word, for it had retreated to depths she would no longer be capable of reaching.

In only a few weeks she realized Tampico was unworthy of her, and so she decided to move on to Ciudad de México, *the* commercial and cultural magnet for the entire region. The railway system had been built more than thirty years before, but the revolution of 1910 impeded its updating, so it took her twenty-eight hours to reach the capital by train. She quickly found room and board, and soon felt embraced by the vigor and enthusiasm of a thriving, Yiddish-speaking Jewish community. Bela quickly realized her potential: she would marry and multiply, prosper and reign.

The Jewish presence in the city was limited to a handful of neighborhoods. A tour today through the downtown Calle Justo Sierra, near the cathedral, where the Sephardic Temple Monte Sinaí still stands, not far from its Ashkenazic counterpart, Nidje Israel, on the adjacent Calle Revillajijedo, allows the visitor to stand on the sites where the Holy Office of the Inquisition publicly burned a handful of crypto-Jews who in 1492, when Cristóbal Colón found an alternative course across the Atlantic in his search for the Indies, sought to escape the intolerance of Spain. These Sephardic immigrants arrived some three centuries before the Ashkenazic newcomers. But is it right to describe them as *inmigrantes judíos*? On the street, Bela and her peers were often described as *rusitos* and *polacos*. Their identity stood out. In contrast, their Iberian counterparts blended more easily: they looked Spanish. The long and fruitful cohabitation of Iberian Jews with Muslims and Christians in the peninsula had darkened their skin and in many cases had also lessened, if not altogether erased, their piety. Their fate was tragic, though. Three hundred years later, what was left of their traditions and costumes? Could many still call themselves Sephardim? Were they familiar with Ladino—Judeo-Spanish, also known as *judesmo*—a dialect that recalls old Spanish and Portuguese but is written in Hebrew characters? How many conversos settled in Nueva España—New Spain, as Mexico was known during colonial times—it is impossible to know. By most historical accounts, the number oscillates between three and four thousand. A substantial minority among them were *marranos* (in Hebrew, *annusim*), conversos whose devotion to the Jewish faith, though kept in secrecy, was still strong.

The Inquisition was a mighty institution in the New

World. Established in 1569, its strength reached a height in Mexico in 1596. So-called Judaizers had settled in the country undisturbed, especially in the northern sections. Roundups began to take place. The most celebrated case against a *marrano* was that of Luis de Carvajal y de la Cueva, the Portuguese-born governor of the New Kingdom of León, whose arrest in 1589 was only the tip of the iceberg. His whole family—including his sister Francisca, his brother-in-law Francisco Rodríguez de Matos, and his nephew Luis de Carvajal "el Mozo"—were tortured and in some cases burned in autos-da-fé. It is to Governor Luis de Carvajal to whom the following Sephardic epigraph is ascribed:

Adiós España, tierra bonita,   *Goodbye to Spain, the tender land,*
tierra de la consolación.   *the land of my consoling.*

By the early years of the seventeenth century, such public cases had diminished but not altogether ceased. Between the time when Marina de Carvajal, one of Luis de Carvajal's sisters, already insane, was burned, and the 1810 independence movement, led by a Catholic priest, Miguel Hidalgo y Castilla, himself a target of the Inquisition for *judaizar,* the crypto-Jews were totally assimilated to the Catholic environment. "Total," of course, is a strong word. Remnants still exist and are traceable, to the savvy eye. When I was growing up, for instance, I remember visiting a Gentile friend whose mother always swept dirt toward the center of the room for fear of passing near the mezuzahs hanging on door frames. She would always change—automatically, I dare say—the tablecloth on Friday night. By the time Bela descended from the boat, the only vestige of their existence was in popular culture. During my childhood, the word *judío*, in devout Catholic circles, was synonymous with "stingy," "abusive," "treacherous." My own home in the Copilco neighborhood was half a mile away from Cerro del Judío, a neighborhood that at one point in the eighteenth century served as a *marrano* enclave. And a legend claims that cabalistic Jews from Spain wandered north to found Monterrey, and its inhabitants, the *regiomontanos*, are well known for their frugality and unscrupulousness. There is also a type of brown bean known in Mexican Spanish as *judías*.

The arrival of the Ashkenazim from Russia and Eastern Europe in the last couple of decades of the nineteenth century was seen as an altogether new beginning. The two waves couldn't have been more different. In the sixteenth century, religious persecution and purity of blood—*la pureza de sangre*—brought them to this *refugio* far away from Europe, but whereas the *marranos* arrived in disguise, and the conversos had already given up their Judaism, their successors, the Ashkenazim, also victimized as a result of their faith, never hid their religious affiliation. They didn't need to. An era of freedom and openness after the 1910 revolution, and the peaceful, fruitful cohabitation of marginalized groups, was the approach taken by the Mexican government. In fact, President Plutarco Elías Calles, in office before the Second World War, approached by the Alliance Israélite Universelle and other international organizations, publicly invited Jews to settle in Mexico. His rationale was simple: Jews were catalysts in emerging capitalist societies, and Mexico, in the first quarter of the twentieth century, after the bloody revolution of 1910, was hoping to leave behind its feudal past and become a stable and strong economy. But the groundwork for Mexico's Jewish community was laid earlier, in distinct periods and from disparate geographies—between 1880 and 1930, when immigrants arrived from Eastern Europe, and in the 1960s and later, when a wave arrived from the Mediterranean (what once was the Ottoman Empire)—Syria, Lebanon, the Balkans, northern Africa, and the Middle East. By the time Bela set foot in Tampico and, subsequently, in Ciudad de México, a thriving community was awaiting her. The first Ashkenazic synagogue and *mikveh* were built in 1890, and Bela discovered the much-needed refuge from her solitude, the hot Club Centro at Calle Tacuba #15, where community activities of all sorts—weddings, balls, parties, theater, poker, and so on—could be planned. Between 1910 and 1920, some three thousand arrived, and the number increased threefold during the next decade. Since most immigrants were socialists, communists, and Bundists, among their first projects was the building of a Yiddish-language day school (which they did in 1924), a Jewish Commintern (aka Der Yiddisher Centraler Comitet), and a number of philanthropic organizations that might allow Eastern European Jews to climb the social ladder. Their success was tremendous: in only a matter of decades, many shtetl dwellers opened a variety of businesses, from jewelry to leather, brewing, and clothing, and became quite wealthy. Culture flourished in every respect, and a couple of Yiddish dailies—*Der Shtime* and *Der Veg*, which I fondly remember reading—served as organs of cohesion.

YIDDISH, *HER* YIDDISH . . . and mine: I remember Bobbe Bela, already a widow, arriving at our home, most likely on Sundays, talking in beautiful Yiddish with my parents and, less consistently, to me. I would listen to her attentively: her uncareful pronunciation of *der mame-loshen*, a bastardized dialect already infused with Spanishisms, mostly culinary: *gefiltefish a la veracruzana, knaydlach en caldo*, and *knishes mit mole*; and, also, expressions including adjectives, such as *portalishe nutniks* and *Indianishe mentshn*. With most of her grandchildren, Bela would use an ungrammatical, heavily accented Spanish, occasionally lapsing into Yiddish; but I always had a particular affection for the Jewish tongue and, when it was appropriate, would respond to her in it. Yiddish, in fact, was the mortar between the bricks of the community. In the 1940s, a nascent Yiddish literary scene, with figures such as poet Jacobo Glantz (the father of essayist Margo Glantz and a distant relative of mine) and journalist Salomón Kahan, established itself at the forefront of Jewish letters in the Southern Hemisphere. Some of these writers maintained correspondence with members of Di Yunge, the Yiddish avant-garde in New York. But literature was a small, almost insignificant token when seen against the larger picture. The Eastern European settlers, secular in their manner, understood language to be the conduit of tradition. They refused to give it up at the speed of their siblings north of the Rio Grande—New York, Philadelphia, Chicago, Detroit. Their offspring, to remain Jewish, needed to be raised in the same verbal tradition. And so language was a tool of continuity, the mechanism through which Bela and her peers managed, magically, to go on living, as it were, in Eastern Europe.

Bela's generation used to refer to the Jewish community as *der yishuv*, the settlement, one not unlike the *shtetelech* in Galicia. In fact, it seems as if they managed to re-create a shtetl in the metropolis, to reghettoize themselves in enclaves with little but business contact with the outside world.

Did she ever fully leave Nowe Brodno? Was she not, as were her peers, a genius in reviving, across the Atlantic, almost the exact same environment—*al pie de la letra*, as the Spanish expression goes, "to the dot"—she had been exiled from? When the time came to choose a career, my father, her Abremele, became an actor in the Yiddish theater and, also and more significantly, in plays translated from the Yiddish and about the Jewish world that was no more.

In her *diario*, Bela describes, in emotional detail, how she met, at Calle Tacuba #15, her beloved Srulek Stavchan-sky, a centavoless Ukrainian immigrant from Khashchevate, a small milling town southwest of Lwów, and of course a Yiddish speaker as well. She remembers the first phone call she received from him, and the sunny Sunday afternoon in Alameda Park when Srulek asked to marry her and kissed her—in her Spanish, *se me declaró*. In my imagination, Diego Rivera's painting *Sunday at the Alameda Central* includes them both, next to each other, just behind José Guadalupe Posada. The description of the kiss is narrated briefly, as if Bela, at the time of writing, was conscious of the potential eroticism of the scene, dirty in her eyes, and thus decided to repress it as best she could. Exactly four moths after her ar-rival, they became engaged. Their marriage took place in 1930, also at the Club Centro at Tacuba #15. Her brother Gil, still in Tampico, was unable to attend the wedding, but helped the young couple financially. Their poverty, nonethe-less, was abysmal. They shared a house with another family and struggled to make ends meet. Zeyde Srulek had arrived with only his most basic belongings, but he was a lucky fel-low: he borrowed money to buy shoelaces and razor blades, and when he sold these, he bought a lottery ticket. He won, and used the money to buy a hardware store on the busy corner of Calles Academia and Corregidor. His luck did not last long, though. Hardship forced him to sell it, and he became an employee of a brother-in-law. They moved to Tampico, where Gil, still on good terms with them, helped him open a children's clothing store. The couple prospered and multiplied. Tío Isaac was born. No *mohel* was available in town, so one had to be brought in from Veracruz to perform the ritual circumcision. After a year, the family returned to Ciudad de México, where Srulek opened an animal-food store, Molino El Venado, the predecessor of the Forrajera Nacional, S.A., which my father would inherit on his father's death. They moved to a newly built home in the eastern section of Colonia Anzures and then to another, more modern one in the nearby Colonia Portales, both Jewish bastions. It wasn't until her children were married that the Jewish community as a whole gravitated north to more affluent neighborhoods like Polanco, Las Lomas, and Tecamachalco, where politicians and the *nouveaux riches* settled.

Bela kept her children close to her. She trained them to be first Jewish and then Mexican, and exhorted them to embrace Spanish as their mother tongue but keep Yiddish as "the Jewish—i.e., intimate—language." As was common, they met Gentiles only in the neighborhood, for kids were sent to Jewish schools and after-school programs. This separation created in them—and in their entire generation—an ambivalent sense of identity. What made them Mexican? And how did they distinguish themselves from other Jews? This duality was, and still is, much more accentuated among Mexican Jews than in their counterparts in the United States, and I daresay, even in Brazil and Argentina. Yiddish, among Ashkenazim, was the umbilical cord with Europe, and was never fully cut. Spanish made them native citizens with full civil rights, but mixed marriages were few, and contact with Catholics and other immigrants was minimal. In short, it was an insular mentality.

All this, needless to say, was destined to change as I was growing up. The ambience persisted, the nostalgia for shtetl life, but the term "shmaltz" had become ubiquitous. It was clear the shtetl had not been a paradise after all. It was crowded with ruffians and criminals. Praying to G–d? Devoting one's whole life to tradition? Well, a portion of the population did, but the place was stern, miserable, cold. At first, the Holocaust, the fatal blow to Yiddish as a living vehicle of communication—how many languages in history have perished so suddenly, in the span of five to six years?—elevated the shtetl to the stature of lost kingdom. But the State of Israel emphasized that Jews were not ethereal beings but flesh-and-blood citizens, militaristic, down-to-earth. And as Mexico struggled to modernize by opening itself up to the world, it was clear Jews could no longer be aloof, unconcerned, apathetic. They were part of the nation, just like everyone else, with misgivings about their *mexicanidad* perhaps—what Mexicans call *malinchismo*—but fully responsible for their actions. None of Bela's children finished a college education, but others in their generation did, my mother included. And though the Jewish day schools, by definition private, keep a close eye on early education, college was the place where exposure to the outside world was inevitable. The result is clear: divorces increased, interreligious marriages were more common (two of Bela's nine grandchildren—my brother, Darián, included—married Gentiles), and the degree of Jewish participation in Mexican public life increased considerably. Whereas not a single Jew of

Bela's generation held a high-ranking government job, several did a generation after, and many more in my own.

The Colegio Israelita de México (aka Der Yiddisher Shule in Mexique), in Colonia del Valle, which I attended from kindergarten to high school—a total of fifteen years—embodied the views on history, education, and culture sustained by Bela's immigrant generation. From outside, nothing about the building signaled its Jewishness: it had no lettered signs, no insignias. It must have had more than a thousand children enrolled. Its ideology was decidedly Bundist: secular in vision, embracing culture as the true religion. Rosh Hashanah, Yom Kippur, Succoth, and other Jewish holidays were celebrated, but in a nonmilitant fashion. What made us Jews, we were told, was not G–d but the intellectual and spiritual legacy carried along for three millennia. The immolation of the Jewish people was not stressed—suffering wasn't a ticket to superiority.

Yiddish class, our link with the past, was obligatory. It met every day, sometimes even twice. At a time when, in the Jewish world at large, the number of speakers, whose average age was around fifty, made it a less used language than Serbo-Croatian, we were taught how to read, write, and speak fluently. Students attended lectures in Yiddish and were assigned history volumes in Yiddish, too. I remember submerging myself in long novels by Israel Joshua Singer, Sholem Asch, and Sholem Aleichem. And I read innumerable Hasidic tales and Holocaust poems as well. Understandably, a majority of the student population saw this as a nuisance: why study Yiddish, a dying tongue? They sat for their exams almost mechanically and quickly forgot what they had learned the moment they left the classroom. But for me Yiddish was a passion: I loved its cadence, its hallucinatory beat. At fifteen or sixteen, I fervently reread passages from *Die Mishpokhe Carnovsky* and *Kiddush ha-Shem* at home and memorized poems. I especially recall a melancholy march by Hirsh Glik that became the hymn of the United Partisan Organization in 1943 and has become a memorial for martyred Jews:

Never say that you are going your last way,
Though lead-filled skies above blot out the blue of day.
The hour for which we long will certainly appear,
The earth shall thunder 'neath our tread that we are here!

זאָג ניט קיין מאָל אַז דו גייסט דעם לעצטן וועג,
כאָטש הימלען בלייענע פֿאַרשטעלן בלויע טעג,
קומען וועט נאָך אונדזער אויסגעבענקטע שעה—
ס'וועט אַ פּויק טאָן אונדזער טראָט—מיר זיינען דאָ!

From lands of green palm trees to lands all white with snow,
We are coming with our pain and with our woe,
And where'er a spurt of our blood did drop,
Our courage will again sprout from that spot.

פֿון גרינעם פּאַלמענלאַנד ביז ווייסן לאַנד פֿון שניי,
מיר קומען אָן מיט אונדזער פּיין, מיט אונדזער וויי,
און וווּ געפֿאַלן ס'איז אַ שפּריץ פֿון אונדזער בלוט,
שפּראָצן וועט דאָרט אונדזער גבֿורה, אונדזער מוט.

For us the morning sun will radiate the day,
And the enemy and past will fade away,

But should the dawn delay or sunrise wait too long,
Then let all future generations sing this song.

ס'וועט די מאָרגנזון באַגילדן אונדז דעם היינט,
און דער נעכטן וועט פֿאַרשווינדן מיטן פֿיינד,
נאָר אויב פֿאַרזאָמען וועט די זון אין דעם קאיאָר—
ווי אַ פּאַראָל זאָל גיין דאָס ליד פֿון דור צו דור.

This song was written with our blood and not with lead,
This is no song of free birds flying overhead,
But a people amid crumbling walls did stand,
They stood and sang this song with rifles held in hand.

דאָס ליד געשריבן איז מיט בלוט און ניט מיט בליי,
ס'איז ניט קיין לידל פֿון אַ פֿויגל אויף דער פֿריי,
דאָס האָט אַ פֿאָלק צווישן פֿאַלנדיקע ווענט —
דאָס ליד געזונגען מיט נאַגאַנעס אין די הענט!

I also sought out Yiddish films of the 1920s, 1930s, and 1940s. If a copy was available, I showed it in a cinema club I organized every Wednesday at the school auditorium. I loved watching Maurice Schwarz and Molly Picon. So fever-ish was my enthusiasm that I began to dream myself into Sholem Aleichem's stories.

Yiddish, for me, was truly the mother tongue, whereas Spanish, the street language, the one I most often used, was the father tongue. The duality was not artificial: Jewishness (though not Judaism, at least not then) was in my heart and soul. There was nothing cerebral about it: it was, I was taught, the source of endurance, the fountain of life. Spanish was also taught at school, of course, and so was Hebrew, although the latter was introduced fairly late. Zionism didn't become the predominant dogma until I was about to leave school. This brought along the slow demise of Yiddish and the triumphant embrace of Hebrew as the language of the Jewish people of today and tomorrow. But Hebrew felt constructed to me, artificial. On Monday mornings, students sang the Mexican and Israeli anthems and pledged allegiance to the two flags. And yet, although I learned it fast, I couldn't quite feel comfortable with its cadence: Zionist patriotism seemed foreign. It wasn't really mine.

So . . . what was the purpose of my whole Yiddish education, its subtext? Was it not an anachronism to teach youngsters about a universe that had disappeared? I left school convinced that Sholem Aleichem, I. L. Peretz, and Theodor Herzl were essential figures of our country. How much did I know about Cuauhtémoc, the last Aztec ruler, and about Benito Juárez? And about thinkers like Alfonso Reyes and Octavio Paz? How many poems by Mexicans like Ramón López Velarde had I read? Not enough, not nearly enough. I had been raised in a bubble, unconscious of the Gentile environment around me. Not long ago, as I passed through Ciudad de México, I did what every memoirist dreams of doing but should avoid: I revisited my old school. The dilapidated building was sold to the government in the mid-1980s and houses offices for some unspecified ministry. A guard allowed me in through the back door, and I wandered around the corridors, hunting for the ghosts of my childhood and adolescence. The shock was great: the bubble was empty, its pupils gone, along with the ideals that shaped them. The socialist dream nurtured inside those four walls with us as its guinea pigs has been replaced by sheer individualism. My old friends, of course, are, like me, parents; they send their own kids to the new Yiddisher Shule, a flamboyant, architecturally innovative building in the northern section of the city. Bela's generation is no longer in command, so nostalgic Jewishness tied to Eastern Europe has been replaced by American pop culture. Yiddish—Bela's Yiddish, *my* Yiddish—has almost totally faded from the curriculum, replaced by English and French. On my way out, the guard told me the government is planning to tear down the place in the near future. I'm not surprised. Wasn't the school already scheduled for demolition in my last year there, when Israeli *shlikhim*, pedagogical envoys, described it as "unfit for progressive education"?

BOBBE BELA'S JOURNEY parades slowly in front of my eyes, as if I were watching the long video movie made when she turned eighty. Smiles, tears, feuds—the melodrama of everyday life. Tío Isaac first became a travel agent, then a jeweler, and finally a respected painter; Tía Elenita, Bela's daughter, married a leather manufacturer; a grandson became a physicist in Israel's Weitzman Institute; a granddaughter had an early fight against cancer; two grandchildren divorced; one became a kabbalist. The turning point for her was Zeyde Srulek's death in 1965. The passages about it in her *diario* are the ones where fear—*el miedo*—is felt most tangibly. But her family brought her back to life and kept her busy. Srulek's death, in fact, is the closest Bela comes to addressing pain—pain and tragedy. There is no reference in her narrative to her lost siblings, killed by the Nazis, or to the memory of her parents. Each time I reread it, I experience the same ambivalence toward her. Though Bobbe Bela is an enviably active person, she remains a Pole in Mexico, one who refused to speak a single word of Polish ever, ever again but only halfheartedly adopted the Spanish language—a hybrid, an in-between. The last pages of her narrative are dry, tense, and not descriptive. There is a feeling of uneasiness to them, as if the reader has been prepared for a monumental revelation in them, but the revelation, the denouement, is somehow evaded. Or is it? *"Mi último deseo,"* she writes, her last wish: to leave behind a financial legacy—real estate—in three equal shares, one for each of her children. No favoritism, she suggests. And, more important, she begs her heirs not to fight but to be in peace, with themselves and the others. She lists her properties: three lots and one apartment. "Be honest," she says. *Sean honestos.*

Honesty: a most elusive word. Can we be honest about what we *don't* see and understand? As time went by, Bela struggled to keep up with the pace of changes around her. *Ya pertenezco a la vieja guardia*, I remember her telling me while still in her late fifties, implying she was already a mummy, a relic of an age long defunct. The twentieth century had moved faster than she was able to digest. A clear sign of this, in my memory, was her refusal to alter her hairstyle or wardrobe: she always wore a fluffy, lacquered do, which she protected overnight with a delicate, almost invisible net. She would put on her elegant wool and silk dresses à la Golda Meier, her high-heeled black shoes, and her cat-shaped plastic-frame glasses. A stoic, she neither smoked nor drank. And she wasn't interested in sharing the sexual and intellectual energy emanating from the United States in the 1960s. It wasn't for her. Though she tried repeatedly to learn English and, less strenuously, Hebrew (her youthful Zionism never diminished, even if she never truly contemplated *aliyah*), she was always more attuned to the past.

ILÁN, POR FAVOR, escríbele. . . . Quiere saber qué piensas de lo que te mandó. My father tells me again by phone to send a note to my grandmother. And what do I *really* think? *Sé honesto,* my father adds. What can I write to her? Any attempt at criticism would be misplaced, for Bela is my grandmother; objectivity is obviously not within reach. Besides, I have not been asked to critique her diary but to inherit it, to digest its memories and to make them mine, to be a link in the chain of generations, to pass along the torch. I should wholeheartedly applaud her effort. I should write to thank her, should I not?

I struggle to draft the first words of my response. Isn't there an element of comedy *and* tragedy in her? After all, she survived the xenophobia of her native Poland, emigrated to Mexico, and thrived; but she also helped build a community on the margins of history, one unconcerned with *lo mexicano,* things Mexican—an anachronistic enclave, disdainful of the rest of the world. Once again, I think of Yiddish, her portable ghetto. What am I going to say when I see her?

It strikes me, suddenly, that Bobbe Bela's *diario* is a control mechanism specifically directed at me, that she is anxious to learn my reaction, to hear—not from her Abremele, but from me directly—that I have read it conscientiously, processed it, and have no qualms about its main storyline. In the past year or so, I have been telling my family about my desire (or, better, my "intention") to write a memoir about my own upbringing in Mexico and my emigration to America. How soon it is likely to happen, I do not say. The English-language readership that surrounds me is infatuated with autobiography as a literary form: to shape one's life into narrative has become a sport of sorts. My aim, although I dare not say it too loud, is to produce one in a few years, which makes accuracy as such, objective truth, questionable. For how much of what we are, what we know about ourselves, is really *true*? We are merely a sum of viewpoints, and human memory is treacherous and inconsistent.

Life is experienced through language, isn't it? Gestures, voices, words. As I read and reread Bela's *diario*, time and again, the word "inauthentic" comes back to me. I try to imagine how Bela would have written to me in her *true* tongue: Yiddish. I conjure the warm, gentle sounds articulated in its sentences, the magic of re-creating Nowe Brodno as it felt to her. By translating it for me, has she injected it with a dose of nostalgia? In seeking words absent from her childhood (simple forms: *se me declaró, un malparido, Puerco Judío*), has she amended her own past? I think of the challenge ahead of me. I'm aware that crafting my memoir in English will, in and of itself, be a form of treason. For shouldn't it be written in at least three if not four languages (Yiddish, Spanish, Hebrew, and English), the four tongues in which—and through which—I've experienced life? But no publisher in his right mind would endorse such an endeavor. It is perhaps an unrealistic dream, and ridiculous, too. My aim, nonetheless, is to convey not my nationality but my *translationality*. To succeed, the original ought to read as if written already *in* translation—a translation without an original. I think of the segments in Anglicized Yiddish in Henry Roth's *Call It Sleep*, and those in "transliterated slang" in Richard Wright's *Native Son;* they appeal to me because they are bastardized forms of language, polluted, compromised. And an illegitimate language is exactly what I seek.

Bela, of course, has no clue as to my thoughts. She simply knows I'm ready—or getting ready—to write a memoir; to reflect on the family's past and evaluate its present; to single out, as all autobiographers do, members of the family not only through a hierarchy of anecdotes but by means of what Martin Buber once called "comparative morality"—e.g., the standing each member has vis-à-vis the rest of the group. And she knows—how can she not?—that she, Bela, is likely to share center stage with my father, *her* Abremele, as well as with my brother Darián, the Stavchansky trio whose influence on my *Weltanschauung* is most decisive. And so, before memory fails her, before it is too late, she makes up her mind: modestly yet decisively, she will write a memoir herself. Not a full-scale, multivolume memoir, like the one fashioned by Sholem Aleichem, *In the Country Fair*, or the one by Israel Joshua Singer, *Iron and Steel*. No, Bela's will be a plain, simple narrative whose main objective is to set the record straight.

Straight? As I try to compose my response to her *diario*, I realize she has produced it mainly for me—and, through me, for the rest of the world—to get "the correct impression" of who she is. In all honesty, she is not the only one that has expressed concern. There is nothing to denounce in my life, no one to ridicule—except myself, of course. Still, the moment news went out that I was contemplating an autobiography, family members on both sides came to me with requests, people obsessed with their place in family history. But only Bobbe Bela has gone out of her way to put down her version of the events, and to send it to me, through my father. She is concerned about the record. Or is she? Am I imagining secret motives behind the innocent memories of a mature woman? Am I falsifying her message? Who cares if the story in her *diario* is a pack of lies, where Tío David, to name just one relative against whom Bela directed her merciless fist, is not even mentioned? Whose autobiography isn't far-fetched? Will I, when I'm finally courageous enough to speak my turn, be ready to face my own foibles, my own hypocrisies? Isn't the genre of autobiography about redefinition and redemption?

And so I send her a quick note—in Spanish, how else?—via e-mail, to my father's address. I've done it before many times. Mexico's postal service is a disaster. Besides, Bela loves to be read messages by phone. Every Sunday, when she is brought to my parents' home in Colonia Cuicuilco, in the Insurgentes Sur neighborhood, she asks to be connected to the Internet, and without further delay writes to me. My mother usually types while she dictates. I've asked her numerous questions about Białolenska Street in Nowe Brodno, about her arrival in Tampico on the *Sparndam*, about the Club Centro at Calle Tacuba #15. In fact, as she responds to me and my imagination is stimulated, I feel that the excruciating process of drafting my own memoir has begun.

"It's here, *suegra*," my mother tells her. "Ilan sent you a message."

"Really?" She smiles. Minutes later she sits in front of the screen. "The Internet . . . We could not have imagined it in our shtetl!"

"You were never in a shtetl, Mamá," my father replies. Soon after, my mother reads out loud.

Querida Bobe:
Mil gracias por tu hermoso diario. I admire you. Your memories are mine already.

Te amo, I.S.

{ 3 }

Under the Spotlight

> **Selfishness is not living
> as one wishes to live,
> it is asking others to live
> as one wishes to live.**
>
> **—OSCAR WILDE**

A PLEASANT SUNDAY afternoon. It must be late May, perhaps early June. It's breezy outdoors. The pollution isn't heavy, since heavy rainstorms descended in April. Spring has arrived: trees are robust, flowers bloom. It has rained a bit, though not too much. My Bar Mitzvah took place a few weeks before, and I'm thoroughly relieved. How did I overcome the feeling of unworthiness that swept over me while on the synagogue's *bimah*? I remember thinking: This is a nightmare from which I must wake up at once, or I will be trapped in it forever. *¡Hasta la eternidad!* Why was I so unhappy? I had memorized the Brakhoth, my portion of the Haftorah, and had drafted a speech, to be delivered at the end of the service. A banquet was held after the ceremony.

Bobbe Miriam herself made the wine—*el famoso vino de la Bobe*—as she did every season, buying boxes of grapes, cleaning them, placing bunches in buckets, and smooshing them with her feet. . . . I was quite ready, was I not? What was the source of my misery?

I have no answer. The fact that it is now history delights me. I did what was expected of me. Did I shine? No, I don't believe I did. Still, everyone congratulates my parents. "Time flies, Abremele," an old lady tells my father while I stand nearby. "Your first child, eh? Already a Bar Mitzvah *bocher*!" My father smiles while holding my hand. A grown-up: I'm a grown-up, at least according to the Jewish religion. But it is my father who is congratulated.

"Mazel tov, Abrum!"

Abraham, Abremele, Abrum, Abramzsykle: he parades his pride around. Or, better, he exudes *amor, mucho amor*. For me his love is a fountain of joy, but also a curse: I adore him, but I also feel overwhelmed by him.

What is it that makes me so ambivalent? He is utterly charismatic. Toward his wife and children, he manifests a kind of passion verging on the obsessive. He loves too much and he knows it.

Why? Is it a façade?

Not that I should complain. How many of Mexico's children are fatherless? Mine embraces me with such strength, to the point that it hurts. Or does it?

"Might your son become an actor, just like his father?" someone whispers. "I see the same talent in him."

"Well, he is surely temperamental," my father replies.

I'm stunned. An actor? Actors are selfish, volatile. And I thought I had given a lousy performance. . . .

Now, more than a month later, I think about it again. An actor? Not the slightest chance.

It is close to 4 P.M. We have just finished a late lunch, as the family often does on Sundays. Bobbe Bela and Bobbe Miriam are invited, my brother plays the piano, everyone talks for hours while munching *jícama* with lemon, salt, and a type of dried chili pepper known among children as *chile piquín*. My father's nap is part of the routine. Occasionally, he convinces me to snoooze with him. I am seldom tired, but the treat of being hugged by his warmth, of resting at his side, is hard to resist. During the week he is too busy with his business, Forrajera Nacional, S.A. He comes back at 3 P.M., eats a late lunch, and disappears into his bedroom, only to re-emerge close to 5 P.M., ready to seize the night, his favorite time of day. Between his arrival from work and his reappearance, his temper is flammable. Not a word can be uttered, for he is likely to retaliate.

"*No estoy de humor, Ilán,*" he might tell me, "I'm tired and in a bad mood."

This afternoon I've decided to join him for a nap. My sister is outside, riding her bike. My brother is away at a friend's house. I don't generally take siestas—not at thirteen, for sure. I'd rather be outside playing soccer, riding my bicycle, inviting the neighborhood children to be part of a play I want to direct in the backyard. But today I want to be next to him. In a little while we'll go together to Teatro Orientación. He is in the play, *Un frágil equilibrio*, a Spanish adaptation of *A Delicate Balance* by Edward Albee, directed by Rafael López Miarnau.

It's my turn to go with him, and I'm proud. But I also feel uncertain. Seeing him onstage inspires me, yes, although it also fills me with tremendous fear. Fear and envy. Fear of losing him—what if he becomes the character he is impersonating once and for all and doesn't return to his own personality? And envy of the audience who will get his full attention, not me.

We jump into bed. My father hugs me, and his deep breathing rhythms soon start. I let myself be overwhelmed by it. The entire room seems to enlarge and contract as he exhales and inhales. Soon I fall asleep. Or am I hypnotized?

I have an uncomfortable relationship with him. He is the older sibling I don't have: inflexible, dogmatic, yet encouraging. Selfish. Like all true actors, he *is* selfish; his Self—with a capital "S"—is the center not only of his life but of the whole family. People love him; or, rather, they *love* to love him. He is the one that matters. I'm known as "the actor's oldest child." For him, an eternal charmer, life itself is a stage.

In my dreams I imagine my father dressed up as Hercule Poirot—slicked-down hair, mustache, British raincoat. I have seen him on TV a thousand times: dressed up like a priest, a disloyal husband in Baltimore, a Brechtian moneylender (a miserable Jewish caricature), a Vietnam soldier, a clown, a farcical police detective. Which of all these personalities is truly my father's? How can I be sure he is not a con man? Where does the stage end for him and life begin? As his son, I often wonder, for I perceive an oversentimental side to his character, a tendency to dramatize everything around him. Is this my own misperception? Do others share the same impression? Or is it only me? I have yet to discuss this with my siblings. I wouldn't dare, not in a thousand years, to articulate it to my friends. It is too intimate a thought, too personal.

Hercule Poirot, or should it be James Bond, in one of whose films—*License to Kill*, with Timothy Dalton—he eventually had a small role? In my imagination, my father is a secret agent. Under his raincoat, a walkie-talkie at low volume allows him to communicate with the Mossad. A Nazi criminal entered Mexico decades ago, a collaborator of Adolf Eichmann, and has lived incognito in Colonia Hipódromo, not far from Bobbe Bela's apartment, across the street from Parque México. As a trained hunter, he must find him: follow him, tape his phone conversations, watch his acquaintances. My father's rhythmical breathing accelerates. Is he about to capture the enemy? He walks through a park, enters an old building, climbs up the stairs, reaches the roof, and waits. He waits patiently. What's his next move? Where is the Nazi criminal? His puts his right hand inside his raincoat. A gun? The same gun stored in the safe-deposit box?

I blink and wake up. Nothing has changed. I'm not alone. We are still in my room. The curtain is drawn. My father's deep breathing has slowed down; he is still asleep. I look at his epidermis, the shape of his chin, his eyebrows, his nose. The nose: in his view, it is too pointed, too long. "If only I had plastic surgery when I was a young man," he often tells me, "I would have been *un galán*, another James Dean. Many more roles would have come my way, don't you think, Ilan?" I smile. Probably, but perhaps not.

His glasses have left dents on both sides of his nose. An old man? He is only in his early forties. And yet he *is* afraid of senility, and very soon—half a decade later at most—he will begin dyeing his incipient white hair. An actor's body is a canvas, a work of art, so he spends a lot of time manipulating it, hiding its handicaps, embellishing its edges.

I look at him and think to myself: I can't stand actors—they are so shallow, so lighthearted. When my father organizes his late-night parties at home, to which he invites numerous friends (Manolo Fábregas, Zero Mostel, Dennis Weaver, Libertad Lamarque, Silvia Pinal, etc.), I study their frivolity. Laughter, wine, drugs, sex. With few exceptions, they live in a world of kitsch and artificiality. My resistance is not straightforward, though: I am a fan of pop culture, of melodrama; I allow myself to be swept up by it on TV and film with the same intensity with which I listen to Anton Dvořák's *New World* Symphony. But I don't like it in our house, as part of our family life. For actors, only applause matters. They change spouses as often as underwear; they refuse to attend the theater unless they are personally invited, and when they do, they invariably eulogize what they see, aware that a friend, any friend, is always a potential source of income. Was it Saul Bellow who once said that writers never wish each other well? But his maxim is too tame to describe actors, for as a rule they are envious and self-aggrandizing, epicurean in the extreme.

On the other hand, there is also an enviable honesty in actors, and my father is a prime example. *Envidia*, envy: the word comes up again. Yes, actors might be greedy and jealous, and their place in Dante's Seventh Circle of Hell might be forever secure, but as I explore the feelings I have toward my father, I realize how unlike his colleagues he is at home: benign, comforting, affectionate, inspiring. In fact, I *envy* his probity and candor, his joie de vivre. His self inflates like a balloon when in the company of strangers, but in the intimacy of daily life it shrinks to an almost regular size. You can read his thoughts before he utters them, so crystalline are they, so undisguised.

"Do you love me, Ilan?" he often asks. Do I? Yes, of course, and he knows it well. But he needs constant reassurance.

I admire him, but I fear he perceives me as his rival. I began dreaming of a career in film thanks to him. In my early teens he frequently took me to foreign and Hollywood movies, sometimes three to four times a week. *National Velvet, Chitty Chitty Bang Bang, Mary Poppins, The Planet of the Apes,* and *The Time Machine,* but also Alain Resnais's *Night and Fog,* Woody Allen's *Bananas,* Fellini's *8½,* even Ingmar Bergman's *Scenes from a Marriage.* The plots often left me in the dark, but I didn't care: the movies were a form of dialogue between him and me, an encounter. (I particularly recollect one early Czech film, whose title I can only invoke in Spanish: *Otra vez brincó sobre los charcos.* It is the dramatic account of an equestrian accident in which a little boy becomes paralyzed. I remember crying out loud and discussing it endlessly with my father. For years I've tried to track it down, but without success.) He introduced me to Truffaut, Satyajit Ray, and my adolescent hero, Luis Buñuel. My siblings were far less interested in the moving image, so it was I who frequently went with him to theater premiers, film openings, and even an occasional art exhibit.

His art had once been daring, but it had grown more complacent and imitative as he matured. Ticket sales and not radical aesthetics are what attracted him as an adult. The years when he participated in student protests and experimental theater were past. More often than not, his shows were adaptations from Broadway hits. Money and time permitting, at least once a year he and my mother—and later on I as well—traveled to Manhattan to see a slew of current musicals and commercial plays. He needed to see them before anyone else south of the Rio Grande, and perhaps might even buy the rights to them. He had become satisfied as the entertainer for the ever-volatile middle class at a period—the mid-1970s—when a Faustian Mexico sold its soul to the devil: American pop culture. Theater was his sole passion: he and he alone monopolized the thespian realm. So, when I began suggesting, around my Bar Mitzvah, that I, too, was working on various story ideas, perhaps for a play of my own if not for a film script, he took me half seriously. "I don't doubt your talents, *querido hijo mío*," he said, "but I'm sure others can do it better."

How come? *Estoy furibundo:* I get irritated. Isn't this what was uniquely mine after all these years of apprenticeship? Shouldn't a father be more supportive? What, if anything, has been the purpose of my education in the arts?

He wakes up from the nap. "Time to go," he says, and disappears into his bathroom.

I go downstairs.

"Where are the car keys? *Ya nos vamos.* . . . We're about to go," he tells my mother.

She looks at her clock: past 3 P.M. "Isn't it a bit late?" The keys are next to the kitchen sink, where they always are. My mother hands them to me.

Is it really late? No, not really. My father's first performance on Sunday is at 5 P.M. and the theater is only a couple of miles north on the highway. Besides, traffic is slow at this hour. But we should hurry, just in case.

I get myself ready, too. The two of us kiss the grandmothers goodbye, hug my brother and sister, and walk toward the door with my mother. We discuss the evening plans: she and my siblings will arrive at the theater at 9 P.M. and we'll all go for tacos.

But something is meant to go wrong today—I sense it. "¿*Y las llaves?* Where are the keys?"

HE TURNS THE engine on. Our Rambler wagon is uncomfortable—cold leather seats, side windows difficult to roll down, undependable gear—but the mind travels faster than the body, which makes the automobile ride ahead of me among my favorite times in the week. In the next half-hour, my father will undergo a profound transformation, like that of Dr. Jekyll and Mr. Hyde: slowly, he will cease to be the person I know, the one loving me to death. I will experience the loss of his becoming someone else—a cancer patient, a Holocaust survivor, a priest.

Do I have one father or many? I wonder. In daily life, very often he forgets he is not acting. Especially when he is among strangers, he emphasizes certain aspects of his personality, he becomes more himself than he really is—a bit like Don Quixote. And sometimes his character prevails and he assumes at midday the persona of one of his creations. Schizophrenia? No, he is a normal fellow. He simply loves theater too much and can't wait to return to the stage. Impatient. Perhaps the whole universe is his stage, like Calderón de la Barca's Segismundo in the Golden Age drama *Life Is a Dream*. Or like Shakespeare's Hamlet.

While on the road to the Teatro Orientación, inside Chapultepec Park, he and I talk. And talk and talk . . . The session is delicious. I have my father all to myself: no interruptions, no subterfuges. What do we talk about? *Todo y nada*, a million topics. I feel I am his best companion, perhaps even his favorite son, although the thought makes me uncomfortable. Why is he so unresponsive to my early drafts of plays? Am I too young? Will the day come when I shall write one for him? Is he confident of my future?

I've submitted short stories and screenplays to him, mostly in Spanish. How many in total? Impossible to say.

"*Tienes una ortografía espantosa*," he says, invariably. Instead of valuing them for their content, he criticizes my spelling.

He is right, of course. Isn't he always? Why haven't I learned to spell properly? Was it learning one too many languages? Not really, because my brother was a master speller from an early age. At any rate, I cannot distinguish between a "z," an "s," and a "c." Nor do I really know where to place the accents. Why does Spanish need to be so labyrinthine? I always get the sense of imminent danger. Still, I experiment with style, although I am mainly concerned with characterization and the denouement. At this stage, I'm not even remotely convinced the literary path should be mine.

"It is *perversión*, not *perverción*. And neither is it *Parangaricutirimiquaro*."

To ease my discomfort, I recite the famous Mexican tongue-twister, a verbal game from a small town in the state of Colima:

El rey de Parangaricutirimícuaro,
Se quiere desparangaricutirimicuarizar.
El que lo logre desparangaricutirimicuarizar,
Será un gran desparangaricutirimicuarizador.

I repeat the tongue-twister once, twice, five times. I understand the lesson but am confused by his lack of support.

He is a Chekhovian character. Almost any Russian type fits him like a glove: in spite of his pronounced nose—or because of it—he would do wonders with an adaptation of Gogol's "The Nose." He is perfect in Turgenev's *Fathers and Sons*, and could make Dostoevski's Raskolnikov come fully to life. He is the incarnation of these characters. His mustache, a hybrid of Charlie Chaplin's and Carlos Fuentes's, can make him look severe, but he is huggable like a teddy bear, and is remarkably sociable and affectionate. People meeting him for the first time feel they have known him for years. He was the first openly Jewish actor on Mexico's professional stage; his first exercises were in Yiddish at the CDI. His repertoire included *Der Fargangener Taij*, a melodrama, loosely translated as *The Hidden River*, by the prolific nineteenth-century playwright Abraham Goldfaden, whose many plays—almost as numerous, and surely as popular, as those of Lope de Vega in the Spanish Golden Age—were performed by itinerant troupes that delighted audiences all over Eastern Europe.

Though my father's true calling is the theater (*su pasión*, his obsession), TV has put bread on the family table. "For money, my dear. I do it for money, like a thousand other colleagues," he says. He has been cast in dozens of soap operas, from *El amor tiene cara de mujer* and *Barata de primavera* to *La sonrisa del diablo*, and for a while had his own variety show on prime time, called *Antojitos mexicanos*. On the street he is stopped for autographs. But TV is too easy, too manipulative for his taste, whereas theater is serious business. In the studio at home, next to my brother's piano, underneath an old stereo system of my home, my father kept albums with news clippings, programs, cables, and telegrams, yellowish photographs, all dated chronologically. I would sneak a peak at them, alone, mesmerized by the many personalities he had mimicked. He had begun acting at the age of eighteen, and among his roles in Spanish was that of Motl Kamtzoyl in *Fiddler on the Roof*, as well as Peter in *Diary of Anne Frank*, a vehicle for the diva of Hispanic theater, María Teresa Montoya.

He easily hyperventilates, particularly when Bobbe Bela is around, for she always placed the most challenging obstacles in front of him. And she did it by means of a simple, nefarious strategy: she withheld her love from him. Not to express her affection, to manipulate people, to make others feel they are undeserving of her love. Perhaps that's why my father loves so much—as a reaction. *Yo amo, tu amas, él ama* . . .

In truth, Bobbe Bela is only one of the difficulties he has had to combat. He is rebellious by nature. For decades he refused, as vehemently as he could, to accommodate himself to the status quo of the Jewish community. He criticized its members as flimsy, materialistic, and comfort-driven. Academic excellence was never his stock, either. In Der Yiddisher Shule he was known as a clown, *un payaso*—perhaps one Sid Caesar might have adored, one destined for stand-up comedy. To this day his impersonations and childhood pranks are famous. He was also known as a rascal, *un pillo*: with his friends, he had competitions to see who could pee and spit the farthest in the school yard; and he was also known, like my brother, Darián, decades later, for kissing the girls without inhibition.

Understandably, Bobbe Bela was often called in by teachers to discuss his conduct: Abremele the troublemaker, Abremele the terrorist.

She taught him, at home and in school, to speak Yiddish

and Spanish. And sent him to the United States to learn English. My father mastered these tongues, but his true vehicle of communication is the body, not the word. Physical language.

Still, in Yiddish he made people laugh as in no other tongue. "Do you know the joke about the Jewish Red Riding Hood, Caperucita Finkelstein?" his friends still ask him when their paths cross at social reunions. "You mean the one whose nose is bigger than the wolf's?" And ha-ha-ha—they all laugh uncontrollably.

His passion, he soon realized, was theater. *El teatro puro y el puro teatro*. Upon hearing the news, his mother was horrified. "Theater and prostitution are companion careers," she used to say. "One denigrates the body, the other the soul." She frequently ran out of pejorative adjectives: actors, she shrieked, are irresponsible, capricious, volatile, alcohol-driven, reckless parents . . . blah-blah-blah. This litany, I'm convinced, intensified his neurosis. What he liked most was to lose himself in the darkness of the movie theater. Every time he attended the nearby Cine Lido to watch his models Spencer Tracy and Humphrey Bogart, Bobbe Bela would worry to the point of sickness. "*Dem shlekhtn veg,*" the wrong path. "*Du velts zayn a fargangener,*" you will become a lost soul. My father's dream triumphed, though. He read literature avidly, especially plays. I inherited his library: Ibsen, O'Neill, Arthur Miller, and, yes, Calderón de la Barca's *Life Is a Dream* in a cheap, yellowish edition printed in Buenos Aires, along with the work of Mexican playwrights such as Xavier Villaurrutia and Rodolfo Usigli. But he knew the written word was not his vehicle.

His generation rebelled against their immigrant parents in a number of ways. For one thing, they sought education and wealth as stabilizing factors. But they were also spiritually poorer, throwing tradition out the window. My father never much cared about Jewishness. Not in his adolescence. Not until he met my mother.

He felt suffocated in Der Yiddisher Shule, so he called it quits after junior high to enroll in a two-year accounting program. He found the outside world liberating: Jews were not daring enough. He found *shkotzim* aplenty, sincere, endearing Gentiles to be friends with. Bobbe Bela boycotted him, but it was better to be *sólo y sin apoyo*, alone amid the true Mexicans. He didn't need Jews. As far as he was concerned, the reclusiveness of his Yiddish-speaking immigrant forebears was a mistake. Why reject the conviviality of the nation's majority population?

Still, he was possessed by doubts. Would he ever meet *una chica judía*, a nice Jewish girl? He wasn't yet ready for marriage. Marriage was too easy a way out, too bourgeois a solution to the ongoing quest of an artist in search of his own place in society. He needed to test himself, to challenge his vision, to become a hungry artist. He was young—only twenty-one, hardly a grown man. Life was full of possibilities. He surely wouldn't starve, would he? Besides, poverty is a gift to the soul, isn't it? It purifies, it allows one to reach higher levels.

Love and social acceptance. His circle of *goyish* friends slowly expanded. He began to go to plays, conferences, concerts. He was not an inspired speaker, like the ones he heard in public lectures on art and theater in the Palacio de Bellas Artes and the Museo del Chopo. He admired their arguments and, even more, their performances, and thought about the chemistry between speaker and audience. Then, in mid-1953, he met Seki Sano, a Japanese political refugee and master stage director, in whose workshops my father spent many hours. He began to associate with young actors, playwrights, producers, and theater people (Jorge Ibargüengoitia, Arnold Belkin, Soledad Ruíz, Humberto Almazán, Ana Ofelia Murguía, María Eugenia Ríos, and, later, Adriana Roel and Beatríz Sheridan). He talked so often of Seki in my childhood and adolescence, I was convinced he was a mythical figure not unlike the Prophet Elijah.

Seki this, Seki that . . . I remember him talking nonstop about his master. *El maestro que enseñó a actuar.* It would be many years before I figured out who the person behind the name was. To read about Seki, to watch clips from a trashy film he made in 1948, *Han matado a Tongolele,* was, in many ways, to reconfigure my father's apprenticeship in his early twenties. My father must have approached him the way I later approached Franz Rosenzweig and Irving Howe: as idols, as torch carriers.

The fact that Seki Sano was an immigrant, I'm convinced, is significant: not a *mexicano hecho y derecho* but a foreigner, a wanderer, just like my father. To judge from all I've read—biographies, eulogies, critical appraisals—he was a visionary, the Platonic model of a restless soul that makes good with his talent wherever he goes. His experimental technique in theater, which was inspired by Meyerhold and began after the earthquake in Kanto in 1923, always managed to find a way into the heart of the drama onstage, to make it purer and more meaningful. He had been born in 1905 in Tientsin, in China, and studied at the Imperial University of Tokyo. In 1931, he left for Hawaii and California, where he worked for Paramount Pictures, and came into contact with Michael Gold and also with the Group Theatre. He then moved to France and Germany, and, eventually, to the U.S.S.R., where he collaborated on, among other endeavors, Alexander Dovzhenko's film *Aerograd*. He then returned to New York, where he successfully directed Lope de Vega's *Fuenteovejuna* with the Group Theatre, finding a way to breach the cultural gap between the Iberian and Anglo-Saxon worlds. At that point he met the painter Rufino Tamayo, who helped him get an invitation to Mexico.

I've seen a myriad of black-and-white snapshots of his globe-trotting odyssey. He arrived in Veracruz—not far from Bobbe Bela's Tampico—in 1939, just as the Second World War was about to break out, and immediately created the Teatro de las Artes. Soon he was translating Stanislavski into Spanish, with the help of Ignacio Retes. He was praised in Hollywood and on Broadway in due course as a first-rate pedagogue. His staging of Clifford Odets's *Waiting for Lefty*, Tennessee Williams's *A Streetcar Named Desire*, Chekhov's *The Bear*, Usigli's *Corona de sombra*, and Mozart's *The Magic Flute* left an indelible mark on many an artistic generation in Mexico, for Seki's style was unadulterated, politically committed, asking actors to search deep inside themselves for the motives that made their characters come alive.

Sometimes I wished I possessed a supernatural gadget to go back in time just once and be present at a single adaptation of Seki—that of Arnold Perl's *The World of Sholem Aleichem*. It was Brechtian in every respect: it didn't invoke the Eastern European shtetl through nostalgia; instead, it portrayed it as merciless, a place of poverty and despair. As such, it was the opposite of the Broadway approach, reproduced years later in Mexico by Manolo Fábregas. Seki's vision was uncondescending, heavy-hearted, cheerless—much as, I'm convinced, the shtetl was, in spite of Sholem Aleichem's liberating humor. Otherwise, how do you explain the emigration of millions of its dwellers to America and elsewhere?

Had Seki spent his mature years in New York or London, I'm convinced his legacy would be known worldwide. But he ended up in peripheral Mexico, where audiences embraced him, but where the international spotlight hardly ever shines. Did he regret in later years the route fate had assigned him? I've never come across a diary by Seki, nor have I found a companion that knew him intimately, so I don't know. What is unquestionable is that he concentrated on shaping the gifted young in Ciudad de México, and my father was among the lucky few he nurtured with inexhaustible care. My father made his debut with Seki in 1955, in *Cinco preciosidades francesas*, an adaptation, by playwright Jorge Ibargüengoitia—and with a set design by the promising painter Arnold Belkin (who would later on court my father's sister Tía Elenita)—of five medieval French tales, written between 1464 and 1515. And he was also part of Seki's versions of Miller's *The Crucible*, as well as of Paddy Chayefsky's *The Tenth Man*, the latter staged at CDI. To celebrate, my father decided to change his name. "Stavchansky" was too unpronounceably Eastern European; instead, he chose "Stavans," which was *kurtz und sharf*: short, unromantic, and serious. Tío Isaac was attempting a career in painting already, and also used the same abbreviated form. (Years later, as I began as a writer, I opted for "Stavans" to continue the genealogy.)

El joven talento, a burgeoning artist destined to become

my father. How handsome he looked in the photographs of the era. How daring in his artistic poses! Was my father meant to be another Anthony Quinn (original name: Antonio Reyna)? "Be careful, for talent is easily spoiled," Seki used to tease him. These were words of caution. The photographs signal a road not taken. My father never quite achieved stardom. He says it was his lingering nose and his Jewishness, but it might have been something else: his hesitation to embrace his career wholeheartedly from early on. Still, in those days of limitless possibility, he was—and is today, in spite of the regrets—happy, happy, happy. What I envy most is his complete communion with his audience in the theater. Only actors and dancers and musicians performing live enjoy this extraordinary experience. Other forms of art are too remote, too indirect. But actors, like priests, do establish a tête-à-tête, which, though ephemeral, makes their craft semireligious.

Egotism, selflessness.

My father's performances in Seki's plays, I've heard from people who saw them, were ritual acts. He still longs to relive them, to bring back the mysticism they evoked. The theater was a temple. People who attended talk of "the perfect balance" he and the rest of the cast reached. Through a Japanese émigré my father found enlightenment.

And love. The love of other immigrant—Bobbe Bela— never offered him unconditionally.

I NEVER MET Seki Sano. He died in 1966, at the age of sixty-one, of a series of heart attacks, when I was five years old. I have photographs of him, passed along by my father: a profile of Seki, his cigarette on the left side of his mouth, his right hand moving a piece of chalk across a classroom board; Seki in front of a microphone, delivering a lecture in 1965; Seki in glasses and with a pipe, looking pensive. His death was a blow to my father. But he didn't work with Seki all the way to the end. No, he left him when opportunity rang its bell.

Stardom . . . Destination: New York. And in the back of his mind, Seki's maxim, "Be careful, for talent is easily spoiled, especially in America."

In 1956, still in his early twenties, he was accepted as an *oyente*, a student observer, in Lee Strasberg's Actors Studio. Frantic excitement. The institution had a worldwide reputation as a superb school for serious actors. Would this be his chance to redeem himself from having been born on the periphery of global culture? Could New York lead to Hollywood? Surely this would be just at the vortex of experimental theater, where things happened.

To this day, when I walk the streets of midtown Manhattan, I visualize him in the company of Marilyn Monroe and Marlon Brando, who were enrolled in the class before his.

How sweet the image: my father talking to sexy Marilyn. Neither Arthur Miller nor Joe DiMaggio, but Bobbe Bela's Abremele, perhaps shoulder to shoulder with gorgeous Marlon.

Bobbe Bela, of course, opposed his north-of-the-border sojourn. But nothing stopped him. Zeyde Srulek had relatives in Brooklyn: Uncle Jack and Aunt Betty Futoran, on Snyder Avenue. They had three children and a grocery store and were more than willing to accommodate another person, especially from the beloved Mexican wing of the *mishpocheh*.

The nine months he spent with them were decisive. He

took a five-day bus ride by Greyhound from Ciudad de México to Manhattan. Zeyde Srulek used to send him a little money—*debajo de la mesa*, as the Spanish say, surreptitiously and without Bobbe Bela's approval. In her view, the less he had, the faster he would return—not only to Mexico but to his senses, i.e., relinquishing his hopes of being an actor.

But he didn't.

Exhilarated to be near Strasberg and Monroe and Brando and the whole gang, he daydreamed about auditions and about hitting it big on Broadway.

He used to take long subway rides in the morning to West 54th Street, where the Actors Studio was located, and make it back to Snyder Avenue just in time for dinner. It wasn't easy, though. As a student observer, he had no actual place in the class and wasn't allowed to participate in exercises, workshops, or rehearsals, only to listen. *Oir sin hablar.* The passivity made him melancholic. Listening has never been easy for him: as he struggles with impatience, his mind wanders and his facial expressions betray him.

More than anything, he missed home—his friends, his brother and sister, and especially Zeyde Srulek and Bobbe Bela. Could he really master American culture to become its stepchild? he pondered. Was he meant to be an immigrant like his parents and Seki?

He had his doubts, and so do I today. His English was infinitely better than mine when I myself left for New York. (The first place I stayed—for almost a week—when I moved north, in 1985, was at the Long Island house of Jack and Betty's oldest daughter, Libby Rosenberg.) The tools of acting are first and foremost physical and emotional. He loved his Brooklyn cousins—Libby, Francine, Stanley—young

American Jews whose place in society was more secure than that of their parents: eventually, they went into the food industry, married and divorced up-and-coming lawyers, and moved to Long Island. But they were goal-oriented; worse, they were less affectionate, or at least failed to express themselves as openly as he did. Mexican Jews, in his view, had a richer inner life; and Mexico as a nation, though less stable politically and financially, was infinitely more interesting than the U.S. In New York, on the other hand, he was in his element, but isn't that the feeling it specializes in, to make people comfortable but only for a short while?

Not enough love.

I REMEMBER AS an adolescent at home seeing several copies of Stanislavski's *An Actor Prepares*—in English and Spanish, and perhaps even in Japanese, part of Seki's legacy. The book was my father's bible. He memorized its passages. In our daily life, he would, on occasion, invoke a sentence to make an aspect of reality clearer. And he admired people who were ruled by their inner ghosts, just as Stanislavski suggests for actors. I still see him talking about *la cuarta pared*, a stage's invisible fourth wall.

"It is the keyhole's eye, Ilan," he would tell me. Acting, he believed, doesn't stop when you leave the stage. "By the sheer repetition of affection, I have convinced you I'm your father, have I not? I try to act my part as best I can. But someone else could do it better."

The thought, of course, frightened me a lot. If everything is an act, who are we? What is behind the mask each of us wears? What demons do people nurture?

Click, cliiick, cliiiiick. This Sunday afternoon, inside the Rambler, I look at—am almost hypnotized by—the rhythmic movement of the keys hanging behind the wheel. *Máscaras y demonios.*

He is anxious about the audience: *¿Habrá público, Ilán?* Will there be enough people?

The question is always the same, and he asks it whenever a performance is about to start. So I wonder: Why do people decide to leave the comfort of their homes on a gorgeous day like this and hide themselves in the darkness of a theater? Why are they ready to put a sudden stop to their routine and submerge themselves in the life of others? Indiscretion—what else is theater about? Yes, it is such a bizarre spectacle, the audience sitting patiently for a couple of hours. Why is the ritual so enticing? Well, they are—we all are—enthralled by life summarized and deconstructed, by the need to extricate the trivial and highlight the dramatic. Onstage, people talk, eat, drink, and sleep, mechanical human acts we hardly pay any attention to in real life. But when they are sheer pretense, when they are staged for us with a purpose, when artificiality gives room to meaning, then we sit quietly and applaud.

But these metaphysical queries do not trouble my father. He is too much of a down-to-earth and here-and-now guy. In his mind the question is simpler: will he be applauded this afternoon?

Fortunately, in spite of his fears, his show this season is a success, even on Sunday afternoons. There is a long line waiting for the box office to open. I see it from the parking lot, where he leaves the Rambler wagon.

My father smiles. "It will be worth it, then."

Of course it will be worth it: without his daily dose of stage bliss, he is miserable, in a stage of depression, for his is a self akin to depression if love and applause are not around.

To be and not to be: a delicate balance.

Depression and nostalgia. Beaten by them, he returned from New York to Mexico in 1957. He says he had a TV offer: a stellar role for Televisa, the privately owned communications empire, in *Puerta al suspenso*, a popular mystery series. He thought it was the door to success. But the truth is he was homesick: *asolapado*. He had tested himself abroad and had come to realize that the little things home is made of were too important to him. How much farther did he need to go? Mexico was good enough for him. He was ready to build his career there, and maybe a life as well.

A couple of years later, in 1959, after a series of dead-end outings with other female friends, he met my mother, Ofelia Slomianski. Their encounter was a blind date orchestrated by a cousin of hers.

The romance of one's parents cannot be fully seized by memory. Something stops me. Was it love at first sight? Did they make love right away? I'm not interested in the answer. What matters to me is the outcome: a family. Yes, I've seen pictures of them from before I was born: their wedding, just a few months after they first met; my mother pregnant with me; the apartment in Condesa where I was born, my house in Copilco, not far from Coyoacán, before construction was completed in the mid-1960s under the supervision of architect Elías Fischer. *My* world, without me. But it's unappealing.

What does intrigue me is the reason my father married: the need to build a nest where stability might encourage love, or vice versa. Bobbe Bela's dictum—theater and prostitution as companion careers, one denigrating the body and the other the soul—filled him with fear, but it was also an existential challenge. Could he prove her wrong? Would he be able to devote himself to his career and at the same time build a real home? *Un desafío*, a challenge. What he sought in a woman, it is clear, was love and determination.

They married in a lavish ceremony before four hundred guests at CDI in July 1960—he was twenty-six and wore a hat acquired in the fashionable downtown store Sambreros Tardán, she was nineteen and wore an elegant but unpretentious bridal gown. They traveled to Europe on their honeymoon.

OFELIA, OFELIA—I'VE always distrusted Freud, but I cannot fail to see her as a continuation of Bobbe Bela. They were very different women, no doubt, but with some shared characteristics: iron-willed, undefeatable, and unforgiving.

In the eyes of many, the relationship was doomed from the outset. Not only did my maternal grandfather, Zeyde Jaime, a wealthy leather-factory owner, thoroughly disapprove of the match, but he never hesitated to make his displeasure evident. Whenever Abraham came for dinner, Zeyde Jaime was rude, incommunicative, coercive.

"What kind of support will he provide?" he repeatedly asked Ofelia. Financial fortune, in his view, should be every Jew's objective.

"He has performed in a Goldfaden play—in Yiddish," his daughter would reply, as if to stress her boyfriend's faith, a factor she knew her father approved of.

"Bah . . . Yiddish, shmiddish. From the *mame loshen* he plans to make a living? Nobody does it any longer."

Bobbe Miriam, although quite strict and stubbornly conservative, was slightly more welcoming: she was polite and well mannered, conversing with him without reservations; and she cooked my father chicken when he came for lunch, because he disliked fish. Perhaps she realized it was no use ignoring the love in her daughter's eyes and figured it was easier to accept right away rather than to reject a suitor who would ultimately prevail. At least Abraham Stavchansky was no *shaygets*, although he did come from a problematic family, not religious enough and surely on the fringes of society.

At least he was not a *shajato*, as Sephardim from the Middle East are known in Mexico; in those days, an interracial Jewish marriage was worse than one with a Gentile.

Also Bobbe Miriam's own relationship with Ofelia, her youngest daughter, had always been rocky. Just after Ofelia's birth, Bobbe Miriam suffered from phlebitis and was immobilized for four months, her legs held up in a vertical position. The baby—my mother—had to be sent away to an aunt's house. My mother didn't find this out until she was in her teens, but when she did, the separation helped to explain the ambivalence she felt toward Bobbe Miriam.

The Slomianskis, by all accounts, led a far more Orthodox life in their home in Colonia Portales, on the city's East Side. Sabbath candles were lit every Friday, and the nearby synagogue was attended on high and minor holidays. A photograph taken at Nidje Israel of Bobbe Miriam's father, a book peddler and a *tzaddik*, makes him look pensive and robust. People say I resemble him.

Ofelia was an honors student: intelligent, resourceful.

She enjoyed food and was on the heavy side as a girl. She dreamed of becoming a psychotherapist one day.

But motherhood kept her busy for years. It wasn't until her second child—Darián—was born that she received her bachelor's degree. (Rumor has it that she almost didn't make it to her final exam because she was on her way to the hospital to deliver my brother.)

More than anything, she adored Abraham. For her, he represented a flamboyant life-style. But her love was not about superficialities: he was a *mensh*, a Latin lover, and an incredibly talented artist. What else could she want?

LOVE WAS FORTHCOMING indeed, but not a livelihood. Once I was born, my father hesitated: could acting really provide the means of family support? He didn't want to embarrass anyone—let alone Bobbe Bela—so he began working for Zeyde Srulek in his animal-food warehouse: Forrajera Nacional, S.A., a dusty and smelly factory where large quantities of corn and wheat were processed and packaged daily and shipped out all over Ciudad de México. *Una mierda.* Nothing made him more unhappy. But at least it was only during the day; in the evenings, after a quick siesta, he pursued his career, performing in variety shows, doing TV, dubbing American sitcoms. The arrangement, he kept telling himself, was temporary. Soon he would find the courage to devote himself in full to his passion.

Though my mother endorsed this compromise, their life was at a standstill, and she kept wishing for a way out of it. Would fortune knock at the door and alleviate their misery? Parenting is synonymous with sacrifice, is it not? The family comes first. But until when? Is an unhappy father a good role model?

In late 1963, Zeyde Srulek was diagnosed with cancer. At sixty-one, he was weak, increasingly incapacitated by performing his duties. The business he had built from scratch, Forrajera Nacional, S.A., had never quite achieved the financial success everyone wished for, but at least it put food on the table. Now *alguien, alguno de los hijos quizás*, someone needed to be in charge of it. Tío Isaac worked at his father-in-law's jewelry store while Tía Elenita, their younger sister, was still a teenager. So my father volunteered.

But did he really? More likely, he was volunteered—by sheer family pressure, mainly from Bobbe Bela, whose opportunity to force her Abremele onto a serious path in life had finally arrived.

My grandfather's agony lasted a total of eighteen months. It was a dark period, one in which old partners took advantage of him. One of them stole his savings and ran away to Israel, leaving the Stavchanskys unable to pay the medical bills. Years later, after one of my public lectures, my father came across the oldest child of the thief—an adult by then, a bit older than himself. They recognized each other by name. "Your father was a scoundrel. He left mine in smisery while cancer was taking its course," he told him. "But I have nothing against you; children are not responsible for their parent's mistakes." And he left him standing there.

My father adored Zeyde Srulek, who was generous, honest, a devoted husband and father. "He gave you your first tricycle, Ilan. But you were three or four years old when he died." And he often repeated: "At the cemetery, as the corpse was being cleaned, someone approached me and said, 'You have a lot to live up to, Abraham!' The statement never left me. It is always with me, especially when I am with you and your siblings." In my Manichean view, his passion and compassion for Zeyde Srulek compensates for his ambivalence toward Bobbe Bela.

At any rate, after the death of Zeyde Srulek, Forrajera Nacional, S.A. fell into my father's hands: he inherited it, and with it the responsibility for feeding Bobbe Bela (through rental payments; she owned the real estate) as well as his own wife and children. He did his best by relocating it on Calzada de Tlalpan, selling eggs, dog and bird food, furnishing a handsome if cavernous office for himself, and pretending to be happy. But he couldn't. Despite his acting talents, he couldn't find a way to lie to himself. He hated the place. Every morning for seventeen years, he woke up early, showered, dressed, and went to work. His father had come from Khaschevate, in the Ukraine, famous for its white and wheat bread. Windmills were the recurrent feature in the landscape. In Mexico, he again surrounded himself with mills, though this time they were food-processing factories. His financial knowledge was adequate: he had transformed himself from a poor immigrant to a small middle-class businessman. From him my father inherited the discipline, but not a grain of sagacity. Throughout my upbringing, it was unclear how much longer Forrajera Nacional, S.A., would go on, for it was always on the brink of bankruptcy, a business with not much business. My father would often take my siblings and me along with him. While he sold the animal food, we played hide-and-seek behind the mills, ending up dirty from head to foot. He was invariably somber and even mournful, a bit tyrannical, as if he wasn't in his own element, a fish out of water.

Would there be enough for the weekend? Could a small vacation in Acapulco be afforded? Although we sometimes heard how the savings account was depleted, we enjoyed all the technology newly available in the 1960s—color TV, freezer, blender, Turmix, Tupperware. The family lived as if it were rich—at least that was the impression Abraham and Ofelia wanted to present. "As if," of course, is what the actor's trade is all about: to pretend being what we're not. Was that attitude yet another side effect of Bobbe Bela's outright rejection of the theater? True to form, it would take many years—until she was in her early seventies and my father in his fifties—for her even to acknowledge his success in TV commercials for Vodka Nikolai and Zest soap and in soap operas like *No todo lo que brilla es oro*. (Translation, with a hint of prophecy: "Not everything that glistens is gold.")

Within the family, a feeling of inadequacy prevailed. How often were we on the brink of economic disaster? Did my parents have to ask for one loan too many from Bobbe Miriam, the wealthy forebear, whose fishy fortune was made when her husband, Zeyde Jaime, "accidentally" burned down his own leather factory and then got a large check from the insurance company? I don't know the answer. What I do know is that the make-believe instilled in me a particular world-view: a distrust for what I see. School tuition was too high, vacations had to be taken, and all the other middle-class bills had to be paid. To make ends meet, my mother enrolled for a degree in psychology at the UNAM. She was among the first Ashkenazic women of her generation to do so. She also sold homemade yogurt and, years later, with a degree in hand, taught private classes to mothers trying to understand their small children. Bizarrely, the family economics did not preclude having a permanent maid at home—Inés López Caballero, a mestiza from Texcoco. She and her daughter Victoria stayed for over two decades—and sometimes she even employed an assistant. This, I believe, was part of the pretense: not rich enough, but almost.

UNTIL MY MOTHER said, "*Shoyn genug*," enough is enough, *ya es suficiente*.

My father was a middle-aged man whose time to take true risks had come. A swift transition was required to put an end to the stalemate. My mother's plan was to sell Forrajera Nacional, S.A. My father needed to embrace the theater wholeheartedly; and she needed to finish her doctorate. But would there be enough money? What was required was action, and it came, albeit slowly. Selling the business involved letting go of Zeyde Srulek. It took enormous mental energy: putting the delivery trucks on the market, stopping the sale of eggs to longtime customers, hiring a company to remove a safe-deposit box as heavy as an elephant in order for the next tenant to build a garage, and so on.

This time my father was not mournful. Quite the contrary, he was as upbeat as possible. Finally, he was ready to become a full-time actor. Would producers call him as often as he wished? Would . . . It didn't really matter to him; even if he worked little, he was immensely happy to have made the decision.

In the end, things turned out all right. He didn't get as

many phone calls as he wished, but he did find steady work. His career never reached the apex people had foreseen when he was a young man, but, then again, how many of us live up to youthful expectations? Isn't the art of growing up also the art of revamping our dreams?

A delicate balance.

Over the years he played a leading role in Stephen Sondheim's *Sweeney Todd*, did cabaret, and was part of many Broadway shows adapted into Spanish in Ciudad de México.

His struggle for self-definition paid off when the Mexican-Jewish community began to recognize him as a role model. After all, he was among the first successful Jewish actors to switch from amateur Jewish theater to the professional stage. Self-aggrandizing pride. "*Ya era hora*," he would say. "Finally, they appreciate what it takes to become an artist. Although they'll never recognize the many obstacles they place ahead of the talented young."

He began to get invited by CDI to stage plays in the very theater where Seki Sano had directed him. At first he refused, but eventually gave in and orchestrated a revival of *Fiddler on the Roof*. Also, at my insistence, he directed an adaptation of Bashevis Singer's "Yentl: The Yeshiva Boy," and I assisted him. It was the first collaboration between us, done in 1983, after years of little encouragement on his part and mistrust on mine.

BUT ALL OF that would take place years after the fateful Sunday afternoon, as my father drives his Rambler to Teatro Orientación. He is still a hostage to his own condition, miserable in the morning, exhilarated in the evening, a man kidnapped by his family legacy and struggling desperately to be happy.

Teatro Orientación is a cold two-hundred-seat auditorium known for its bold dramatic experiments. Its architecture is stamped with the 1960s style: sharp edges, a plethora of square windows on its façade, its interior decorated in an American style. It has a playground in the backyard: swings, slides, a sandbox. My father greets other members of the cast, recounts an anecdote, and talks about the latest political crisis in Mexico. He then greets someone from the staff, to whom he introduces me.

"*Hola Juan, ¿qué tal? ¿Cómo está tu esposa?*"

"Everyone is fine."

I'm holding the Rambler keys in my left hand, playing nervously with them.

He is pure charisma.

"*¿Tu hijo?*" asks Valentina Vargas, a delegate from ANDA, the Mexican Actors' Union, who is devoted to filling out bureaucratic forms about the length of a play, the number of curtain calls, etc. She is obese, in her early sixties, and wears a wig and thick glasses.

"Yes," he replies. "And I need to ask you a favor: while I'm onstage, please keep an eye on him. *Échale un ojo, por favor.*"

Why? I'm thirteen years old, aren't I?

My father's mastery at re-enacting jokes is stimulated. He tells the delegate one that suits him to perfection and has in some way become his trademark. It is about a neurotic hypochondriac—like him—who, while shaving early in the morning, realizes he has cut himself slightly.

"*Me corté,*" I cut myself, he says, astonished. But rather than stopping, he goes on masochistically—"*Me corté, me corté, me corté*"—injuring himself further simply because, once the damage is done, what else is there to do but to dramatize it? The joke tells so much about him: his intensity, his emphatic behavior.

The delegate laughs. My somber mood is becoming overwhelming. Envy, ambivalence. I know my father is about to lose himself on stage, to become someone else. Will I get him back?

Not long ago, I asked him how he would prefer to die: "Onstage, obviously," he replied, "right in the middle of things." The answer was indeed obvious, but it nonetheless shocked me: why die at the precise instant when you aren't yourself? Selfishness. Or is it selflessness?

And what about my *own* self? Why is losing him to an audience so challenging for me? Don't I feel ambivalence when I have him around? He hardly ever acknowledges my talents.

"But don't talk about death, Ilan," he tells me. He always seems to pour out his soul when uttering sentences like this one.

Theater, theater: does he actually know where the stage ends and life begins? As a Bar Mitzvah gift I got a copy of *Alice in Wonderland* in Spanish. I haven't made myself read it from beginning to end, but while browsing through its illustrations I came across a quote:

> Let me think: was I the same when I got up this morning? . . . But if I'm not the same, the next question is, Who in the world am I? . . . "I'm sure I'm not Ada," she said, "for her hair goes in such long ringlets, and mine doesn't go in ringlets at all; and I'm sure I can't be Mabel, for I know all sorts of things, and she, oh! she knows such

a very little! Besides, *she's* she and I'm I, and—oh dear, how puzzling it all is! I'll try if I know all the things I used to know. . . ." her eyes filled with tears. . . . "I must be Mabel after all, and I shall have to go and live in that poky little house, and have next to no toys to play with, and oh!—ever so many lessons to learn! No, I've made up my mind about it; if I'm Mabel, I'll stay down here! . . ."

My mind keeps spinning. I've gone out to the playground with Valentina Vargas, but I'm thinking of him. An actor prepares: I know he is looking at himself in a mirror, becoming a ghost, a chimera. Years later, I will read a sentence by W. H. Auden: "No other human activity seems as completely gratuitous as 'acting'; games are gratuitous acts, but it can be argued that they have value—they develop the muscle or sharpen the wits of those who play them—but what conceivable purpose could one human being have for imitating another?" But Auden is nearsighted, for the phenomenon is astonishing. And don't other artists do the same? Doesn't a novelist imitate other people through his characters? And what about a sculptor, whose task it is to re-form and deform the edge of reality? And doesn't the dancer also strive for a technique through which imitation becomes renovation? To imitate—it is the first clearly defined social form of communication a child engages in; and throughout life we do little else but imitate: we become the people we are by stealing from others and then stamping our own character onto a certain attitude, a mannerism, a viewpoint. What an astonishing phenomenon, the actor's trade! For, inasmuch as I suffer seeing him lose himself to another personality—my fear of not getting him back is constant—I'm tantalized by the sheer magic of it all. And I'm aware—yes, even at thirteen years of age—of the envy I feel. Why can't I do it as well, why can't I have what he has? To accommodate such radical alteration, human nature needs to be incredibly plastic. But are all of us really as plastic, as malleable as he is? No, the magic is his and his alone.

"Te amo, Ilán," he said to me before I went outdoors. I love you. "And you, do you love me, too?"

I climb a ladder and let myself go on the slide. Valentina Vargas talks to me about her seven-year-old stepdaughter, María de la Luz.

"Oh, yeah," I say. "Wasn't she around last Sunday? My brother might have played with her."

I take the car keys from my pocket and throw them down the slide. I let myself go, too, pick them up, sit on a swing, and pretend to drive my own Rambler wagon away from the Teatro Orientación. Where to?

My own private theater.

Un payaso, a clown.

I climb the ladder again, and slide again, each time at greater speed. Then I hang myself like Spiderman from a swing. Am I acting my age? Am I now supposed to be an adolescent already? Have I regressed to my childhood?

My movements are almost frantic. Could I attract my father's attention from this far?

> *El rey de Parangaricutirimícuaro,*
> *Se quiere desparangaricutirimicuarizar. . . .*

Valentina Vargas is oblivious, until—kabooooooooom. Blood is pouring from my chin. I've fallen on the ground, my face right on top of the car keys. I open my eyes to focus on a pebble in front of me. I'm hurt.

Shock. Valentina Vargas realizes I've fallen. She approaches me. I obviously need stitches, so she cries for help. Someone arrives, and I'm hurried backstage.

Am I pretending? Theater, theater. Is the pain really as excruciating as I make it sound? Is it possible that I might also become an actor, as people dared to say at my Bar Mitzvah?

So far I've always been a healthy and gregarious child, although a bit irritable. "Temperamental" is the word my father uses. And he also says I fail to express my emotions. Fail to manifest my love for the world. Do I really?

"Tienes un corazón de piedra," he says: You have a heart of stone.

My father, in between scenes, rushes to my side. He is utterly distressed. He complains to Valentina, *"Pero mujer, pensé que lo estabas cuidando."*

But yes: I've got him back. I'm quite proud of my accomplishment. Mazel tov, Ilan!

{ 4 }

On My Brother's Trail

It's not possible that you won't be happy. . . .
It's not possible that you won't be happier than I.

—ISAAC BABEL, "KARL-YANKL"

FOR YEARS THE mid-size black-and-white photo hung proudly on the staircase at home. Later my mother stored it away. When every one of her children had finally moved away, it resurfaced in her studio. In it Darián, approximately sixteen months old, is standing up, his delicate hands on the windowsill. He wears dark overalls, long white socks, and boots with shoelaces neatly tied. And his hair is neatly brushed. He seems terrified. He isn't looking away but straight into the camera, ready to confront the moment. His deep fear, his anxiety, tells it all: I, the older brother by about eighteen months, rude and merciless, am nowhere to be seen; but even in my absence, I'm a power broker, a menace Darián must always reckon with. I am feared. I am the one person he hates to love.

I remember the photograph without a hint of nostalgia but with much—far too much—remorse. In my mind, two qualities have always characterized Darián: *la música y las palabras*. He is a stutterer, and his medium is music. Words were an impediment for him, the unavoidable obstacles he needed to overcome to be with others, to function in the community. The only time I can remember them serving him well—or, better, doing him a favor—was when, like all young Mexican males, Darián was called up to enlist in the nation's army. After a quick medical checkup, his *cartilla militar* was stamped with a release form that read: *inútil a la patria*, useless to the country. His stuttering, the lieutenant concluded, might put others in danger.

Impossible guttural syllables made him flounder: "br," "ppss," "bbbsss"; *bbrrazo, prrrrograma* . . . Sometimes reaching the end of a brief, insignificant sentence would become an ordeal, as torturous a task as climbing Mount Popocatépetl. In a matter of seconds he would travel from nervousness to fury to self-defeat. Were I and those around him the cause of that self-defeat? As I remember my reaction to his stuttering, I am overwhelmed by a limitless feeling of remorse. Remorse and grief. No sooner was Darián's tongue paralyzed than I would make an impatient gesture, a sign of expectation and hopelessness. Why couldn't he reach the end of the sentence? Time and again his verbal stumbling defeated him. How cruel of me! How ungenerous! What a lack of tolerance I displayed! And whenever Darián managed to finish what he wanted to say, I saw it as anticlimactic. I had already given up and nothing, *absolutamente nada*, my brother would do could make me regain my confidence in him.

But in music, he was completely free—free and undisputed.

Through it he defended himself against the merciless-
ness of those around him. He never stuttered when singing,
or when music was in the background. I am shamelessly
tuneless: I cannot, for the life of me, maintain a simple melody. Not even "Twinkle, twinkle . . ." or a lullaby, although
I'm told that, as if by magic, I can sing Yiddish songs—"*As
der rebbe Elimelech . . .*" and "*Oifn pripetchink . . .*"—with perfect pitch. Do I really? I also don't know how to dress. Darián, on the other hand, is harmonious in his whole being.
When he passes by, people comment on his meticulous ele-
gance and refinement, his obedient hairstyle and his chic
clothes. *Todo un caballero*, they are likely to utter, a gentleman
hecho y derecho.

Darián: no one else, not a single person, awakens in me
so much guilt. Or is it only discomfort? We shared a splen-
did childhood: played in our bathing suits with the water
hose, orchestrated epic battles with toy soldiers, kicked the
soccer ball up and down around the garden, and built so-
phisticated fortresses with Legos and Duplos; we laughed
and cried and fought and throughout our preadolescent
years remained simply inseparable—*como uña y carne*, as the
Spanish popular saying goes, or, in its English counterpart:
"joined at the hip."

But somewhere along the way, *nel mezzo del cammin di
nostra vita*—kaboom—everything fell apart. Communication stopped. Words collapsed. The music ceased. Was I the
culprit? Had the family dynamics turned us into scapegoats?
Or was it only Darián who needed help? True, his instability
began to manifest itself early on, but my parents chose to ignore it. Or, rather, they attempted to assuage it with our
daily routine. Having grown up in the 1960s, I now see how
they misread the signs and mistreated their judgment. The

weak individual is always the repository of collective anguish, they said to themselves; we must protect Darián, we must bring about his psychological health.

JUMPS, SOMERSAULTS, INCESSANT activity: always nudging, always bouncing around. Darián was a hyperkinetic boy. He got his precious fingers into any dangerous situation—a blender, the toilet, a pencil sharpener, a bicycle pedal— much, much faster than the eye could see. What patience my parents needed! What stamina and resignation! But he was utterly captivating. People laughed at his pranks. They delighted in and applauded his behavior. Darián the genius, Darián the piano virtuoso, Darián the *simpático*, Darián this and that . . . Was his constant motion a way to compensate for, perhaps even to hide, his slowness of speech? My parents, I'm told, detected the verbal impediment the moment he began talking, at around fifteen months of age—more or less when the haunting black-and-white photograph was framed and hung on the staircase. Were they worried? I'm sure, as all normal folks would be. They talked to friends and acquaintances, to their own parents, about what to do. How does one treat stuttering? What are the latest scientific theories about it? Is it a sickness or a symptom? Yes, stuttering—*tartamudear* (in Spanish the words is already a tongue-twister, *un trabalenguas*)—is an impediment, but it also carries a stigma for which there is no cure.

It is, to be sure, a well-known problem. Famous stutterers range from Moses of Egypt to Lewis Carroll and John Updike. I know my parents consulted one too many specialists, and from each and every one they received a disparate, often contradictory response, some of them not different from Demosthenes' explanation in the fifth century B.C. "It is the result of the disparity between mind and body," said one, "for it appears in individuals, mostly schizophrenics and idiots, whose minds travel at one speed and mouths at another." No, another doctor pronounced, "it is a sign of the misbehavior of the tongue," and suggested, by way of a cure, to tie it tightly for a couple of hours a day. I also heard of other, equally nefarious treatments applied to other patients, including electroshock. Finally, my parents were told by a top neurophysiologist to connect speech and psychology.

A specialist asked Darián to perform a series of ridiculous tasks, most of them physical exercises that, looking back, seem denigrating. Were they helpful? I especially remember what I used to call "yin-yang gymnastics"—his crawling like a baby after a doctor established that my brother's stuttering was the outcome of a last-minute anatomical shift inside his mother's womb. Darián, we were told, had been destined to be left-handed, but just before birth he had become right-handed. The result was an "indirect physical scar," which manifested itself in his incapacity to speak fluently. In other words, his left side was unhappy with his right side. The medical recommendation was simple: he needed to be more balanced, reaffirm his two sides, and to do so he needed to regress to a pre-bipedal status—to crawl again, at least half an hour a day, every day. I have no clue how established this yin-yang theory was in the profession, but it seemed nothing less than ludicrous. Still, it might have some truth to it, Darián became convinced, simply because he regularly suffered from other ailments on the left side of his body: his left leg, his left testicle, his left eye, his left ear, etc. No matter how radical a treatment doctors applied—at one time he even underwent surgery on his testicles—the pain was undeniable. It came and went like a furious thunder cracking in the sky. His body, he knew, was a minefield, and an unbalanced one. So, every afternoon for fifteen minutes, he went on all fours in circles in his bedroom.

My mother believes Darián's stuttering is indeed connected to the strange pregnancy that ultimately brought him into the world. Shortly before he was born, she was told that the placenta surrounding the embryo had grown deformed and the umbilical cord, instead of functioning as a center of gravity and nutrition, moved toward the right hemisphere, resulting in an unequal distribution of food. In the end, the baby was delivered on time but small—six and a half pounds—though not small enough to be placed in an incubator. Did this amount to an explanation? Or had one of the many luminaries in the field managed to convince my knowledge-hungry mother that it had to be so, that the source of the problem was physical?

At any rate, everyone talked of "correcting the problem" by means of methodical strategies. One doctor—a tall, bearded man whose eyes invariably looked at you with pity— suggested weekly sessions of speech therapy. Indeed, I remember Darián attending his office regularly for forty-five minutes to an hour at a time, being asked to utter the same word a thousand times at different speeds: *millón, mi-llón, mmmiii—lllllllllóóóóóóóóóóóóóóónnnnnn*. These sessions, if memory serves me well, were part of his life at various periods, often with different physicians. Skinnerian therapists shifted their focus to techniques of self-control. As years went by, Darián felt a bit less frustrated—only a bit, though. The sessions proved effective, for, by the time he reached twelve or thirteen, the trick, as far as he was concerned, was rather simple: to be able to control his vocabulary, to select his words carefully, to listen to his own voice before it came out his mouth, to be ahead of his speech, as in TV soaps. Control, control, control ... Darián had to teach the world to be patient with him. And the only way to do so was through self-regulation. He learned to evade—to bypass—troublesome syllables, to master the art of synonyms, to be a *vocabulista*.

Still, public attention was always bestowed upon him. It was he, not I, whose talents were manifest. Would he become an actor, like my father? Unlikely. Probably he was destined for an illustrious career in music, for only in and through music could he relax, and when he did it was as if the heavens had opened their doors for the angels to descend. The piano was my brother's true friend, his means of expressing himself. The house must have had one from early on, but I fail to recall it. I remember the day, in the early 1970s or perhaps a bit earlier, when, with a sizable endowment from Bobbe Miriam, the whole family went to a Yamaha store on Avenida Insurgentes, in Colonia del Valle, to buy him the instrument. Darián was as proud as he could be, his fingers caressing its keyboard, experiencing their porcelain softness. He was worshipping his idol, praying for it to inspire the great talent he knew he kept inside himself. Soon afterwards, Tía Malvina—wife to Tío Isaac and a neighbor, just around the block—began to teach him to play in earnest through Béla Bartók's manual for children, *Aprendiendo a mover los deditos*. Frustration gave way to excitement. Darián played magically: any tune, no matter how complicated, was easily turned into a full-blown concerto. Music was his panacea. People visiting us at home always asked to have him play. At first he said no, but in the end he complied. He loved performing, for clearly he was in his element. My father would invariably interrupt a spontaneous conversation between guests and gather everyone in the downstairs studio. Darián would sit on his bench and—*uno, dos, tres*—produce enchanting music. He would play ("entertain" is too earthly a word) for twenty to thirty minutes. In the end, applause and adulation: my father, imperious in his manner, would conclude by talking for several more minutes about Darián's talent, his future, the euphoria the whole family felt.

DARIÁN'S PRECARIOUS SENSE of self was built around his *tartamudez*. In spite of his charisma, in spite of his enviable skills as a pianist, he saw himself—how could he not?—as the black sheep, the ugly duckling: *el patito feo*.

His rage intensified, often pushing him to perform insane, self-hating acts: deliberately cutting himself with a pair of scissors, putting a needle through a finger, his left foot through a moving bicycle wheel. Sometimes he targeted others. On one occasion he tried to drown my sister, Liora, in the bathtub. On a schoolbus ride he once exhibited his penis in front of the girls. He had a violent sexual encounter with a cousin in the darkness of a closet.

He had little interest in languages, of course. (For him Yiddish and Hebrew are interchangeable.) And history and civics he disowned. Only in his music lesson did he thrive. His overall grades were barely acceptable, but that was the least of the problems. My parents were frequently called by the school principal to discuss the matter: his aggression, his lack of control, his frantic states of mind. All of it, it seems, was exacerbated in the presence of the opposite sex. *Las niñas*—the girls drove him crazy. He pushed them around, declared his passion for them, then threw objects at them. But by then my father and mother had taken what I am tempted to describe as "the socialist approach": Darián's dilemma was collective; they believed society needed to change as much as the individual in question. Repeated attempts were made by the school—three teachers and the principal together, a teacher and several sets of involved parents—to persuade my incredulous parents to find more effective treatment for their second child. Rebellious as they are by nature, they blatantly ignored these pleas: Darián had to live *in society*, not away from it; he needed to learn to adapt, to behave, to be like everyone else. This was their answer: "Don't like him? Buzz off, please. . . ." At one point, for instance, his current and previous teachers at Der Yiddisher Shule met with my parents and told them that Darián's conduct was dangerous: *un peligro*. They used the term "mental illness," which, although clear to many, was anathema to my parents. His teachers recommended placing him in another school, or at least having a special teacher at his side most of the time, working with him very closely. Many years later, I talked to one of these teachers. She described how my parents listened carefully to all that was said, and then, when the time came for them to reply, simply stated that Darián was a very creative child—a genius—and that to put him under some sort of strict medical supervision would hamper, even annihilate his artistic drive. They concluded by simply walking out of the meeting. Were they right? My instinct tells me no. As a father today, I understand the intense suffering they must have experienced: a child's challenge is also his parents'; a drastic measure could easily backfire. But they were also too hopeful. Explosive individuals ought to be treated as such, even though society must learn to accommodate their handicap. My brother clashed more and more frequently with the status quo. On every occasion there was much noise *and* suffering.

The passive approach—"let him be"—became my parents' motto. But let him be *with* music, to the point of saturation. His loving family would rescue Darián; each of us (my father and mother, my sister and I) would help him become as useful and adaptable a citizen as possible by simply allowing him his daily dose of drugs: music and more music. In truth, though, the family was shaping itself into a spiderweb, and doing it through words. My parents were convinced that Darián's dilemma might best be handled through verbalization, so conversation was encouraged to the point of exhaustion. An incessant blah-blah-blah. Every action, every feeling, every experience waited to be verbalized, reflected upon, analyzed in all its facets. *Digito ergo sum*. We talked for and about Darián. And we didn't just talk, we talked about the act of talking.

Do other families talk so much? Do they partake in so much self-examination? Was it only my *Jewish* family? My *neurotic* Jewish family? Words descend upon us like a Biblical deluge. Was speech not a subterfuge, a form of deception? I am still transfixed by the long—very long—afternoons of undirected family therapy, in which my parents stubbornly sat us down together to talk. About what? To what end? Simply to discuss our affection, our need for each other. Darián was not the center of these conversations, for placing him in the spotlight all the time would surely have backfired. No, the topic was life in general. Or, better, each and every one of us as an important participant in it. I, of course, hated these sessions. Did they really have a purpose? What did they have to do with me? The irony was unavoidable: Darián had trouble speaking, whereas everyone else in the family suffered from an overabundance of speech. This verbalization, in my view, sprang from our Jewishness, and I wondered, did G–d deliberately endow us Jews with a tendency not to stop shvitzing and shmoozing? How could I suddenly shut up without offending everyone else around me? Would I cease to be me if I fell silent for a minute?

Years went by. The family group sessions moved to VIPS, Sanborn's, Denny's, and other popular cafeterias where Mexico's middle and upper-middle class often met. Nothing was sacred, no secrets were kept—everything was talked about, time and again: Liora's first menstruation, my first marijuana joint, Darián's announcement that he planned to pursue a musical career at Juilliard. . . . Everything was known to everybody at all times. How exhausting it all was! How intimidating! But each of us pretended it was just as well, perhaps because we knew of no alternative. Darián's handicap had given way to *verborrea*, unstoppable talk. I think of Bartleby the Scrivener: "Ah, the family, ah humanity!"

I HAVE SAID it already: I love Darián wholeheartedly, in spite of the misery. He is *my* brother, an integral part of me. Our inner natures are inseparably linked: I always knew where he was and he knew where I was. At times, this dependency took a bizarre—I am tempted to say "supernatural"—twist. A couple of recollections should suffice.

Once Darián was scheduled to spend the whole day at a

friend's house. My mother was putting on mascara in front of a mirror when I told her it didn't seem a good idea to allow my brother to go to his *amiguito*. "He might have an accident," I said. She sighed, and the conversation ended. In the evening, though, she rushed to the hospital, where she picked Darián up, his left arm in a cast. He had fallen while climbing an Aztec ruin, a pyramid he and his friend had gone to visit.

In school I struggled to convince my friends to allow him to play soccer, by far my favorite sport. I feared for his safety, and although when together I invariably tormented him—the black-and-white photograph, did it describe or prescribe our relationship?—I was also his bodyguard. How to sort out my ambivalence toward him? We slept in the same room, went to the same school, played the same games. . . . I remember the day I found the courage to ask my parents for my own private bedroom. It must have been shortly after my Bar Mitzvah. Originally the second floor of our Copilco house was built as a huge playroom. But when Liora was born, a wall was raised to divide it in two. Darián and I had one of these half-size rooms; the other was reserved for toys. With time, the walls in the playroom were completely covered with watercolor paints, the rug was sticky with glue, and the furniture we had climbed all over was scratched. My hope was to be granted permission to renovate this room in my own taste. I would plaster it, clean the rug with a rented machine, polish the old furniture by hand. I didn't mean it to be a luxurious room, but it would be mine and mine alone.

Permission was granted. I began work right away. It took me almost a week to complete the job. I can still invoke the feelings of accomplishment and independence: my room, my habitat. I no longer shared space with Darián; I had the sense I was about to redefine myself, to begin anew, to shape my own character independently from his. Freedom—its taste was magnificent. Within a few days, I felt as if a fog had been lifted from my eyes. I was able to think more clearly, to know more decisively what I liked. And what *did* I like? First and foremost, to be left alone, to live autonomously. This gave me the opportunity to see my brother from a different perspective. Was he a genius? Was he another wunderkind, like Mozart? Another Chopin or Debussy? And what did I, in contrast, have to offer the world? My brother was lucky to have his piano. It made him a celestial creature, a champion. I didn't know what to do with myself. I loved film and theater but hated reading. I enjoyed chess, comic strips, and outdoor sports, none of which compared to Darián's odyssey as a young Arthur Rubinstein on the road to Carnegie Hall. Yes, I, too, was convinced he was destined to be a master. Aren't all artists erratic in their behavior, incapable of conducting themselves in a civilized manner?

Art and chaos: is there a worse cliché? Its roots are in Romanticism—in Goethe's *Young Werther.* In private, I understood art not as an excuse for rotten conduct but as a dignified gesture of the intellect. And so what to make of my brother? I wondered. How long would it be before he fell to pieces?

IN ADOLESCENCE, OUR roles began to reverse themselves. Much as I try, I cannot think of a more troubled adolescence than Darián's. He had—and still has—a striking physical resemblance to my father, to the point where people called him, without a hint of doubt, *dem kleinem Abremele:* young Abraham. As time went by, though, the resemblance became a conviction and then an obsession. He was indeed a youthful version of my father, Darián told himself, and he began to model his life as if my father were reliving his, step by step. He insisted, for instance, on describing his own difficulties in school as nothing but a mirror image of my father's three decades before; and he portrayed himself as a rascal, a rebel, an eccentric, whose future sanity depended solely on building himself a suitable home. The exit from the quagmire was a woman, one exactly like my mother—intelligent, strong-willed, uncompromising—whose own life would be devoted to *his* art.

Darián had been a slim child with unruly hair, but in his teens he inflated in size: his neck became unusually large and his round belly made him resemble a childish Buddha. He hated sports and other forms of physical activity. Books were not for him, either. Only music and more music. While he convalesced at home from mononucleosis, he spent his mornings in pajamas, listening to popular radio stations. His idols were Elton John, Barry Manilow, and the Bee Gees. I would come back from school to find him tucked in his bed. He had a phone next to him and called radio stations to request a favorite song and, should his call be the first, to win the latest LP by Olivia Newton-John. Nothing in Mexican music attracted him: *rancheras*, mariachis, *corridos*, *baladas*, these were all lower-class rhythms, *música naca*, not art but artifacts. This, I'm convinced, was the result of our segregated Jewish upbringing; Julio Iglesias, Emmanuel, Rafael, and Juan Gabriel were sheer kitsch as far as he was concerned, and so, by the way, was Klezmer music, which he perceived as overly sentimental. No, what he enjoyed were the ballads of mainstream American icons. Was this his way of asserting himself among the young, refusing the classical-music education my parents envisioned for him? American Muzak symbolized escape, and escape is what he longed for.

Escapism also came in the form of an infatuation with *la mujer ideal*, the ideal woman. It was in the early 1970s—Darián was in bed with mononucleosis—when, as I recall, a cheap Hollywood melodrama, *Melody*, with actor Mark Lester of *Oliver!* fame, targeted to youngsters, premiered at Cine Manacar, some seven miles north of our neighborhood. My brother heard the theme music on the radio and immediately fell in love—with the tune, with the movie he had not yet seen. I remember him returning home from the cinema—his first time out after a three-week convalescence, a rendezvous with my father which my mother strictly opposed—talking nonstop—*¡qué belleza!* and *¡qué calidad!* and *¡qué actuación!*—about the leading female star, a second-rate actress whose career seemed to founder after this movie. In the next weeks, he returned to the theater, without exaggeration, some ten, twelve, eighteen times, usually early enough to scrutinize the publicity photos in the entry hallway. At first he had company, but then he happily went on his own and arrived completely enraptured. "*Ay, Melody*," Darián would sigh. The movie was a romance, and Melody was the name of the heroine. Did a more stunning angel walk on the face of the earth, Darián wondered? If only he could travel to Hollywood to find her and tell her in a tête-à-tête how much he admired her, how much he loved everything about her: her eyes, her lips, her holy presence. He understood the dialogue in the movie through subtitles. It was not the message but the messenger that he was truly after, though: the ring of her voice, her gracefulness. Darián's infatuation quickly developed into an obsession. He rang the film distributor in Mexico and asked if there were any stills, publicity photos, a poster he could acquire. He was in desperate need to have Melody next to him. He was told there were none available. The movie was actually a commercial flop; it was not expected to last long—one or two more weeks, at the most. In the United States, it had already been forgotten. This did not deter Darián. Often he was alone, or almost alone, in the theater, but the Talmud states it forcefully: a man is a universe unto himself. The producer's negative reply didn't stop him. He borrowed my father's camera and, while inside the theater, took pictures himself. He also photographed the publicity stills in the entrance. A couple across the aisle gave him a perplexed look, an angry viewer asked him to cut it out, and finally an employee asked him either to stop or to leave the theater for good. By then he had a whole roll. The quality, of course, was deplorable, but did he care? Darián had Melody with him, constantly at his side. He hung the images next to his bed and studied them with enormous concentration. I remember him staring: each of these pictures allowed him to relive the film yet again, or perhaps to reinvent it so as to include himself as its protagonist. Yes, the character played by Mark Lester was erased from the print in his memory, and he, Darián Stavchansky, proudly replaced him. He imagined himself kissing Melody time and again, taking her for long walks in the park, drinking milkshakes with her in an ice-cream parlor. His days brightened up. He looked happier, stimulated, a young man at peace with the world.

The crush lasted months. Darián never quite got himself out of the affair. I remember him sitting in the afternoons on the wooden windowsill, staring for long hours at the outside world while listening to pop music. Complete concentration, physical immobility. It was obvious he enjoyed his solitude tremendously. He had few friends, most of them male. His attraction of the opposite sex frequently had explosive consequences: he hurled his sexuality at them, kissing them against their will, pulling his pants down, getting them pregnant and ending up in abortion clinics. Secretly, I admired these escapades, his courage to be physical. I was envious. How could I not be? Since my Bar Mitzvah, I had suffered from a skin disease—a merciless invasion of abscesses—that had a strong impact on my self-esteem. Those awful abscesses . . . No, "pimples" is a better word, better than "abscesses," "carbuncles," "pustules," and "swellings"; it is the most recognizable. But I can't use it, so tormenting are its echoes. In a matter of weeks, I was totally overwhelmed by them: my nose, cheeks, neck, forehead, my back and even my crotch reconfigured by them. I was turned into a monster. Or, more precisely, to a medieval gargoyle.

How I longed to exchange my body for a less vulnerable, more appealing one, like Darián's. I finally came to terms with the skin disease, but for a long, long time, it was a source of public shame. What did others think of me? What did they say behind my back? Why was I the one inflicted by this? I had many skin-related nightmares, but nothing was more unbearable than the daily routine. I looked for ways to hide the problem: I wore turtlenecks, had saunas weekly, avoided displaying my torso in public, and swam wearing a T-shirt. And I avoided mirrors everywhere, in the home, in the bathroom, in department stores and restaurants. I tried every remedy to cure my illness: weekly doses of antibiotic, a diet reduced in calories with no nuts or chocolates. I even visited a *curandera*, a quack, in the state of Morelos, whose prescription—inhaling a potion made of wild herbs—seemed to release me temporarily from the psychological pain. The theories were manifold: oil secretion in my epidermis, too many sexual encounters, unholiness (which a rabbi endorsed), and, of course, heredity. My mother told me Zeyde Jaime, her father, also had trouble with his skin and on occasion suffered from swellings.

The nightmares still cling to me. One I distinctly remember had the texture of a Czech film: slow motion, sepia-color interiors, visceral language. I was in the Warsaw Ghetto. Not long before, I had read about the diaries of Janusz Korczak, the doctor and advocate of children's rights in an orphanage in Warsaw in the 1930s. I had seen pictures of Korczak in a long, heavy, worn black coat, and in my dream I wore that very coat. I was lonely and alone in a small cubicle, nothing but a prison cell, with a bed, a scratched wooden table, and some painting equipment: oil tubes, brushes, a pair of canvases. The first image I remember is of me asleep next to a painting. Then another one, waking up in the middle of the night. As soon as I was conscious, I automatically touched parts of my face—my mouth, an ear—to make sure they were still in place. I quickly discovered my nose had moved. An inch, two perhaps. It was no longer at the center of my face. Or was it? I tried to bring it back, slowly, carefully. No success. No sooner did I change its position than it moved again. And again. *Otra vez. Y otra vez, y otra . . .* I stood up, looking for my coat. When I finally found it, I covered not my body but my face with it.

The passing of real time makes it difficult for me to retain the sequence of the scenes. I do remember, though, that at one point my nose disappears from my face. It appears in my left armpit, behind my right ear, in my crotch. Then it appears in my mouth. . . . The more the dream unravels, the less in control I am of my facial features.

A second nightmare was even more dramatic. I had it several years earlier, at the house of Bobbe Bela. I remember waking up terrified and soaking in sweat. She calmed me down and gave me a glass of water, but I was afraid to return to sleep. In the dream my entire immediate family—my parents, Darián, Bobbe Miriam, and Bobbe Bela herself, but not my sister, Liora—is in an old Peugeot my father once owned. He is at the wheel, and the atmosphere inside the vehicle is tense. We are on Avenida Copilco, half a block away from home, but we don't make the right turn and continue on. Suddenly, Liora, not more than six years old at the time, crosses the street, and the Peugeot runs her over. We feel only a slight bump. The accident decapitates Liora. Her head rolls under the car. I turn around to look from the rear window and notice acne on her bloody face. The dream abruptly concludes with Bobbe Bela saying, *Me kent nicht veinen*—in Yiddish, One shouldn't cry.

The skin disease deeply affected my sense of maleness. In my wildest dreams, I, too, wanted to kiss girls, but was reduced to smart conversation with them, for I feared any manifestation of intimacy. I was sure they would be repelled.

At one point, for instance, I was attracted to a brainless classroom beauty, Jenny N. For days I agonized about how to attract her attention, but without any success. After much deliberation, I stopped her during recess and asked, simply: *¿Quieres ser mi novia?* Would you be my sweetheart? She laughed, of course. I was unattractive, not one of the "hot items" in the class. I felt ashamed, denigrated. I shouldn't have asked, I told myself. Darián was far better at this daunting business. Still, I tried my luck with another girl, Gina T., again without happy results. Darián at least got his way. Sure, he jumped in too fast, but girls were attracted to him. Did I have a defined, clear-cut, convincing personality of my own? I wasn't sure, although those around me thought so. Deep inside, I wanted what my brother possessed. Yes, he was often out of control, but so what? Darián often got into trouble, serious trouble, making adults furious, but at least he had guts, didn't he? I had none. Or not enough. And if I did, they brought no satisfaction, nothing I could be proud of.

In our environment, maleness was a virtue and a weapon. Macho males were strong, handsome: conquerors. Women were trophies, captives, the terrain on which the male left his mark. The appeal of men was based on their roughness, their muscular power. Too much attention on one's own cleanliness and dress was considered a sign of femininity: *maricón*, *puto*, a female male—*faygeleh* in Yiddish. How on earth would I be able to attract a wife? Sex was the challenge. On a Saturday afternoon when I was sixteen, I was taken by a group of close friends, a few of them older, to a whorehouse in Colonia Roma. I have no clear recollection of the arrangements, but somehow I got the impression my father had been informed about, and approved of, my visit to a harlot. It was a rite of passage: so many before me had undergone the same ritual; as soon as the male Mexican adolescent reaches his teens, talk of *desvirginación* becomes ubiquitous. To reach the age of thirteen and still be a *quintito*, uninitiated, untouched, is a source of laughter. Other men are able to tell, in the blink of an eye, who is or isn't a real *hombre* in the way the adolescent walks and talks, in the way he behaves toward his peers.

I had gotten a phone call the night before. Everything was set: the initiation would take place around 4:30 P.M. An acquaintance could meet me and some friends at a restaurant a couple of blocks away from the apartment where we were going. I shouldn't be nervous, the voice on the phone said: the whole affair—a brief chat and a turn for all four of us—would last a couple of hours, perhaps less. I hung up the phone and decided to take an almost unbearably hot bath. Boiling water would clean my skin. It would purify me. Yes, I was exceedingly nervous. Would I be able to have an erection? How would I know where to put my penis? And what if I peed inside her? Would she get aroused at the sight of my naked body? Would it disgust her?

I remember the day vividly. I told my parents I had a date at a friend's house. My mother drove me to Colonia Hipódromo, where I met two of the other four bachelors about to be initiated. We spent the morning discussing expectations and cracking jokes. We speculated about who had the longest penis. We walked to a nearby newsstand and browsed through pornographic magazines. Our fathers had surely followed a similar pattern, but not our fathers' fathers, for ours was a strictly Mexican rite of passage. Or was it? A test of virility in a civilization obsessed with sexual potency. We took a bus to Colonia Roma to find our "tour guide." On the way, every single young woman we saw as a potential candidate for a future adventure. Soon we would have the necessary knowledge to conquer and possess. By then it had become clear that the words "conquest" and "possession" were essential to the understanding of all sexual games around us. Men "occupy" women, *las poseen*. In Mexico the term for the verb "to fornicate" is *cojer*: to take over, *echarse a una mujer*, to subdue a woman. These views might prevail in most of Western civilization, but south of the Rio Grande they acquire a unique historical connotation. The Spanish conquistadors came and conquered: *nos cojieron*.

The Spanish word for "whorehouse" is *prostíbulo*, a syllabic unit that makes me think of a bubble bath. The apartment we entered was dark and decrepit. In the living room were a couple of run-down Art Nouveau sofas and several folding chairs. Other customers had come in that same day, and five young men were sitting patiently, either waiting for their own turns or simply waiting for others to finish so they could all leave. Near them, eight or nine young prostitutes, some barely fifteen years old, looked at us. Theirs was the look of temptation. They might have been young, but they were clearly on their turf. One, a mestiza beauty, looked at me almost immediately. Her skin was bronze. She had long braids and a tight dress that showed off her figure. She smiled, and I looked away. I saw one of my friends, Meni Meshulam, a hyperactive adolescent—like Darián—of Middle Eastern descent. In the school's circle of male friends, Meni was known as an insatiable masturbator (*el gran sobador*), and as an even more unappeasable fornicator. Had he already performed the heroic act? He smiled at me and, with a nod of his head, suggested the girl I should conquer—the same Indian beauty I had just evaded. Were they in cahoots? I looked at her again, and in less than a minute we were both inside a yellow bedroom.

The curtains were closed; the bed had just been remade. Yolanda: *la mujer fácil*. I asked her a few personal questions. Where was she from? How long had she been working in this apartment? How many men did she . . . go through in a single afternoon? She was from Oaxaca, where her family still lived. . . .

"But have you come to talk?"

I was terrified.

She proceeded to undress herself and unbutton me. Suddenly, I became conscious of her skin color. Our racial encounter was a replica of the hierarchy in Mexican society: white on top of mestizo, mestizo on top of mulatto. . . .

Her tongue began to excite me. And what did I feel? Dizziness. How many mouths had she kissed? She began licking my neck, then my chest. In a quick, unforeseen move, she was behind me, facing my back, fully aware of my skin disease. I tried to turn around. Yolanda had found out my secret: she knew I was repulsive—or, at least, that I had a repulsive side to me.

Had I been a fool?

She said nothing, not for a while at least. I was not her lover. Ours was just a business transaction. But I was a teenager, oblivious to such realities. She was my first and only mistress, my goddess of Eros. And so I interpreted her *silencio sepulcral* as acceptance. As I look back, though, I'm aware of her generosity. She didn't spoil my first sexual encounter.

I remember closing my eyes in shame. After a while, she gave in and asked, "Do you apply any ointment to the injured spots?" And then she pulled out the dagger: Did I mind fornicating—no, she used the expression *hacer el amor*, to make love—with a towel on top of the sheets? You see, the house matron forces us to keep our rooms impeccable, to be clean, to avoid infections by . . . Anyway, how about using a towel to prevent leaving spots (pus, blood) on the bed?

Hhhhh . . . Was Yolanda about to pull out of the game? I took a few seconds to respond, and after a deep breath confidently said: "Sure, why not? I don't mind at all. I'm rather used to it."

The rest of our exchange is foggy. I only remember that I did penetrate her. Or, rather, that I entered her and then got lost, submerged in ecstasy, oblivious to words and the world around me, to my skin disease, and to Yolanda. I was . . . where? I don't know, but I felt warm and cold at once, and mostly bestial, but truly alive and mystical.

Then it was over. I had performed my duty, but I had also achieved something else: the recognition that, beyond the suffering it inflicted, I was also capable of physical pleasure.

Yolanda got dressed and I did, too. I repeated to myself: *Fornico, fulmino, fabrico*—I had become *un hombre*. And I felt dizzy again.

But it had been painful. If only I could be as handsome as Darián, as unafraid of intimacy . . . He was probably still a *quintito*. Or was he not? Had he outdone me in this area, too?

Yes, no doubt about it. I never dared to ask him, though.

DARIÁN'S LOVE OF popular ballads increasingly led him to try his luck at song composition—*un cantautor*. He began to fancy himself a *baladista*, one capable of wide recognition. If stuttering was a hindrance, a barrier even, his music would be his ticket to fame. It took no time for us to realize that he was indeed an astonishing composer. His songs of love and longing, of solitude and despair, mesmerized audiences. Not an inspiring singer, he found a way to join sentimental lyrics happily with piano accompaniment. I teased him regularly: "Darián, you're the next Julio Iglesias! Your future is in Viña del Mar," a popular Chilean tourist spot on the Pacific Coast that hosted an annual international favorite-song competition televised across the globe. He laughed but was somehow enamored with the idea. Suddenly, he sympathized with icons like Emmanuel and listed the favorite light pianist Richard Clayderman as a symbol of achievement. It was then, I think, that Darián moved from Melody to a real-life darling, Jacky K., a precocious classmate of my younger sister, Liora, hardly fourteen years of age at the time. The relationship started normally: a smile, a passing word, a phone call, a lunch date, a movie engagement. . . .

Soon they saw each other twice a week, and eventually every day. He was at her house or on the phone with her for hours. And she was also at our place, often alone with him in his room. Darián composed several melodies for her, which coincided with his early attempts at performing in public, a sort of coming-out for him, since his stuttering had always made him feel insecure on stage. But with Jacky K., he seemed like a new person. He registered for several competitions, one of them in the CDI. It had various categories, and Darián soon became the favorite candidate for "Spotting the Young Composer," for which contestants submitted a single original song, which they then performed in front of an audience of approximately three hundred people. Judges selected three out of the group, who performed again, after which the winner was announced. I distinctly remember the loud applause he got after he played. But the entire theater was kept waiting half an hour for the judges to finish. Apparently, something was wrong. I sat next to my brother, cracking our fingers, until the news finally came that he had been disqualified. His song, the judges claimed, was too close to the second movement of Beethoven's Sixth Symphony, the so-called *Pastoral*.

I still carry Darián's tune in my mind: pah, pah-pah, paaaaaah, pah. I liked the *melody*, and so did the crowd. Everyone—myself included, of course—was utterly shocked. Did he plagiarize? Yes, no doubt. But aren't popular songs by definition derivative and unoriginal? Don't all songs by Barry Manilow sound like remakes of those by Engelbert Humperdinck and Tom Jones? Isn't Elton John his own worst imitator? Why penalize a youngster whose inspiration is Beethoven? Then again: why not? Shouldn't a devotee of Beethoven and Sibelius and Mendelssohn be committed to a higher standard, even if he has given up his faith in the classics? And what is originality, anyway? Isn't the Xerox machine among our most revered deities? Aren't we all copies of copies? Jacky tried to encourage him, and so did others. But Darián took it as a rejection of his own essence. He hated himself and promised never to compose songs again. Strangely, his was an unexpected reaction. Instead of abandoning music altogether or, perhaps less radically, hating Beethoven, Darián decided he was oversaturated with kitsch. No more melodrama, no more second-rate art. Soon he sold his LP collection: no more Muzak, he said.

He needed to get serious, and he did. He slowly began to buy classical records—Herbert von Karajan, Leonard Bernstein, Zubin Mehta; Arthur Rubinstein and Alicia de la Rocha; Jascha Heifetz, Isaac Stern, and Pinchas Zuckerman; all of Mozart and Mendelssohn, Sibelius and Dvořák. And he began to compose again. His piano lessons had taken him so far, he announced. It was time to try his own luck. He soon found out about concerts in Ciudad de México and often invited Jacky to the Palacio de Bellas Artes and the nearby Sala Netzahualcóyotl.

Music and the girl—nothing else mattered. His obsession increased. Darián needed to be with the girl all the time. My parents felt confident about the relationship, for it seemed to make Darián more confident as a young man, less insecure about his speech. There were no more accusations of sexual assault, no more erratic behavior in the classroom. But the girl's parents were less enthusiastic. They liked my brother and even recognized his talents as a musician, but they also felt their daughter became increasingly suffocated, remote from friends and family. They wanted her to be open to other friendships, not aloof and diffident, which they blamed on Darián's incessant passion. They sensed, too, that Jacky's relationship was potentially explosive. They wanted her to taste freedom.

She was in love, though, *locamente enamorada*, and didn't want to hear about it, not a single word. . . . So Jacky's parents talked to mine, to no avail. They tried everything in their power: forbidding her to see him and sending her to family abroad, etc. Finally, in desperation, they took the most radical road available: they moved to the United States. The father, I believe, was an engineer. He found a suitable job in Massachusetts, somewhere near Boston. This piece of news was devastating to Darián. Their liaison had lasted a couple of years. He had invested his whole self in it. What could the future hold without her?

All of this happened rather quickly. Suddenly, Darián was left alone. Alone and lonely and deprived of his *only* love.

My parents, ever patient—oh, how much I admired and even was jealous of their patience!—persuaded him to go into therapy. But he was not fully committed. The long-distance phone bill reached sky-high: he spent hours on the phone talking to her when her parents were not at home. Then, out of the blue, he plotted a trip to visit Jacky, bought himself a cheap plane ticket, and off he went to Logan Airport, his very first international journey alone. Was he eighteen already? The voyage was a disaster. I cannot imagine it otherwise, even though my father's cousin from Long Island took him in for a few days. Darián conveyed the whole sad story to me in retrospect. He flew to New York, where he found family comfort, but then landed in Boston in the middle of a terrible snowstorm. He had to find his way to Jacky's home. The taxi driver, a moody, intolerant man, dropped him a block away. When Darián finally arrived, sneezing, his fingers and toes half frozen, the girl's parents refused to open the door. Apparently, they were alerted to his trip and were furious. In spite of her tantrums and his petitions for clemency, they refused to let him in. He returned to Ciudad de México downhearted, without a will to live, *con el rabo entre las piernas*.

She did slip a photo through her window: Jacky as a cheerleader. He showed it to me. "Darián, I can't believe it," I said. "*Ya es una gringa. . . .*" He thought about it for a second. "Yeah. No longer my Jacky."

DEPRESSION. DESPERATION AND silence. It was clear something was terribly wrong.

One afternoon I found Darián in his room, on his own.

On the stereo was Mendelssohn's Third Symphony, known as *Scottish*. No Barry Manilow, no Bee Gees. Was he in a specially dark mood? I came closer and realized he was pale and crying. I found out he had tried to commit suicide by throwing himself out his bedroom window. His room, like mine, was on the house's second floor, at a maximum height of not more than thirty feet. He described the attempt to me. "I felt dizzy, Ilan, without the will to live, not knowing who I am. . . . But I held on to the sill." A few days before, he confessed, he had hit the bathroom mirror with his right fist. Mirrors were as daunting to him as they were to me, but his masochism turned them into dangerous objects. He had broken the mirror in anger, and blood came out. "I hate myself—*Mmmeee o-dio prrrrofunddddddddamente.*"

JACKY, JACKY, JACKY. The obsession was endless. I tried to console him, but it wasn't easy. We talked, and talked, and talked. . . . Only gibberish, I think today. Was I capable of giving him some hope? Was all this sheer acting? Was he shouting for affection? My mother came in. She was very worried. He needed therapy, she said. Quickly. The family's verbal pump-ups were insufficient.

I was fed up with the whole affair. Weren't we all guilty? And I thought to myself: Could Darián kill himself? Had he attempted suicide before? How much did I know about his internal plight? And how could I help him? Even though we were closer to each other than to anyone else around, I sensed I did not know who he was. Would therapy be the solution? I was scared. I was blind. I just didn't see a solution: my brother was riotous, indomitable, a caged beast ready to break out. All along people applauded his genius, but no one knew how to react to his monstrous side.

Deep inside me, I wished I had not found him in so deplorable a situation. I wished I had not known about the attempted suicide, about the calamitous Boston odyssey, about Jacky K. and Melody and everything else.

In the next few months my parents watched him closely, but I felt the need—the urgency—to distance myself from him. As much as possible. Not that I was abandoning him, at least not deliberately. I tried to talk to him, to be friendly, but I felt he was the center of a staged farce. And I found myself increasingly uncomfortable, yearning for more harmonious childhood years. Why was I so reluctant to embrace him? To applaud him? I had trouble explaining my ambiguity, not least to myself. My mother intuited it. In one of the blah-blah sessions at VIPS, she interrogated me: "Why this . . . ? Why that . . . ?" I found no answers. Words simply didn't convey my complex feelings. Had the moment not come to become adults, each of us independently and not in a symbiotic relationship that often made me crave fresh air? But how do you explain the need for freedom if not by seizing it?

Did I act responsibly? I trust I did. Darián began therapy, but I made it my duty not to find out about it. The family, *my* family, was too interfering in our individual lives. Each of us needed privacy, didn't we? I was disoriented. And guilty . . . Could my reluctance accelerate Darián's downfall? Did I hold the key to his stability?

LONG THERAPEUTIC CONSULTATIONS. First one doctor, then another.

Darián calmed down. *Se tranquilizó*, at least a little. The stuttering became less problematic. His physical appearance changed dramatically: he lost a substantial amount of weight, and his neck shrunk. He communicated well in his environment, even though the number of his friends did not increase. His future seemed under control: in time, Jacky K. slowly faded from the picture, the way Melody had; she was replaced by a wholehearted devotion to classical music, which translated itself into daily sessions of Tchaikovsky, Bach, Vivaldi, as well as established Mexican masters such as Moncayo, Carlos Mérida. Long-distance calls to Massachusetts were few and far between. They seemed to cease just as Darián began to ridicule Jacky's cheerleading career.

"By letter she tells me of a boyfriend," Darián told me. "Jack is his name—a football player. Can you believe it? It is over." He paused. "Jack and Jill went up the hill. . . . What in G–d's eyes did she see in me? How can she go from a composer to such a rough, unpolished type?"

In rapid succession, he finished several concertos for piano and orchestra and a full-fledged symphony. And he had a vision for a professional career. Soon after finishing high school, he said, he planned to enroll in an American music school, perhaps the New England Conservatory. That the institution was in Boston was received with uneasiness by many around, of course. Was it another ploy by a slender, refurbished Darián? And how would he pay the tuition? His answer was brave: with talent. He planned to write to several internationally renowned conductors, including Zubin Mehta, Ricardo Mutis, and Eduardo Mata, enclosing his symphony with the letters. They would open the doors themselves, for sure. ¿Y por qué no? No reason why they shouldn't, was there? It was simply a matter of time.

Meanwhile, I myself began to mature. Magically, the

moment I reached my twenties, I was seized by a feeling of certitude: I knew who I was, or at least I thought so; and I also understood what I had been born to do. It wasn't that easy, of course—I crashed one too many times—but Darián's disorientation served as a counterpoint: I was, I needed to be, what he was not. Filmmaking was my true passion, so I began to write screenplays and film reviews. How does a film director get his first job? By experimenting, I told myself. Next I invested all my savings in a Super 8–millimeter camera and made one short documentary after another about a myriad of subjects: chess, homeless orphans, the architecture of bridges. The titles were uninspired: *Sin niñez*, *El juego mental*. . . . I also engaged in a short metaphysical movie about space à la Stanley Kubrick, *Grepsonita Pytuitariax*, which won an amateurs' prize. (For want of state-of-the-art technology in special effects, I painted my whole room black and decorated it like the Milky Way with tinfoil and toilet paper.) My intellectual restlessness took me to Israel, northern Africa, Europe, and Central America. Home was too oppressive a place. Too much talk. Too much guilt.

Each time I returned, I found a more somber and compromising Darián. Therapy made him feel better about himself. What he was impatient about was my parents; their hypocrisy; their never-ending histrionics. And he idolized me: "You're free, Ilan, with no roots—you're made of stone." I knew the way, he thought; perhaps he, too, should plot an escape.

Was my presence unnerving? Was I the reason for his recurring instability? We sucked each other's blood: I found clarity in his confusion, and he sought comfort in my vigor.

Evasion, avoidance. A short time later, Darián booked a

ticket to Paris, where my mother's cousin Rosa, usually in Canada, was temporarily living. Darián's plan was to stay with her for a month, explore the city, and then travel to Vienna to visit Beethoven's tombstone; he wanted to explore Europe. But as soon as he arrived, he regressed to childhood. He was frightened, paralyzed. Solitude was scary, especially when he was so very far away from home; strangers were lofty, menacing to him. Rosa had errands to run—her children were in school, her husband needed a lift to his job downtown—and she offered to drop Darián at a suitable location and pick him up in the evening. It didn't work, though. Long long-distance calls followed: to Mexico, to Boston again.

He returned to Ciudad de México and once more fell into a deep depression.

More therapy.

Did he need my support? Or was it better for him not to have me around? I don't know, frankly. His anger translated itself into pure hostility. He fought constantly with my mother, less so with my father. The cycle was predictable yet uncontrollable: stuttering, shrieks, offenses, followed by melodramatic reconciliations and the promise of eternal love. His unhappiness, he thought, resulted from a flawed sense of self and a misleading education: no, he was not a genius, nor did our family belong to the bourgeoisie.

Bourgeoisie? "Ilan, we were raised like the rich, but the bank accounts were empty." Was he hallucinating? I failed to understand. Ours was, is, a middle-class family, with all the worries of the almost-halves but also the almost-have-nots. It struck me that Darián was the victim of a Marxist-oriented therapist. He told me all this at a VIPS, then repeated his obsessions. "Mamá is too domineering, too castrating," he claimed. "She always insisted that I behave like Papá." He paused: "*Me jjjj-odieron*, Ilan. Papá and Mamá injured me so much. And so they really owe me the world . . . *e-e-e-el mundo e-e-e-enntero*."

Sadness: I was overwhelmed with sadness.

The fallacy of words.

MONEY, MONEY . . . IT became Darián's new obsession, the key to success. How would he support himself? Through small business deals, until fame descended upon him. The options were minimal, though. First he had a part-time job with a computer specialist, then he sold his whole record collection (around 550 titles) to my parents, only to buy it back at a considerably lower price, which they agreed to out of compassion. Meanwhile, he enrolled at the Escuela Nacional de Música, a public music school nearby where prominent violin and piano soloists from Mexico and the Southern Hemisphere taught. He found it terribly mediocre. In his view, the teachers were of very low quality and the lack of artistic rigor was simply shameful. He stayed on, though. The institution was in Coyoacán, only about a mile from our house, allowing him to remain at home. His piano skills developed tremendously. Every single day, for four to five hours, in the morning and evening, he practiced a set of Chopin's Nocturnes, Beethoven's *Moonlight* Sonata, pieces by Bach, Ravel, and Mozart.

Darián taught me how to listen to music. After long sessions at the piano, we sat together in his room, relaxing as we listened to record after record, comparing tempos, discussing directorial styles, analyzing a particular movement to exhaustion—Brahms and Mendelssohn, but also Verdi's *Requiem* and the melancholic Chopin. How I cherished these encounters! My brother was my Virgil, walking me confidently through his music. Not naturally disposed to rhythm, he taught me to recognize moods, to let my imagination flow freely without the interference of graphic images. Those sessions were in sharp contrast to the repetitiveness of his practice periods, for which, I'm ashamed to confess, I had little patience. Too little. The same nocturne by Chopin, repeated twenty, thirty, forty times, perhaps more. I sat in my upstairs room alone, reading Borges's *Other Inquisitions*, Bashevis Singer's *The Slave*, Gabriel García Marquez's *One Hundred Years of Solitude*, Italo Calvino's *If on a Winter's Night a Traveler*, hearing, time and again, the same variations. My books, I thought, were an escape; but Darián's piano-playing didn't really allow them to take me captive. Often—too often—I felt I was about to go out of my mind.

Remorse, again. And impatience. Is Darián to blame? Of course not. What is technique if not the art of reiteration? And what do a musician and a reader sharing the same roof need except patience? Books beg to be cherished in silence, isolation, intimacy, their imaginative universe coming alive only when this world is frozen, disregarded, betrayed; music, instead, is expansive and outgoing, an attempt to amend our environment through sound. But in moments of desperation, I descended the staircase in a rage, hurled a few words at him, and slammed the door annoyingly behind me.

Months went by, perhaps years. I became very demanding of myself, to the point, as a friend had it, of becoming an Oscar Wilde–like snob. If I was to become a filmmaker, it had to be of a global caliber, like Andrzej Wajda. Why strive for less? I applied to the Centro Universitario de Estudios Cinematográficos, Mexico's film school, the equivalent of Italy's Cinecitá, but was rejected; I also sent inquiry letters to American colleges with prominent film programs—as I recall, the University of Southern California and NYU, among others—but was told no financial aid was available. Concurrently, Darián began to perform concerts, not only at the Escuela Nacional de Música but in the provinces as well: in Guanajuato, Michoacán, Querétaro.

My cruelty was sometimes unforgivable. One evening, during a performance of pieces mainly by Chopin, he stopped several times to correct himself. He looked nervous. I wriggled in my seat, looking away from the stage to avoid the painful scene. "¡*Pobre Darián!*" I repeated to myself. The concert, part of a course, was designed to allow the student to gain public confidence. But he already had that, didn't he? What did he make of the many home sessions when guests applauded him triumphantly?

In the end, in a crowded dressing room, he approached me. "Did you like it?" he asked impatiently.

"It was terrible," I answered. Darián smiled with difficulty. He was obviously offended. In his eyes, I was the strictest judge. He never forgave me. And shouldn't have. What a pretentious bastard I was!

I MOVED TO New York. Darián was dispirited to see me go. Our love was too strong. But I sought a climate other than that of Mexico: I needed intellectual and artistic freedom, a landscape wherein my Jewishness—so essential, so unavoidable—mattered. I believed, though, that my absence would ultimately benefit him; I was too strong a presence, too commanding a figure in his psyche.

In the first few months, we corresponded assiduously. Letters and postcards went back and forth. I also sent him records, a book—tokens of esteem. Gradually, slowly, the flow decreased, to the point where the only news I got about him—progress in school, another symphony to his credit—was through my parents.

"Darián can't stand Mexico, either," my father once said.

"But I thought after his Paris experience he made peace with himself," I replied.

"Well, he is searching. It isn't easy for him, Ilan. He says he wants to move to *los Estados Unidos*, just like you. . . ."

Then, several months later, my father announced that Darián had received an encouraging letter from Boston's New England Conservatory. "They can't wait to have him as a student. He's matured tremendously. Wait and see—I'm convinced his genius will finally flourish."

(Why was Boston always a magnet?)

The news came as a surprise to me. And also as a headache: with Manhattan only a few hours away, I would be entrusted—automatically—with Darián's well-being.

Preparation for his voyage began. Nothing else was discussed in my parents' calls. Just as I had done years before, Darián had a farewell party. He triumphantly announced that his tenure as student at the Escuela Nacional de Música was over. Also, after dating several Jewish girls without success, he made it clear that his misadventures with the Mexican-Jewish community were part of the past. He was determined not to succumb to homesickness again. Success, only success mattered.

He was delighted by the registrar's letter from the New

England Conservatory—which he framed—offering him full tuition and even a small stipend. Other financial support he had to provide himself. He asked Bobbe Miriam for a gift of $10,000 to support his endeavors; when she turned him down, he was furious and ceased speaking to her. He proceeded to solicit small amounts from relatives. My parents volunteered a portion. He sold his record collection yet again and found some freelance jobs. In all, he collected enough for a year.

Darián and my parents arrived at my place in New York and stayed for a couple of weeks. His stuttering, I noticed, was more pronounced than it had been the last time I saw him. He was excited but also nervous, very nervous. I was amazed—I have always been amazed—at how he spoke English. Other languages had never interested him, but Shakespeare's tongue—a symbol of cosmopolitanism, politeness, respectability—attracted him. By now he had mastered it, so much so that at times he even sounded like a native, at least to my ears. I realized that in English Darián stuttered less, perhaps because he constructed his sentences far more patiently. To my surprise, I discovered myself feeling jealous once again. I was already a couple of years into my north-of-the-Río Grande self, but my tongue, my unruly foreign tongue, still contorted when I uttered words like "chaos," which I often pronounced as "cows," and I still could not distinguish between "living" and "leaving." My trouble with prepositions—the difference between "pass out," "pass on," "pass in," and "pass away"—was insurmountable; and metaphorical expressions, such as "space cadet," which I once tried to invoke at the right moment, only to utter "cloudy commander," instead, were a headache. Furthermore, I was mesmerized by the syntactical differences between Spanish and English, to which Darián obviously paid absolutely no attention whatsoever. Would I one day be able to write fluently, even capriciously, the way Henry James did? My brother, it seems, could succeed much faster; how long would it take him in Boston, six months? How to explain the different world-views that collided in me as I accepted my role of U.S. immigrant: the English expression "the facts of life," for instance, with its bizarre Spanish equivalent, *los misterios de la vida*? Was it possible that I, permanently obsessed with puns, was stranded? Much of my time, I realized, had gone into deciphering these linguistic dilemmas. To what avail? In spite of his stuttering, Darián, on the contrary, had reached a point in life at which he approached language as a simply vehicle of communication: in English, at least, he was professorial, civilized.

In a conversation with my father in a café, I used the term "mental illness." He was shocked. "Your view of your brother is antiquated," he said, and added sarcastically: "Grow up, my boy!"

Was he right? Had my departure from Mexico impeded my understanding of a refurbished Darián? The answer came that same evening, when he placed a phone call to Jacky. "We're no longer close," he said, as if to justify his behavior, "but I did want to let her know I'm coming. . . ."

We finally drove from Manhattan to the National Yiddish Book Center, in Amherst, Massachusetts, which I was eager to visit, and then to Boston. Saying goodbye was painful.

What happened next is excruciating to narrate. Darián tried to live his life alone, but his days were grim. He found the student body cold and uninviting, the teachers pompous. Nobody cared much about him. Was the cello his instrument? His symphonies, a tutor suggested, needed work, a lot of work.

He tried to see Jacky K. once, but she failed to show up. So Darián began to look actively for a replacement, a girl-friend to warm up his days. Again, however, the female students appeared uninterested.

I was updated regularly by phone. He told me everything: whom he met, what he heard. First he called every two or three days, then every morning, and finally, as the situation deteriorated, five or six times daily.

"*No sé*—is Boston really for me? The New England Conservatory is really not a world-class school. Its reputation is inflated. People hardly talk to each other. Everyone is on his own."

He decided the dorm wasn't for him: too much noise, too dirty. He found a nearby apartment.

About two weeks into the semester, Darián met a beautiful girl. He told me he enjoyed talking to her in the dining room. Then, one morning, he called in terrible shape, crying inconsolably: "*Ay*, Ilan. You won't believe me. I was beaten up. My cheek hurts. . . . On my way to class, some of the girl's boyfriends approached me. In my dorm. First I saw them from afar, in the hallway, but then I realized they were under my nose. 'Don't fool around with her,' one of them said to me, and gave me *un chingadazo*."

The girl had gone to them in distress. Had Darián harassed her? Had he tried to kiss her without her consent? Had my brother become passionate with her, too passionate?

Un chingadazo y otro y otro más. I tried to console him.

Alison, my future wife, whom I would marry in 1988, also offered support. But Darián appeared irremediably upset. I asked him to take a train to Manhattan; I could meet him at Pennsylvania Station. He took my advice, and we spent the long weekend together. Perhaps the whole idea of moving to the U.S. was a mistake, he said. Did he really need to study at a conservatory? Many great musicians have not even finished primary school. And Boston was not New York: too Waspy, too puritanical. I told him he was quitting too soon: he needed to give the adventure more of a chance.

"Was it hard for you at first, too, Ilan?"

Yes, it had been difficult, I said. But time works in mysterious ways. Routine, sooner or later, makes you forget what you've left behind. You're too busy to think of what's missing. And once you remember it, you realize you really don't miss it any longer.

He returned to Boston on Monday. I didn't hear from him for two or three days. Deep inside, I hoped he was finding his way, but on Wednesday evening he called again. I heard loud noises in the background. His story? Some hours before, while he was studying alone, burglars entered the apartment, tied him up in the bathtub, stole the TV, radio, etc., and left; when the apartment's owners arrived, they called the police. He felt terrible. His arms and legs were hurt, his chin was swollen. He was calling from Logan Airport, on his way to Ciudad de México. Just wanted to say thanks and goodbye.

THANKS AND GOODBYE. Darián and I hardly talked to each other in the next few months. I was angry and disappointed.

Should I have done something? Was my attitude too harsh? Too paternalistic? Should I have behaved more sympathetically? In my eyes, his mental condition was deteriorating dangerously. Often I heard of fights between him and my father, followed by sweeping reconciliations. How much more could they bear? Darián was in trouble, but they refused to recognize it. Would weekly therapy sessions help him? My father always looked for ways to excuse my brother's behavior: his adolescence was difficult, and my father was convinced he'd come out of it. But when? At what point would Darián start conducting himself like an adult?

He was back at my parents' house and had returned to the Escuela Nacional de Música. In the next few months, he cut off all contact with my sister, Liora, and any other family members. He also refused to pay a visit to Bobbe Miriam, whose health was rapidly failing. When she died in 1991, he refused to attend her funeral or sit *shivah*.

My parents halfheartedly reported his ups and downs to me. They knew I felt guilt and sadness and never dwelt on him.

To support himself, Darián extorted money from my father in different ways, always promising to pay it back. "I need money—*Nnnnnecesesssittto ddd-dinero, por favor.*" I knew it was not meant to be returned.

He moved from student to instructor to teacher, offering various courses, at home and in school, on piano and on the history of music.

Among his pupils was Lorena D., a short, slim, impressionable Gentile girl some ten years Darián's junior, from a humble background. I received sporadic news by phone and mail of their relationship, which started professionally but quickly became personal. He began dating her, and within a period of weeks, perhaps a month, the liaison was steady enough for my parents to hear mention of a wedding. While lecturing in Ciudad de México, I met Lorena briefly: not a beauty, but a self-conscious *simpática*. She seemed to emulate my mother's manners, wearing the same type of clothes, an almost identical hairstyle. *"No es judía,"* I heard my father announce. But he suddenly fell silent, as if choosing to allow the cards to play themselves out. My brother looked confident.

Again, events precipitated themselves at an astonishing speed. On my return to New York, my father warned me by phone: "Wait until you see what's in store." Not long after, I received a long handwritten letter from Darián that shocked me to the core. I have it stored somewhere, too afraid to reread it. My father probably prompted him to send it. In it he introduced his sweetheart to my wife and me as the daughter of an Auschwitz survivor whose terrible experience in the Holocaust prompted him to have serious violent fits and succumb to alcohol. Thus, he claimed, Lorena was half Jewish, and fully committed to returning to the tribe. Her love for Darián was only a sign of it. She was committed to undergoing a conversion under the aegis of Mexico's chief rabbi. Her crypto-Jewishness, she realized, was a dead end. She wanted redemption and, with it, approval from her peers. The actual description of her father's survival was horrendous: torture, hunger, depravation, an excruciating adolescence in hiding, a brush with death under Nazi machine guns. . . .

My first reaction was sympathy. Was this true? If so, how horrifying! My brother's problems, I thought, are only likely to get worse. The girl, obviously, was going through a tremendous transformation. Why become her redeemer? Didn't he himself need help? Minutes later, I translated the letter for Alison, who is far more intuitive than I. She knew immediately that it was all a fake. I resisted: Lorena's story had to be true. Why else volunteer such an atrocious destiny? But Alison pointed out the serious inconsistency in the chronology: to begin with, Lorena's father, a man in his early seventies, was too old to have been an adolescent refugee during the Second World War.

My father was equally incredulous. "Lorena's father? *Un borracho de mierda, eso es todo.* A fucking drunk," he said to me. He and my mother had heard the tale a week before but didn't want to influence my reading of it. By now, though, the lie was out. Days before, Darián and Lorena had shown up unexpectedly at my parents' new apartment in the fashionable Insurgentes Sur neighborhood. "She has something to tell you," Darián proclaimed. Soon she was crying inconsolably, requesting their forgiveness. "*Les mentí,*" she said melodramatically, "I lied to you." The whole encounter, as my father described it, sounded like an unbearable TV soap opera. No Auschwitz, no tales of misery under Nazism, no crypto-Jewishness, none of it happened; the only truth she held on to was her plain, crystalline, uncontested love for Darián.

LORENA APPROACHED A rabbi in Mexico, but he declined to convert her. She went to others, including one in Texas, and finally found her soulmate: a Reconstructionist charlatan known for charging high fees to mixed couples.

Darián married Lorena in a private ceremony. My

mother, Liora and her husband, and a few acquaintances attended the civil wedding. I was invited, along with my wife and child, but did not attend.

The last installment of this tormenting saga came in early 1994, when my mother called me once late at night, desperate, in tears.

"You won't believe what just happened, Ilan," she said. Her words were full of grief. "I was alone at home, your father onstage in the downtown theater. Darián and Lorena came by. We talked. An argument erupted. He became very angry and started to destroy the house. If you could only see. Everything is in pieces: the crystal vases, paintings on the floor, the furniture turned upside down. Everything destroyed! Lorena just stood by, looking on, never tried to stop him."

I tried to calm my mother down, but she went on: "He threw things at me. He tried to kill me. Thank G–d he missed, Ilan. I don't want to see him ever again." Her pain was inbearable. "Ever again."

My father arrived a few hours later. He, too, phoned me. I was desperate, thousands of miles away, incapable of helping, thinking only that Darián should be hospitalized soon.

"You must change the lock," I told my father. Suddenly, I remember noticing the black-and-white photo of Darián at sixteen months of age, hanging on the staircase. A significant memento. Who was behind the camera? I continued talking, but was thinking how many times I had invoked the photo in the last couple of decades.

Afar, aloof, alone . . . "Change the lock!" I repeated, realizing that what we were talking about, inevitably, was the severing of an umbilical cord. Can parents and children ever do it successfully? How could I stop myself from speaking to my brother again? But if I spoke to him, what on earth would I say? *Dios mío, ¿que?*

I didn't hear from Darián for a long, long time. Nor did my parents. It was as if darkness had swallowed him up. Actually, not darkness but silence. The silence of pain and incomprehension and violence.

Control, chaos.

A few months later, while in Ciudad de México, I bought a CD of Darián's piano pieces, *Imágenes de amor,* at a VIPS. It contains a lullaby, "Canción de cuna," halfway between Debussy and Richard Clayderman. As I listen to it, it prompts me to review his life as if it were a slow-motion film: his Yamaha piano, his adaptation of Beethoven's *Pastoral,* the stills of *Melody* hanging in his room, Lorena's Holocaust letter. The slow-motion effect doesn't conceal the feeling of having experienced it all at an intense speed. How did it all begin? What came first? Where was I when all these events happened? When Darián broke the bathroom mirror? When he sought out Jacky K. in Boston? When he tried to suffocate Liora? Where was I when he . . .

{ 5 }

Amerika, America

Writers have to have two countries,
the one where they belong and the one in which they live
    really.
The second one is romantic, it is separate from them
    selves, it is not real but it is really there. . . .
Of course sometimes people discover their own country
    as if it were the other.

—GERTRUDE STEIN

M Y PASSPORT, THE loss of my passport.
Robert Graves, in his First World War memoir, *Goodbye to All That*, offers "a passport description of myself," and then, seemingly without effort, "let[s] the items enlarge themselves." I am unable to follow his model, if only because, in my case, as in that of most immigrants, the switch from one passport to another is a dramatic mutation in identity, a metamorphosis by which the immigrant's life is forever defined. I remember Luis Buñuel once arguing with a customs official who had requested to see his passport: "Why do you need it?" Buñuel asked. "*Pero me tienes a mí de frente*. . . . You have me, have you not?" How many times I

have thought of this reply when passing through immigration and pondered uttering similar words. But bureaucrats have no sense of humor. Besides, what are we today without a passport?

And what are we with it? A number, a photograph, a succinct and fraudulent description. My Mexican passport is a masterpiece of concision: date of birth: 7 April 1961; sex: male; place of birth: Distrito Federal; height: 1.58 meters; weight: 170 kilograms; complexion: robust; eyes: brown; hair: blond; distinct features: none. Profession: writer/professor. The polarity has never satisfied me, perhaps because I have never fully made peace with myself as an academic. Still, it helps to say, "professor," since government officials look at you with suspicion when you suggest literature is a way of life. Journalists seldom generate a similar reaction, but they are often asked to show a publisher's letter and a newspaper ID. Better to avoid complications.

Any language? No mention of it in my Mexican passport, even though, in a nation so vast and multifaceted, at least an eighth of the population doesn't use Spanish. Indian languages are alive in the provinces, especially in the southern states of Oaxaca, Yucatán, Chiapas, and Quintana Roo.

I'm holding on to my Mexican passport tightly, aware, of course, that I'm about to lose it. Actually, I'm surprised at how little sadness I feel. Why am I not sorrowful, or even melancholic, about letting my Mexican self go? Around me are some two thousand people from all over the world, invited to this athletic arena, to pledge allegiance to the flag of the United States. Throughout my life I have had my passport reissued in Ciudad de México, a dozen times perhaps. The first one I had was a collective one, for the entire

Stavchansky family. I must have been five years old. My parents requested it; after all, children and toddlers don't travel on their own. Some versions, like the one I used in the early 1980s while I lived in the Middle East, Europe, and Africa—crowded with official stamps, signatures, and visas—I have kept in a special drawer. The only visa not found in this passport is for the United States, because when I was a child Washington, D.C., passed a law establishing that Mexican citizens were allowed to carry a perennial plastic visa in the form of an ID. There was a rush, by Jews in particular, to get these, since they represented, if not a green card per se, an open door to the neighbor up north. A few years later, the U.S. government changed its mind and ceased to issue them. But those already issued remained valid. Mexicans had to be careful about safeguarding the visas. I remember my father obsessing about it every time I was about to embark on a trip: *"La pierdes, Ilán, y quedas expulsado."* Its loss represented, albeit tangentially, a surrender of status: no longer at ease, able to enter any country in the world except the most desirable.

The day I finally surrendered my U.S. visa to a bureaucrat in Manhattan is vivid in my mind. I had been in America for half a decade and had a steady job as a teacher in the City University of New York education system, with the promise of lifelong security, promotions, benefits. I had gotten married not long before, and I applied for a green card as the spouse of an American citizen. Medical exams and blood tests were performed in dungeonlike rooms on 42nd Street, off of Times Square. Extensive legal paperwork had to be sent by mail, along with notarized bank statements, letters of recommendation, family pictures, fingerprints, and, of course, perfect black-and-white photographs. After interviews, an officer gave me a resident-alien card in exchange for my old U.S. visa issued in Mexico. I was downhearted at letting it go, after keeping it close to me for two decades.

Years later, the inevitable loss of my Mexican passport makes me less fearful. After all, what is a green card but a permit, rescinded the moment you leave the country for more than 365 days? A Mexican passport, on the other hand, means you carry the country with you everywhere, but your share of it, your claim of ownership, has been severed. Am I ready to renounce my Mexican citizenship? Sure—why long for a past I felt only accidentally attached to? I have fulfilled my obligations and am ready to become an American. But will I be able to hand in my Mexican passport in exchange?

The ceremony, I am told, normally lasts some forty-five minutes. But on this Wednesday in the early summer of 1994, it will surely take longer, since never in the history of the state have so many immigrants been sworn in. I arrive with a Cuban friend and fellow writer some thirty years my senior. He has persuaded me to embark on the immigration process with him. His legal status is problematic: a political refugee since 1981, he has had his Cuban passport canceled. But he had not applied for a U.S. passport, afraid of rejection and perhaps because, although he consistently denied it, deep inside he nurtured the dream of returning to his native island with the ousting of Fidel Castro's tyrannical regime. The two of us submitted the paperwork more or less at the same time. His was acknowledged first, and his personal interview with the INS bureaucrat also took place first. Applicants were told they needed to respond satisfactorily to random questions about the American government (its branches, its powers, and so on), and especially on the nation's history. He memorized the pertinent booklet, arrived on time for his interview, and proceeded to respond to the questions. The first was about Pearl Harbor. Then came Normandy, followed by the Bay of Pigs. Then my friend was treated to a litany on how Cuban émigrés have taken over Florida and parts of the Northeast, why they should be sent back, and how mistaken the U.S. government is in granting refugee status to exiles who clearly have not given up communism altogether. Naturally, he got nervous and began to stutter. The bureaucrat was suspicious. Eventually, he told him he had passed the test but suggested he take English classes.

My own case was drastically different. The day before, Mexico's presidential candidate Luis Donaldo Colosio, the designated successor of the leading party, had been assassinated in the northern part of the country. Instead of studying, I had written an opinion piece, syndicated nationally. It was published in the *Boston Globe* the morning of my interview. The immigration official had noticed it, and we spent almost thirty minutes in a friendly dialogue on politics south of the Rio Grande. In the end, he did ask me a couple of questions about the federal and executive branches of the government, and about D-Day. It was, as it turned out, a most pleasant encounter, if also a bit embarrassing. I was told America benefited greatly from the brain drain that brought people like me to this country, and was applauded for my command of English. My passport, the officer concluded, would be ready for pickup in June at a collective event where I, and scores of others, would pledge allegiance. Aware of what my Cuban friend was exposed to, I felt honored but also disgusted.

Shortly after my arrival at the arena, I noticed people sitting happily in the bleachers. Many had relatives nearby with cameras ready for the climactic moment. And many, too, especially those aged fifty and older, had interpreters at their side. Their English was deficient, if not nonexistent. Their applications were surely accompanied by their children's requests for their naturalization. I remember a mature Japanese woman carrying an umbrella, which at one point she inadvertently dropped. I picked it up and delivered it to her. She smiled graciously and said: *"Taka! Taka!"* I obviously took this expression to be one of gratitude.

The incident puzzled me. What does it mean to be an American? English was not, as I had heard, the great equalizer, at least not at the moment when a citizen is sworn in. Is immigration not, first and foremost, about reinventing oneself in a different land, not only socially and culturally but also verbally? What did my own experience entail? Transplanting oneself in the soil of another tongue, finding some degree of comfort in a foreign language, I told myself, leads at first to a sense of deterioration rather than improvement, of loss rather than gain. One gets the impression of ceasing to be—in Spanish, the feeling of *no estar del todo*. The immigrant feels trapped in the space in between words and in the intricacies of the journey. *Taka! Taka!* But sooner or later, loss is transformed into gain: the immigrant is born again—rejuvenated, enriched by the voyage. Robert Frost might have been right when he said that poetry is what gets lost in translation, but in my own view, the successful immigrant feels the fusion of tongues as an addition rather than a subtraction. His life is what gives poetry its meaning—the voyage in search of rebirth.

At least that's the sensation I got. But obviously not everyone at the ceremony shared it. Amerika, America . . . The immigration process turns the mythical "k" into a standard "c," it makes the utopia an earthly, temporal site. The country has been good to me—very good indeed. I came in search of the Garden of Eden.

EDEN—UTOPIA. IT was Quevedo, that sublime Spanish Golden Age poet but also a shameless anti-Semite, who called attention to its Greek meaning: "There is no such place."

I had spent my entire youth in search of that nonexistent place. My need to find it, to seize upon it, was, I'm convinced, deeply rooted in my Yiddish-language education south of the Rio Grande. Mexico's Jewish community lives frozen in time, self-marginalized, unconcerned with either national or international matters. This isolation, this sense of being on the margins of history, was a source of great distress for me, even though today I cherish it as an asset, for it gave me the world-view I have as a diaspora Jew: a chameleon. Since kindergarten, I had been surrounded by the same circle of acquaintances. But college meant, for me at least, direct exposure to the miseries around me: poverty, injustice, absence of intellectual freedom. It all erupted in my consciousness during the last years of high school, as I began to break away from my suffocating circle in search of contacts with the larger world. I began to attend screenings at the Centro Universitario Cultural, a film club a few blocks away from home. I also began drafting screenplays, reading biographies of Hitchcock and Eisentein, and attending parties with radical neighborhood friends, mostly male, whom I had known for years but never taken seriously. I remember them only by their names and, in some cases, also by their nicknames: Foncho "Grilla," Pepe *el futbolero*, Javier *el palillo*. . . . They served as a bridge, introducing me to intellectual and political figures like Italy's Marxist theoretician Antonio Gramsci and Chile's martyred president Salvador Allende and mythical Mexicans such as former Minister of Education José Vasconcelos and the seventeenth-century proto-feminist nun Sor Juana Inés de la Cruz. They also invited me, through trips to the provinces and charged discussions, to learn about facets of my native country of which I was ignorant, such as its insurmountable poverty and pervasive corruption.

The shock of recognition was too strong, and I felt deeply angry. Why had I not heard a word during my education about left-wing activists like the brothers Flores Magón? What was the point in teaching me so much about Jewishness when it was clear the Jews were less than 1 percent of the total population? And why learn Yiddish, a language that, to put it simply, felt like an anachronism, in a reality ambivalent about its connection to Spain but remote from Eastern Europe in every sense? Not surprisingly, I felt I had been thrown out of paradise and left to wonder: Where do I fit in modern Mexico? Is there a way to link my Hebraic ancestry to my day-to-day life? My first, most instinctive solution to the dilemma was a cowardly one, but one that, ironically, opened my eyes in ways I could not have foreseen. Shortly before turning twenty, I packed my luggage and sought a more permanent home in Israel, where I decided I should try to live, at least for a while. My education had stressed difference: as a Jew, I was a guest in Mexico; I rented a room, aware, all along, that I could never own it. An unfair status, no doubt: Wasn't I like any Mexican? Did I not have the same rights and privileges? What made me different? I knew the best way to answer these questions was to enroll in a public college, befriending Gentiles, studying the nation's history in its own terms and tongue. But I was afraid; I couldn't face the challenge—not yet, at least. Why not try first to live in a place just like my Jewish day school, only as large as the state of Rhode Island? Why not be a full-fledged citizen, feel comfortable, lead a "normal" Jewish life?

Normality, *normalidad*. I had heard the word a thousand times.

"In Israel, Jews have finally come down to earth," said Lerer Saul Lockier, my Yiddish teacher, a Bundist in most things except when it came to Ysröel, concerning which he automatically became a fervent Zionist. His sentences, I remember, always played upon the word "home": to be homeless, to build a home.

"We no longer need permission to live, to move around, to be who we are."

I asked him why he hadn't made *aliyah*. His answer was sheer evasion, of the sort most Mexican Jews indulged in daily. *"Mexique is ver ich choib myn shtibele. Es is shoin main cheim,"* he announced. "I'm an adult, fully settled, with a job. But you, Ilan, are still a young man. Your life is ahead of you. Individual decisions are easier to make when no one else's life is in question."

He paused, and then acknowledged: "Herzl is the closest we have to a Biblical prophet, a modern Samuel."

My curiosity about Israel was ignited in 1978, when, at the height of Palestinian terrorist attacks in Europe and the Middle East and war threats against the Jewish State by

Syria and Jordan, Mexico's infamous President Luis Eche-verría Álvarez, at a United Nations assembly, had famously equated Zionism with racism. With grandiose Fidel Castro–like eloquence, he lectured the globe: *El Sionismo es una foma de racismo.* (Why is "Zionism" spelled in English with a "Z" and in Spanish with an "S"?) His proclamation, of course, was a hideous anachronism, for his own rule of law in Mexico was based on repression. He stands out in history textbooks as the politico who on October 2, 1968, ordered the massacre of students in Tlatelolco Square with tanks, helicopters, and heavy artillery, just as the Olympic Games were about to take place in Mexico. Some six thousand people are estimated to have died. How repulsive to listen to a criminal condemning crime.

But the response by the Jewish community, as expected, was not adequate. Typically, it was more symbolic than real, a ridiculous show of support for a nation with enough intelligence and weapons to defend itself alone. Flashy pins adorned with flowers were handed out at school, rejecting the statement. This reaction left me puzzled: it was sheer passivity. How much longer would we resist commitment? I wondered. "It may be," Isaiah Berlin once said, "that no minority that has preserved its own cultural tradition or religious or racial characteristics can indefinitely tolerate the prospect of remaining a minority forever." Perhaps, but Mexican Jews thus did not exhibit signs of life. Content with their place on the margins, they refused to be disturbed. Or at least that's the impression I got. Shortly afterward, I found out about various kibbutzim near Jerusalem and, further north, in Tiberias. A few friends from school were ready for Israel, too. A number of Israeli teachers, *shlikhim*, arrogant, self-righteous missionaries in Mexico (and in Brazil, Argentina, Venezuela, and Colombia, too) to encourage immigration, offered themselves as liaisons. They made contacts, established routes, and offered advice. In Hebrew the whole enterprise was called Hakhsharah.

MY FIRST LITERARY experiments—in Yiddish—belong to that time. In mid-1979, I staged a play of mine, *Genesis 2000*, loosely based on Antoine de Saint-Exupéry's *The Little Prince*, with a cast of twenty-five. It was favorably reviewed in the weekly *Der Shtime*. The public reaction mystified me. I was described as "a young Pirandello," "a promising voice," "a promising artist capable of digesting Brecht's lessons to the core." The problem: I had heard of Pirandello's *Six Characters in Search of an Author* but had not read it, let alone anything else by him; and likewise with Brecht. Before I attempted anything more in the theater, shouldn't I first find out what their legacy was about? To many, my engagement with the stage seemed inevitable: my father had studiously paved the road I could now travel. But I wasn't so sure. For one thing, the communal experience in theater exasperated me; actors—especially amateur ones—were not people I was convinced I could spend my life with. I also wrote a pair of short stories in Yiddish, one of them a thriller that emulated the Hemingway of "The Killers," which I sent to *Die Goldene Keyt* in Israel, the only Yiddish literary magazine of some distinction published anywhere. I remember retyping them several times on a stolen typewriter with Hebrew characters, which I had borrowed from a friend and refused to return. (A new one would have to be imported from Israel and was thus too expensive.)

All this literary activity didn't make me feel happy. Yiddish wasn't truly mine. I asked the unavoidable question: why use Sholem Aleichem's language when its only readers are all in the geriatric ward? My voyage to Israel, I convinced myself, would offer some answers. It would provide room for self-knowledge. In my imagination, I pictured Israel in its entirety at the apex of Mount Sinai. Hence my excitement at the *ascendance* (*aliyah*, in Hebrew) I was about to achieve. The Promised Land: it symbolized redemption for millenarian Jews. But modern Israel, I knew from photographs and books, was less sacred, more mundane and obsessed with politics. It boasted telephones, chic cafés, fast-food joints, and French-style department stores. History had not only been erased, it had become ubiquitous: every site was a landmark of heroism, every stone a focus for pride and grief for Jews active in the battlefield. I was in love with the country's kitschy image: endless postcards of sunsets at the Damascus Gate, Palestinians pulling donkeys, and fashionable hotels in Eilat; melodramatic songs by Naomi Shemer: *kovah tenbl* and army fatigues sold to tourists to promulgate a view of Israel as a secure homeland and an agricultural miracle; and college dance troupes jumping to the rhythms of Zionist propaganda music. Even the "Hatikvah," Israel's national anthem, with its Soviet-style indoctrination, rang in my ears as a tacky annunciation of the end of the Jewish dispersion. I was innocent at the time and failed to see the ideology of opportunism behind it all. In my eyes, Jews had been eternal pariahs, time travelers, and Israel brought them back to earth. I remember reading on the plane *The Burning Question*, a thought-provoking volume by Eliezer Ben-Yehuda, the lexicographer responsible, to a large extent, for the revival of the Hebrew language in modern times. It excited me to be able to spend a year in a land that reinvented itself linguistically. How many other nations had fully revamped an ancient tongue so as to make it their own yet again, a *reconquista* without parallel?

Deep inside, though, Zionism scared me just as much as Mexico did. It represented the perfect triumph of nineteenth-century nationalism: a people destined to become its own ruler. But it also exemplified the need to fight against ghettoized life, for what was Israel but a larger-than-life Jewish ghetto at the heart of the Arab Middle East? Had Jews in the diaspora, by definition, not been "unlike" their Gentile peers? Israel brought the Jews into the present by allowing them to be worldly—i.e., nationalistic, materialistic—like any other nations. I thought of the debacle, at the end of the nineteenth century, between Yiddishists and Hebraists, pundits forcing language to become a political asset. Which of the two is the true Jewish tongue? Which in the future should become the official language of the Promised Land? In Eastern Europe, Yiddish was the language of the masses; Hebrew was still the property of the synagogue, a vehicle of intense scholastic debate in yeshivas among rabbinical authorities. But what about the rest of the world? What of the other Jewish tongues: Ladino, Judeo-Italian, Judeo-Portuguese, Judeo-Arabic? Israel, from its inception, had been the dream of Ashkenazi Jews. It excluded not only the Arabs living in Palestine at the time but also other Jewish communities.

Of course, Herzl and Ben-Yehuda turned Hebrew into the champion. Had it been the right decision? The more I thought about it, on my El Al flight, the more I felt puzzled. The plane was delayed at Kennedy Airport for nine hours. Israeli security, to defy terrorists, preferred not to follow a strict schedule of departures and arrivals; this made it harder for Arab fundamentalists to plant bombs. Hand luggage was checked time and again, and patience was tested to the limit. When it finally took off, at 3 A.M., I was utterly exhausted, but I began a silent tradition I perform to this day every time my aircraft takes off. (I also sing it to my children, when I have them around.) I sang repeatedly, to myself, to G–d—in Hebrew, the divine language, the *lashon ha-kodesh*. To me the literal translation is besides the point. In the Sacred Tongue, the words hypnotize me:

Adon olam asher malakh, b'terem kol ye-tzir nivra.
L'eit na-asah ve-heftzo kol, azai melekh sh'mo nikra.
Ve'aharei kikhlot hakol, l'vado yimlokh nora.
V'hu hayah v'hu hoveh, v'hu yih-yeh b'tifarah.
V'hu ehad v'ein shei-ni, l'hamshil lo l'hahbirah.
B'li rei-sheet b'li takhleet, v'lo ha-oz v'ha-misrah.
V'hu Eili v'hai go-ali, v'tzur hevli b'eit tzarah.
V'hu nisi u-manos li, m'nat kosi b'yom ekra.
B'yado afkid ruhi, b'eit ishan v'a-irah.
V'im ruhi g'vi-yati, Adonai li v'lo ira.

בְּטֶרֶם כָּל יְצִיר נִבְרָא.   אֲדוֹן עוֹלָם אֲשֶׁר מָלָךְ,
אֲזַי מֶלֶךְ שְׁמוֹ נִקְרָא.   לְעֵת נַעֲשָׂה בְחֶפְצוֹ כֹּל,
לְבַדּוֹ יִמְלוֹךְ נוֹרָא.   וְאַחֲרֵי כִּכְלוֹת הַכֹּל,
וְהוּא יִהְיֶה בְּתִפְאָרָה.   וְהוּא הָיָה וְהוּא הֹוֶה,
לְהַמְשִׁיל לוֹ לְהַחְבִּירָה.   וְהוּא אֶחָד וְאֵין שֵׁנִי,
וְלוֹ הָעֹז וְהַמִּשְׂרָה.   בְּלִי רֵאשִׁית בְּלִי תַכְלִית,
וְצוּר חֶבְלִי בְּעֵת צָרָה.   וְהוּא אֵלִי וְחַי גֹּאֲלִי,
מְנָת כּוֹסִי בְּיוֹם אֶקְרָא.   וְהוּא נִסִּי וּמָנוֹס לִי,
בְּעֵת אִישַׁן וְאָעִירָה.   בְּיָדוֹ אַפְקִיד רוּחִי,
יהוה לִי וְלֹא אִירָא.   וְעִם רוּחִי גְּוִיָּתִי,

I SPENT SIX months in Tel-Katzir, a kibbutz near Tiberias, near the banks of Lake Kinneret—feeding chickens, milking and calving cows, and picking bananas. I lived in a small room on a hill, where I devoted many leisure hours to correspondence. The routine was stimulating at first: I was called to work with my hands, to become a peasant; and I shared most things, from food to the toilet. It all made me reflect on the contrasts of modern Jewish life. On the one hand, Mexican Jews lived lavishly, trotting around the world, attended by servants, dismissing *campesinos* as lowly creatures; on the other, idealists, at a time when the kibbutz as a communal institution was already in steep decline, perceived themselves as the breeders of the future. The diaspora, in their eyes, was doomed.

Within a couple of months, I was bored. I improved my Hebrew after a friend gave me some poems by Saul Tchernichowsky and Chaim Nakhman Bialik and lent me a Hebrew translation of *One Hundred Years of Solitude*, which I still have. I read as much as I could with the help of a dictionary. My dream was to be fluent enough to read Shmuel Yosef Agnon, the Hebrew master known for *The Bridal Canopy* and *Days of Awe* and awarded the Nobel Prize in Literature in 1966, in the original. But after intense hours of work in the fields and with the animals, my mind would wander around, and I would fall asleep at 6 P.M. My wake-up call was around 2 A.M., the time to milk the first cow. As a dutiful outsider, I marveled at the achievements of Israel. Not literature, but the agricultural and urban achievements of the young state were what truly captured my imagination: its irrigation system, its spreading forests, its highways, and especially its cosmopolitanism—in Tel Aviv, Haifa, and even in dark-suited Jerusalem. Was I courageous enough to make the leap of faith, to *ascend*, once and for all? On a trip to the Wailing Wall, I was kidnapped by proselytizing Hasidim, who for a few days attempted to indoctrinate me in religious practices, persuading me to put on *tefillin*, the phylacteries, and to pray ecstatically. I easily gave in to their plea: my search led me in different directions, and religion was a crucial one. I became convinced that my Jewish-Mexican education had been an exercise in deception. Not only had it kept me away from Mexico's native population, but it had failed to initiate me into faith as an essential component of Jewish life.

But as much as I tried, Orthodoxy repelled me. I disliked the Hasidim that surrounded me: their untidiness, their neuroses. The only aspect of their daily life I enjoyed was the midrashic debate, to which I gave my full attention whenever I was invited to participate. But these Jews had something I didn't: an absence of existential doubt. They were not in the least skeptical. For them, G–d's presence was everywhere and was evident in every realm of life. I, on the contrary, seriously doubted that the universe was under a single omnipotent command. Still, to this day, I am ambivalent about my brief stay in a yeshiva. In a contradictory swing, I sometimes surprise myself by expressing admiration for Orthodox Jews—their resilience, their uncompromising faith. (Several cousins on my mother's side have closed the gap between secularism and full commitment.) Engaging in Talmudic debates, I felt happy and in the right place. Still, these intense moments were an all-too-brief intellectual stimulus. The dark-suited men—"ravens," *cuervos*, is what

Mexican Jews call them—that surrounded me seemed celestial in their theological pursuit but despicable in their extremism. I needed them, however, and if I could have ignored their inefficacy in the modern world, I would have joined them. I couldn't, though; Orthodox Jews, I told myself, are an essential component of my people. They represent one end of the Jewish spectrum, assimilated Jews the other. I stand in between, thinking every day about the opposite ends that serve me as ·book covers and wondering whether I should move in one or the other direction. In the end, I always seem to be able to persuade myself that life in the middle ground, though a never-ending negotiation, is what makes me, to a large extent, the Jew I am.

While in Israel, I had an affair with an angelic female soldier, Revital K., only two months before her betrothal. She arrived in Tel-Katzir with her battalion to do volunteer work. Her beauty was the subject of discussion and envy, and my relationship with her, I thought in my youthful mind, made me a David of sorts. Why hadn't she fallen for any of the Israelis in the kibbutz? Why not for any of the dozen foreign volunteers from Norway, Denmark, Holland, or elsewhere in the Americas? What did she see in me? I don't remember her clearly, aside from her beautiful facial gestures and the freshness of her body. I do know that it was with her that I learned to play down my skin condition, hypnotizing her through ideas and words. Revital worked in the banana fields with me. I doubt we were together for more than a month, but we had plenty of time to discuss intellectual matters, books we read, ourselves. Her future husband was in the textile industry. She talked little about him, and even less about her prospects as a wife and mother. I remember the first time we made love—under a clear sky, at the top of the hill, behind an old tree, where no one ever came at night. We began a casual conversation. Suddenly, I felt the urge to embrace her, kiss her, lick her neck. Soon our clothes were loosened, unbuttoned, unzipped. It was a mystical moment, a sexual encounter I cherish—soft, harmonious, sharpened by her pledge to another man and by my total sense of destiny. I was just discovering my freedom, and Revital was about to lose hers. We made love many times before she departed: in the stable where the hay was stored, in my room after a morning's hard work with the cows, after a rendezvous at the movies in the nearby town. Nothing else mattered to me but the moments I shared with her. But then she departed. We both knew no promises were needed. In fact, I never learned her home address.

About six weeks later, she sent me a postcard: the wedding had been a sweet event, and she was off on her honeymoon to Cyprus. Between the Hebrew lines I looked for hints that she missed me, but didn't find any.

THE LONGER I stayed in Israel, the more impatient I grew with Mexican Jews. "Impatient" is too soft a word; "angry" is more accurate. After months in Tel-Katzir, I packed my belongings and left for Jerusalem. Increasingly, freedom for me meant a total lack of attachment: no friends, no acquaintances. Only my parents knew my whereabouts and my longings, from lengthy correspondence—soliloquies, really—that, in the end, spanned many places and moods. These letters were literary exercises; through them I explored my inner state as zealously as I knew how. I spent some time wandering around Hebrew University in Jerusalem, listening to a wide variety of lectures. I also visited Bobbe Miriam's half-brother, Shmuel Meyer, and his wife in Mijmoret, traveled around the Negev, climbed Mount Sinai. When money was short, I volunteered in Ma'ale Ha-Hamisha, a kibbutz very near Jerusalem, which allowed me to be close to urban life even though I again spent my mornings milking cows.

Could I one day make *aliyah*? No, Israel, I concluded, was not for me: it was constantly at war—with its neighbors, with itself through the sharply opposed Jewish and Arab, secular and religious populations. These aspects frightened me. While I was in Tel-Katzir, an emergency drill occurred one night, when news that Palestinians from Jordan had infiltrated Israel reached the kibbutz's main office. The place was put under high alert, children and adolescents were sent to a bunker along with all foreigners, and the rest took out their weapons and, in an orderly fashion, patrolled the area, without a hint of distress. I was frightened to death, as were my friends, but not the children, already used to such nuisances. The bunker was a cold place. Pillows and sheets were available, as well as lamps and table games. A movie projector was available, and a French film—*Le balon rouge*—was shown. Such events made me admire but also recoil from the Israelis: the ubiquitious army fatigues and Uzis I saw in bus stations, the brave and defiant attitude on the one hand, but also their roughness and self-importance. They held themselves in too high esteem, looking down on the Arabs as inferior. It was a society in deep turmoil. It couldn't have been otherwise, of course: from its inception in 1948, the nation lived besieged, shaped by a besieged mentality. Did I want to become a citizen of a state in constant threat? Was it my duty as a Jew? No, I told myself at the end of my sojourn. In spite of my misgivings about Mexican Jews, I was a diaspora creature—and proudly so. I understood that I could thrive only in a non-Jewish environment. Curiously, the longer I stayed in Israel, the more I convinced myself that only in a yeshiva in Jerusalem could I find brief periods of happiness, but that those periods did not amount to a reason strong enough to make me stay.

Hebrew enchanted me. I prolonged my stay in Israel simply to talk—to take a part, however insignificant it was, in the exhilarating revival of the Holy Tongue. How extraordinary, I couldn't help thinking, that just a few decades ago Hebrew had been buried in the Talmudic halls of debate, but today it had words for "telephone," "TV," "dishwasher," "microchip." I went to the movies, listened to the radio, and engaged in endless conversations, always hypnotized by the texture of the guttural Hebrew sounds I uttered. But language alone does not make the man, and when I exhausted my curiosity toward Israel, I also let go of the Holy Tongue and gravitated toward Europe.

El Viejo Mundo: Europe meant total loneliness. Nobody knew me and I knew nobody. In mid-1981, I took an airplane to Munich. From there I began a long pilgrimage with no destination in mind: Switzerland, Luxembourg, Sicily, Germany, Holland, Portugal. I visited Dachau, Anne Frank's secret annex, the Jean Valjan sewers in Paris. I worked in the wineries in southern France, as a brickmaker in Luxembourg and a gardener in England. I slept in train stations and on church doorsteps, taking as much as a week between showers. Long months of anonymity and deep thought, of direct exposure to the human condition. In Zurich, a pair of warmhearted lesbian teachers I met on a train opened their home to me for a week of rest. In London, a black family I met in a McDonald's on Leicester Square—the father a dentist, the mother a housewife in charge of their twelve-year-old daughter and five-year-old son—allowed me to stay in their garden shed for almost a month, while I painted their suburban house.

The full-blown revelation came in España. In Mexico, the perception of Spain and Spanish culture is shadowy. Scores of statues of Montezuma II and Cuauhtémoc stand proudly in plazas and boulevards. Stamps and currency carry their image. More infrequent is the icon of Doña Marina, also known as La Malinche, Hernán Cortés's mistress and interpreter. But Cortés himself, *el villano*, is reviled, and with him his Iberian background. *Vino, saqueó y destruyó* is the maxim. In Madrid, on the other hand, he is a hero—a bridge between the old and the new. His face is in the pool of pop images. A few days into my stay allowed me to go beyond the Manichean perception, for Spain spoke less to me as a Mexican than as a Jew. I spent long days in Toledo, in the Middle Ages home to one of the world's most famous translation centers associated with the Shmuel ibn Tibbon family. And I traveled all over what once was Al Andalus, an ample portion of land where Jews and Arabs lived in peaceful coexistence. In Der Yiddisher Shule I had not been taught much about Iberian Jewry. The easy explanation was the Ashkenazic ancestry of the institution's founders. Was this ignorance—or, rather, a total lack of interest in *el otro lado*, the other side of Jewishness—acceptable? Surely not in an environment such as Ciudad de México, which housed many conversos and crypto-Jews in colonial times. I did not know a single word of Ladino, and as I wandered around, I felt, yet again, angry about the inadequate education I had received.

In Toledo's famous Sinagoga de Tránsito, I met a young bohemian poet, Fernando de Parcas, from Seville. He told me about his passion for poetry, about a series of *tertulias* in his home town, about his fascination with Sephardic civilization, and in the end invited me to travel and stay with him at his place. It was through him that I first heard the first three stanzas of Shlomo Ibn Gabirol's poem about self-loathing:

I am the man who braced himself and
will not desist until he fulfils his vow—
whose heart recoiled from his heart,
whose spirit scorned to dwell in his
flesh, who chose wisdom even as a
youth—though he be tested seven
times in the crucible of Time, though
it pull down whatever he has built,
though it uproot whatever he has
planted and breach all his barriers.

אֲנִי הָאִישׁ אֲשֶׁר שִׁנֵּס אֲזוֹרוֹ
וְלֹא יִרֶף עֲדֵי יָקִים אֲסָרוֹ,
אֲשֶׁר נִבְהַל לְבָבוֹ מִלְּבָבוֹ
וְנַפְשׁוֹ מָאֲסָה לִשְׁכֹּן בִּשְׂרוֹ,
וּבָחַר בַּתְּבוּנָה מִנְּעוּרָיו—
וְאִם פּוּר הַזְּמָן שֶׁבַע בְּחָרוֹ
וְיַהֲרֹס כָּל אֲשֶׁר יִבְנֶה, וְיִתֹּשׁ
אֲשֶׁר יִטַּע, וְיִפְרֹץ אֶת גְּדֵרוֹ. [...]

As I slept—and the skies were spotless—
the radiant, pure-hearted moon led
me over the paths of wisdom, and, as he
led me, instructed me in his light. And
I, fearing some misfortune, was filled
with pity for his light, as a father for
his firstborn son.

בְּעֵת לוּנִי, וְהַשַּׁחַק נְקִי-כָף,
וְהַסָּהַר טָהָר-לַבָב וּבָרוּ,
נְהַגְנִי עֲלֵי אָרְחֵי תְבוּנוֹת
וְהוֹרַנִי בְּאוֹר נָהוֹג וְהוֹרוּ.
וְחָמַלְתִּי, בְּפַחְדִּי מִתְּלָאוֹת,
עֲלֵי אוֹרוֹ כְּאָב עַל בֵּן בְּכוֹרוּ.

And my favorite one by Yehuda Halevi:

My heart is in the East and I am at the
edge of the West. Then how can I taste
what I eat, how can I enjoy it? How
can I fulfill my vows and pledges
while Zion is in the domain of Edom,
and I am in the bonds of Arabia? It
would be easy for me to leave behind
all the good things of Spain; it would
be glorious to see the dust of the
ruined Shrine.

לִבִּי בְמִזְרָח, וְאָנֹכִי בְּסוֹף מַעֲרָב—
אֵיךְ אֶטְעֲמָה אֵת אֲשֶׁר אֹכַל וְאֵיךְ יֶעֱרָב?
אֵיכָה אֲשַׁלֵּם נְדָרַי וָאֱסָרַי, בְּעוֹד
צִיּוֹן בְּחֶבֶל אֱדוֹם וַאֲנִי בְּכֶבֶל עֲרָב?
יֵקַל בְּעֵינַי עֲזֹב כָּל טוּב סְפָרַד, כְּמוֹ
יֵקַר בְּעֵינַי רְאוֹת עַפְרוֹת דְּבִיר נֶחֱרָב.

De Parcas pronounced the Hebrew with extraordinary clarity, and then offered his own translations. He lived with his old mother in an antiquated apartment on Calle de Alfonso XII, near the Museo de Bella Artes, in downtown

Seville. We spent days together visiting sites in the city—I especially remember the Archivo de Indias, where a most impressive collection of documents of the New World is stored—as well as the Guadalquivir Delta, Jeréz de la Frontera, and Cádiz. He had rediscovered his Jewish roots when his dying grandmother uttered a few words in what sounded like Hebrew a month or so before she died. He knew the family was originally from Seville, but for more than a century most of its members had lived in Lima. An ancestor returned in the mid-nineteenth century, first to Cádiz, then to Seville. One generation after another, the feeling toward Spain was always ambivalent, and de Parcas thrived on this ambivalence: *"España es la madre patria y la puta madre,"* he used to sing. We talked a lot about the Spanish Civil War and its exiles in Mexico, and about medieval Hebrew-Spanish poetry in the so-called Golden Age, which, aside from Halevi and Ibn Gabirol, produced giants such as Shmuel Hanagid and Moses Ibn Ezra. In the end, de Parcas gave me inscribed copies of Fernando de Rojas's *La Celestina* and of a Spanish rendition of *Escenas de la vida de Bohemia*, which inspired Puccini's *La Bohème*. It carries the following inscription:

¡Adiós, cruel tierra inconstante!	*Goodbye, cruel unworthy land!*
Azote humano, sol helado	*Human scourge, chilling sun*
Cual solitaria alma errante	*Like a lonesome wondering soul*
Inadvertido habré pasado.	*I'll have passed by you unnoticed.*

I never saw de Parcas again, but it was thanks to his rediscovery of Judaism through poetry that I found a connection between the Spanish language and my Jewish self.

Crossing from Gibraltar to Africa, I meditated on the development of Cervantes's tongue as a refuge for persecuted Sephardim. Years later, while browsing in the *Encyclopedia Judaica*, I came across a paragraph that argued that not until 1910, when the Argentine-Jewish *homme de lettres* Alberto Gerchunoff published *The Jewish Gauchos of the Pampas*, did modern literature express itself *en español*. If so, it had taken more than four centuries since the expulsion in 1492 for the language to embrace Jewishness again. True, the year of the expulsion was when the first Spanish grammar appeared, by lexicographer Antonio de Nebrija. In the Middle Ages, Jews in the Iberian Peninsula knew Arabic and Hebrew, as well as (and depending on their degree of sophistication) Aramaic, Latin, Spanish, and Portuguese—and Ladino, of course. Their liturgical poems, known in Hebrew as *piyutim*, were drafted in Hebrew, and books such as Maimonides' *More Nevukim—The Guide of the Perplexed*—were actually translated into Hebrew from the Arabic (once by Samuel, the son of Judah ibn Tibbon, in twelfth-century Provence), and only later into Latin (*Doctor Perplexorum*), before they reached, much later, the Spanish language. *El español* was not a Jewish literary vehicle, at least not for those open about their Jewishness, even though the historian Américo Castro once argued that it was thanks to the Jews—especially those erudites in the court of Alfonso X, devoted to the craft of translation—that Spain came to find its soul in the Spanish language. Actually, Spanish was—it still is—among the most intolerant of Western tongues, home to Francisco de Quevedo, author of the infamous sonnet "A Man Attached to a Nose": *"Erase un hombre a una naríz pegado, érase una naríz superalativa, érase una alquitara medio viva, érase un peje espada mal barbado. . . ."* On the other hand, crypto-Jews, *marranos*, and conversos, in shaping a literature of their own under vigilant eyes from the fourteenth century on, did use Spanish, albeit in coded form. How often have I heard, since my first visit to the peninsula, the thesis that Santa Teresa de Jesús and San Juan de la Cruz were crypto-Jews? The Jewishness of Fray Luis de León, Fernando de Rojas, and Ludovico Vives, of course, is beyond dispute, but innuendos abound. Some claim Cervantes himself was a *cristiano nuevo*, a New Christian. Spain, of course, ended up suffering much more than its rejected Jews: its economy never fully recovered from the blow, nor did its society, in which a deep xenophobia became *the* pattern. And this intolerance, this provincialism, also manifested itself in its language, alien in its core to the Jewish sensibility until well into the twentieth century.

In Barcelona, I was visited by a dream in which a rabbi, standing outside a movie theater and dressed in a yellow tunic, kept on repeating: *"Morirás lejos, muy lejos . . . ,"* thou shalt die in a distant land . . . ! The image remained with me for days, if not weeks. It was symbolic to me that the dream had come while I was in Spain, for, as infatuated as I was with the country—I returned to it from Morocco and Algiers, and then again after a long stay in Paris—it was obviously not a landscape in which I could settle. The past was there, but not the future. The country felt stilted. Anti-Semitism was subtle yet unequivocal. No, I needed to return to Ciudad de México. The Promised Land was within me. Utopia was an empty vessel, filled with romantic dreams inherited from my past. Zionism was no longer a hope but a reality, and it didn't speak loudly to me. And the rest of the globe also seemed alien to me, what Ciro Alegría once described as "*ancho y ajeno*": outlandish—or, better, eccentric, literally without its center.

Ancho y ajeno.

MY SECOND RETURN to Mexico was painful: *una dura sambullida en la realidad*, a diving-into-reality. My goal was to move far away from the Jewish community, to allow myself to get to Méjico, the old-fashioned one, the one spelled with the "j," the rough-and-tumble landscape forbidden to me with my education. My teens were over: adulthood was ahead of me. The road led, inevitably, to UNAM and then to the more radical Universidad Autónoma Metropolitana, known by its acronym UAM-X, a niche for Marxist activism. In the late 1960s, just as the Olympic Games were about to take place in Ciudad de México, students from UNAM and its rival the Instituto Politécnico Nacional, housewives, and urban workers organized against the ruling Partido Revolucionario Institucional (aka PRI), known for stealing every single presidential election since its founding in 1929 until 2000. Mass demonstrations were held in the Zócalo, the heart of the city, next to the Basílica de Guadalupe and the Palacio Nacional. It is then that President Gustavo Díaz Ordaz, advised by his future successor, Luis Echeverría, ordered the massacre in Tlatelolco Square. Shortly after, Echeverría, by then president, established that the tragedy had taken place because students, by all accounts the prime movers behind the demonstrations, were mostly concentrated in UNAM and Politécnico, located at strategic places in the metropolis. The best way to prevent another confrontation was to reduce the size of both institutions and create a third public university with three campuses far away from one another. Thus the UAM was born.

And so was I—as *homo politicus*—the moment I entered its classrooms. At UAM-X I met extraordinary friends: photographer Edgar Ladrón de Guevara, film director Fernando Sariñana, anthropologist Jiganny Lomelí. (The last, a niece of Fidel Castro, was actually enrolled at the Instituto de Antropología e Historia, but moved in our circle.) Ahead of us was Rafael Sebastían Guillén Vicente, who eventually stunned the Mexican government and the world at large as a masked guerrilla fighter and Zapatista leader in the state of Chiapas named Subcomandante Marcos. I still wanted to become a filmmaker, even though the seed of literature was already growing inside me, so I made a tacit agreement with my father: in exchange for his support to become some kind of artist, I would graduate with a degree in psychology. This would give me the necessary training should the career prove too difficult, as he felt his had been. He didn't want me to repeat the mistake he had made.

I immediately began to read *Das Kapital*, Herbert Marcuse, Noam Chomsky, and Felix Guatari, and to return to the brothers Flores Magón and José Vasconcelos in earnest. Communism, I could sense in the air, was what Mexico was positively about: José Clemente Orozco and José Revueltas, Frida Kahlo and even the French Surrealist André Breton understood it, and so did my generation. Our duty as middle- and upper-middle-class citizens was to use our knowledge to bring about justice and equality to a nation torn by injustice, by a history of *atropellos*, of abuse and exploitation.

Today these words—abuse, exploitation—seem empty to me, not because Mexico has finally redeemed itself (not in the least), but because of the way the Mexican left has turned them into mere slogans. But they were meaningful then. I re-member my father telling me about Leon Trotsky's assassina-tion. He had been a child when Zeyde Srulek told him about it. Trotsky died when an ice pick was thrust into his skull by a Spanish traitor in Colonia Coyoacán. Trotsky's corpse was on view to the public in the Palacio de las Bellas Artes. Zeyde Srulek took him to see it. There were long lines.

"Why did he take you?" I asked my father, hoping to find a trace of elusive ideological commitment in my family to justify my present behavior. Zeyde Srulek, as the family described him to be, was never politically *engagé*.

"I don't know," my father replied, undisturbed by my curiosity, and proceeded to describe the terror he felt at see-ing the open casket. "Trotsky's bearded smile—I shall never forget it."

"A smile?" I pondered.

"Yes . . . He looked entirely at peace. *Feliz del todo*, happy as can be."

I asked him to describe the scene in more detail, but my father was dumbfounded. "He lay quietly," he added, "un-aware of who he was."

Revolución: the key word. Classes at UAM-X were pro-gressive, not to say anarchic: a single teacher for the whole trimester, an emphasis on fieldwork, and an insatiable need to assign provocative Mexican literature: Carlos Monsiváis, Elena Poniatowska, Carlos Fuentes. Union strikes occurred every other month, to the point where the entire school had to repeat a trimester because of so many lost days. The result of this constant interruption was extra free time, which I used to form an experimental theater troupe, to travel to the Yucatán Peninsula, and to begin reading in earnest an end-less list of books of world literature—Flaubert, Strindberg,

Maupassant, Chekhov, Tolstoy, Hemingway, Faulkner, Gide—which I realized were essential to anyone dreaming of even a precarious life in the arts.

Theater was not only alluring because of the passion I inherited from my father. I also saw it as a way to merge aesthetics and ideology. Performing in empty lots and run-down factories, on the streets of poor neighborhoods, more than justified the effort: it was not about show business but about awakening the political conscience. To be effective, plays needed to have a spontaneous and nondidactic quality. My Jewish self was absolutely dormant in these efforts, for the whole enterprise was about Mexico—its masses, its future—and not about its wealthy, self-contained minorities. In fact, I remember those years as intensely confrontational, rebelling against my parents and their background. I wanted, as much as I could, to erase my ancestry, to join in, to become *un mexicano hecho y derecho*. I remember an intense dinner conversation at home with my parents and a close friend of theirs, a teacher of mine by the name of Jacqueline Rubinstein (aka La Jacky), when I told them I was embarrassed by the Yiddish instruction I had received. Nobody in UAM-X had ever heard of Sholem Aleichem's Tevye and the litanies by Bashevis Singer on demons and sexual repression. (Actually, I was once asked by a Gentile acquaintance if the author of "Gimpel the Fool" and *Enemies: A Love Story* was the chief executive of the Singer Sewing Machine Company.) What good was it to train your children in the ways of the vanished world of Eastern Europe, to teach them about Benito Juárez in Yiddish, but not to tell them a single word about Lázaro Cárdenas, who in the late 1930s nationalized Mexico's oil industry to save the nation's soul from international companies and imperialistic regimes? *"Judío de madre, judío hasta la muerte,"* La Jacky replied. Once a Jew, always a Jew. It was a deterministic view, one I couldn't accept quietly. So I stormed out of the house, furious, offended.

Acción—my only escape, I thought, was action. With Sariñana I joined political marches in the Zócalo, and with others I attended plenary sessions of the various Marxist political parties active at the time. Every day I felt more and more proud of my communism and less interested in my Jewishness. The authentic Promised Land was Mexico, I realized, and I was needed to help cure its historical injuries. I was infatuated with the adolescent diaries of Ernesto "Che" Guevara and the theater of Jerzy Grotowsky and Tadeuz Kantor. Among my most vivid memories of those years was time spent with a middle-aged Marxist priest, Padre Chinchachoma (aka Chincha, as his followers referred to him), loosely inspired—or so I thought, having read a couple of manifestos—by liberation theology. Over a beer, he told me about the need to save the children, to rescue *la niñez extraviada*, the many destitute kids on the streets of Ciudad de México. "So many orphans . . . Who are they? Why doesn't anyone in this monstrous city offer them the love they need so much?" His mission, he told me (or, better, his calling), was to adopt them, to make them his own, not by bringing them into his life but the other way around: by submerging himself in *their* universe—their pain, their homelessness. I spent a couple of weeks following Chincha from one rundown hotel to another, from a dump to a hospital, experiencing firsthand the children's exposure to crime and prostitution. Only by living with them could he bring some back. And I went along, convinced his assignment was worthwhile.

Nights in the projects, drugs . . . I slept in places I dare not remember, hugged by eight-year-olds for whom death waited around the next corner, saw scenes of unspeakable cruelty, such as when a mother stabbed her daughter for a few pesos to satisfy her addiction. At times I felt as if Chincha were the Messiah incarnate: forthright, belligerent, ready to do anything to save a life. It was as though I were part of Buñuel's *Los olvidados* or Héctor Babenco's *Pixote:* a companion of criminals. But the young criminals were quite innocent, victims of a status quo that refuses to make room for everyone. How much did I have in common with the orphans? Could I learn to love them? Was Chincha's pedagogy a strategy to satisfy his own needs? I never reached any conclusion, because my physical reaction to the work was so strong that one morning I simply collapsed at home, to sleep nonstop for twenty-four hours. When I woke up and looked for the priest and his children in the hotel where I had left them, they had vanished without trace. I could have searched for them, of course, but I didn't want to: though I admired Chincha, I felt I was abusing his generosity. I felt dishonest, because my main goal in following his path was not to help but to survive and one day write about it.

My education naturally led me to Cuba, where I arrived—euphoric, like most of my generation—in 1982. Jiganny Lomelí made arrangements to ease my visit. (*Protektzia* is the Israeli term.) I went with Sariñana and with people from the theater troupe, traveled to Varadero, Santiago, and Matanzas, but of course spent most of the time in Havana, where a pupil of novelist Alejo Carpentier showed me around. I talked to actors and writers. Books were cheaply made—their paper was not much better quality than news-

paper—and unbelievably inexpensive: a two-volume set of
Victor Hugo's *Les Misérables* for the equivalent of a few U.S.
pennies, likewise Carpentier's *La música que llevo dentro*,
Hemingway's *The Old Man and the Sea*, and scores of Spanish-
language "sympathizers" of the Cuban Revolution: Roque
Dalton, Alaide Fopa, Mario Benedetti, Ariel Dorfman. Of
course, José Martí, "Che" Guevara, and Fidel Castro were
ubiquitous, their work almost given away. I returned home
with two large boxes of books. (I didn't realize how heavily
censored they were until I sat down to read them in Ciudad
de México. The translations were manipulative, and entire
sections had disappeared.) I marveled at the low level of illiteracy and the free medical system, but since I chose not to
travel as a tourist but instead stayed in Cuban homes, I was
also astonished by the omniscience of the state at every level
of life: long food lines, electricity shortages, the general decay of the Havana landscape, and the total absence of intellectual freedom. It never crossed my mind to look for a
shrinking Ashkenazi community in Cuba's capital, which at
one point had been almost as important as its Mexican counterpart. But I wasn't looking for missing links in the Jewish
diaspora. What I wanted was a firsthand view of what socialism could accomplish in the Hispanic world, including Mexico. The only sight I got of Castro was while on a bus ride
back from Matanzas, when someone screamed that El
Líder's limousine was passing by. I looked out the window to
see a luxurious automobile with a stream of smoke coming
out of one of its back windows.

The trip to Cuba was meant to energize my political
consciousness, but it had an utterly negative effect on me.
Una bomba: it began a reversal in my enthusiasm toward left-

wing causes, which, I came to realize, not only distorted the truth for its own purposes but had little imagination to speak of. It merely adapted foreign ideas to native soil without questioning their validity. I belonged to a generation in Latin America that still foolishly idealized Fidel Castro. In the 1960s, many were hypnotized by the miracle of Sierra Maestra and the stubbornness of Havana in the face of U.S. aggression. It was the famous Heberto Padilla affair—in which, somewhat as in Arthur Koestler's *Darkness at Noon*, a prominent poet of the revolution was forced to confess in public to dubious crimes—that put the left throughout the Americas at a crossroads. The international reaction to the Padilla scandal was immediate, and its effects were chilling: Octavio Paz, Mario Vargas Llosa, and others began to repent, taking a more center-right position. Cuba, they claimed, was not a model but an antimodel, an autocratic state that should not be endorsed. Their intellectual odyssey paved the way for a refreshing critique, at times nearsighted, of the rebellious forces and progressive political parties from Mexico to Argentina. And the military coup in Chile against Salvador Allende intensified it. The problem is, the Latin American left has a tradition of awkwardness: it is recalcitrant, monolithic, injudicious, and autocratic. Time and again it has failed to live up to its democratic challenges. And by the early 1980s, not much had changed, unfortunately: Castro was still a demigod, a larger-than-life figure whom disenfranchised youngsters sought to emulate. Widespread poverty and injustice help stimulate Marxist views in the middle-class young, of course. But when most nations in the region embraced an open-market economy, not enough people on the extreme left were ready to give up their dreams of subversion and seek peaceful, democratic solutions to urgent problems. (President Echeverría once cryptically said that in Latin America he who isn't a Marxist before the age of twenty-five has a problem; he who continues to be one after that age has no solution.)

When I returned to UAM-X, I grew impatient with the institution's political volatility. My reaction was not common. Many of my friends—who at some point or other also visited not only Cuba but Nicaragua and even the Soviet Union and Peru, where Abimael Guzmán's Shining Path was a strong civil force, came up with a different conclusion: Fidel Castro's style was not the answer, they realized, but an armed struggle was still justified, or at least activism of some sort. A number of them disappeared from the classroom, failing to complete their degrees. We knew some had moved to states like Chiapas and Guerrero, joining underground groups, and others were still incognito in Ciudad de México, joining the workers' struggle and plotting to overthrow the government by peaceful means.

Perhaps my animosity was the result of an unavoidable fact: in the eyes of comrades, I was and always would be *el güerito*, the blondie—a foreigner whose dream of blending in was betrayed by his white-skinned, European physical appearance. Not a mestizo, not even a criollo: simply *un extranjero*. It was during a particularly unruly meeting with a bunch of agitators in which I was asked to administer some funds that someone, not without malice, said, "But why Ilan? He is not one of us. . . ." The comment was followed by a disquisition on the history of Jewish moneylending.

I was silent. Was a statement such as this the reason I never officially joined Mexico's Partido Comunista? For, as much as I tried to deny it, to run away from it, my Jewishness always caught up with me. I saw myself in the larger canvas:

Do Jewish intellectuals, almost by definition, sympathize with lost causes? And aren't they sooner or later thrown out, expelled by virtue of their being foreigners?

Un extranjero: once a Jew, always a Jew.

MY REACTION, YET again, was to burn my bridges, to abandon Mexico once and for all. But with Israel, Spain, and Cuba eliminated, where to go? Before long, I realized I needed to return to the Iberian Peninsula and the Middle East to exorcise their ghosts.

By then I was obsessed with literature. My work with the theater troupe had been interesting, but I was not a team player: I grew irritated by people's slowness, nervous about my lack of total control.

More than halfway through my undergraduate studies, I realized that UAM-X was a nest of ideological intrigue. *"Nisht far yidn,"* Bobbe Bela told me once. And so, where did the *yid* truly belong?

The magic of Spain—yes, I would become a young Hemingway in Madrid. The word was meant to be my home, but first I needed to appropriate it, to become its friend.

In the early 1980s, I fell in love with a Canadian Jew my parents and sister had met accidentally on a car trip, Hoddie K., a modern Orthodox, free-spirited, if somewhat repressed daughter of a Holocaust survivor. (She is the model of the female protagonist in my novella *Talia in Heaven*, set against a backdrop of revolution.) She came to Mexico on a visit, and my parents invited her for dinner. After our initial shyness, we struck a chord, and a provocative ongoing conversation about the Holocaust and Maimonides began. It seems to me significant that, while my friends were moving deeper into political activism, this ·beautiful red-haired woman, slightly older than I, made me look back at my Jewish roots—through love, not through ideology.

I spent only a few brief months with Hoddie in Ciudad de México, because I was determined to leave everything and return to Europe. If I had any talent as a writer, I needed to find out immediately. I found a job as a photographer's assistant that provided me with some money, and sold some belongings. I left for Spain without an itinerary but with a small green portable Olivetti, found myself a cheap room, and began to write.

Write, write, write . . . Not in Yiddish but in *español*, my own tongue. But words betrayed me. Did I really have something to say? A young Hemingway. Why? Didn't the world already have one? What was *my* place as a writer? A novel. I would produce a novel—the great Jewish–Latin American novel, one that could rival Saul Bellow's *Herzog*. I didn't know where to start, and so I crafted letters filled with longing and sadness . . . and I kept dreaming of Hoddie.

An author needs to know who and where his readers are, I repeatedly told myself. For whom was *I* writing? For my friends? But who were my friends? The comrades I had joined in public demonstrations? No, that facet of my life was over. Mexican Jews, perhaps? Truth is, they hardly read at all, and when they do, the last thing they want is a form of criticism of their *Weltanschauung*. I realized that "my second Spanish coming" was an extension of the first one. I was still as disoriented as ever, without a place to call home.

Some weeks after my arrival, Hoddie joined me. We wandered the streets of Madrid and traveled to Salamanca and Toledo. Her Jewishness, I felt, was exhilarating. It wasn't her Jewish-Canadian self that attracted me, but the honesty with which she spoke of her own quest.

In Toledo I bought David Gonzalo Maezo's lucid translation of Maimonides's *Guide of the Perplexed* and read it nonstop for a week with utter delight. What fascinated me the most was the book's coded message, for Maimonides, both a believer and an Aristotelian, had crafted it so that only "secret readers" would truly understand his heretical message.

We spent almost a month with one another, talking and making love. We traveled together to Switzerland. Then, in Geneva, she left. I was hyperkinetic in her eyes, too Hispanic for her taste.

My response was a reawakening of my own Jewishness. I was a Yiddish-speaking Mexican Jew, and it was time I came to terms with that fact. I had little money left. I fled to Israel—why, I still don't know.

This time I stayed in Rehovot, at the apartment of the older child of Tío Isaac, Joel, and his Israeli wife, Anat. I wandered around the country, from Tiberias to Eilat, in a state of agitation and confusion. In the end, I found some peace by realizing that I needed to return to Mexico, even if Mexico was not my true home. Perhaps, I told myself, I would never find that home. What I needed was perhaps to approach my homelessness as an asset, not as a stigma.

I was perplexed, but I was one of Maimonides's pupils. His teaching was clear-cut: I needed to read between the lines.

DEPRESSION. A SHAMEFUL return. I had told friends and family that if I ever returned it would be with a full-length novel in hand. But I had nothing to show, only a vague belief that to complete what I had already started was the right step.

Back to rhetorical UAM-X.

My afternoons were different this time, for I spent them reading voraciously everything I could find on Judaism and Jewishness: Joseph Roth's *The Radetzky March*, Spinoza, Martin Buber, Albert Memmi, and of course the Bible. The issue of translation began to preoccupy me: How could Jews the world over write in so many different tongues? Why did they excel as translators? Jewish philosophy attracted me keenly, especially the magisterial book *The Star of Redemption* by the eloquent German thinker Franz Rosenzweig. I was transfixed by his tragic life, perhaps because, as Nahum N. Glazer said once, Rosenzweig's journey, with its traits of quasi-melodrama, was about rediscovering Judaism. After fruitless attempts at assimilation, to the point of being ready to convert to Christianity, his recognition of what Jewishness is about came during the religious service of Yom Kippur in 1913, when, while listening to the hypnotic prayer Kol Nidre, he decided not only to remain Jewish but to devote his life actively to explaining its mystery. He began writing his magnum opus in 1918, while in the trenches of the Balkan front, where he also contracted malaria. He returned to his home town, Cassel, and in 1919 finished the volume, a couple of years short of the diagnosis of amyotrophic lateral sclerosis, which would leave him immobilized forever.

I remember when I first read Rosenzweig's words, "Everything that happens [in the Jewish world] is ambivalent. . . ." The world itself, and not the Jewish individual, is Jewish—a compelling idea! It suited me to perfection. And

I remember Rosenzweig's ideas on translation—with his friend Martin Buber, Rosenzweig engaged in a German version of the Bible through which the musicality of the original could be heard and the strict syntactical nature of Goethe's tongue was adulterated—and the strong impact they had on me. I can almost repeat them by heart:

> It is a gross misconception to believe that the translator, in order to fulfill his task, must adapt to German usage whatever is alien. If I were a merchant who had received an order from Turkey, I should send it to the translation bureau and expect that kind of translation. But if the communication from Turkey was a letter from a friend, the translation of such a bureau would no longer be adequate. And why? Because it would not be accurate? It would be just as accurate as the translation of the business letter. But that is not the point. It would be German enough; it would not, however, be sufficiently Turkish! I should not hear the man, his special tone, his cast of mind, his heartbeat. But ought this be expected? Is it not demanding the impossible of a language to ask it to reproduce an alien tone in all its alienness, in other words, not to adapt the foreign tongue to German, but German to the foreign tongue?

I read Walter Benjamin at the time as well, and the scholarship of Gershom Scholem on medieval Jewish mysticism stimulated me. I found a serviceable Spanish translation of *On Kabbalah and Its Symbolism* misplaced in a bookstore, and read it in a single afternoon. It prompted me to pursue his work in earnest. But as an emblem, neither Benjamin nor Scholem spoke to me as loudly as Rosenzweig, not at the time. (A decade later, though, I found him irksome, too obtrusively Hegelian.) The mix of theology and philosophy. Had I made a mistake in thinking I was a young Hemingway when, spellbound by *The Star of Redemption*, I should fancy myself as a young Rosenzweig? In my spare time, I decided to write an extended essay on him, which I showed to a priest whom I knew at Universidad Iberoamericana, a Jesuit university where my mother taught psychology. I also told him about a piece I was considering to write about Bayha ibn Paquda, a medieval Jewish mystic responsible for *Sefer Hobot ha-Lebabot*, a popular manual for proper behavior that in my view prophesied the theories developed by Sigmund Freud in nineteenth-century Vienna. The priest, in turn, gave me a copy of Umberto Eco's novel *The Name of the Rose*, which he had just read, and less than a month later invited me to teach a course on Jewish philosophy at his institution.

The invitation flattered me. I had not yet completed my degree at UAM-X, but already my interests were shifting dramatically from those of my classmates. It was then, while on the faculty as a Jewish teacher in a Catholic undergraduate school, that I began my first novel: *El error*, an esoteric tale of human mendacity set against the backdrop of an enclosed Hispanic university. My attempt was not only to explore the tension between dogma and *episteme* and use Franz Rosenzweig as my secret model, but to examine the tension between Judaism and Christianity in the Hispanic orbit. The site of the novel is a fictional South American nation, Paranagua (I borrowed the name from the scholar Yehezkel Kaufmann), where I've often placed my fiction. The female protagonist, an acerbic, mystical middle-aged woman—modeled on my mother—who not only specializes in Jewish esoterism but is a kabbalist herself, is accused by Paranagua's authorities of a major theft: the disappearance of the cathedral's central crucifix, which rumors claim she brought down at night, while the temple was in total darkness, and stored in the basement of the building where her office is located. The fact that she is innocent is not a deterrent: as the authorities, supported by the Jesuit priests of the Universidad de Paranagua, corner her publicly and are ready to expel her, she triumphantly devises a supernatural escape. I'm incapable of even reading the book today. If memory serves me well, the whole storyline was represented as a palimpsest; but it allowed me to reflect on my ambivalence toward Ciudad de México and about my admiration for the magisterial Catedral de Nuestra Señora la Vírgen de Guadalupe. Sections of the novel were set in Toledo, Paris, Israel; Mexico—or the masquerading loci animated by it—figured only tangentially. The protagonist's Jewishness and the way others perceived her were at center stage. I remember trying to present my Spanish as a nonnative language—that is, to articulate the original as if it were already in translation. The novel's fitting title was a statement of its quality. It was courteously rejected by the only publishing house I dared show it to: the small Editorial Artífice. It was dutifully destroyed soon after.

The owner of Editorial Artífice took me out to lunch at Café La Blanca, near the Palacio de Bellas Artes. After explaining the reasons for her rejection, she announced with the utmost tact that behind this failed experiment was a consummate author who, for some unexplained reason, reminded her of Herman Melville, and in particular of his *Moby Dick:* a certain tendency toward the epic, an attempt to portray the clash between religions as a peremptory battle between moral systems, a portrait of a lone mystic as a stubborn "mariner who, as she looks out of her door's keyhole, sees the entire world before her. . . ." The connection surprised me: I had never read *Moby Dick* in full (I didn't even own a copy), nor was I able to grasp the link between my protagonist and Ahab, the captain of the *Pequod*, in his insane, revenge-driven mission to pursue the white whale. But the allusion flattered me. If it had been offered to make the negative news more palatable, its purpose was fulfilled, for, after a few days, once I recovered from the rejection, I told myself: You shall continue. The rejection is inconsequential. And you should read Melville. The more I thought about it, the better I understood that while drafting *El error* I had felt truly human, and its mere existence opened a door for me— yes, literature was the answer—my Promised Land, an authentic home, and a portable one at that, which I was able to carry around with me. Henry Thoreau once wrote, "The art of life . . . is, not having anything to do, to do something." Herein, I concluded, lay the true utopia: finding raison d'être, inventing your own private homeland.

AGAIN I HEAR the hoopla made by the two thousand people around me. Through a microphone, instructions are given to stand on one of several lines, depending on the first letter of the person's surname. I smiled at my Cuban friend and wished him luck, then proceeded—my Mexican passport in hand—to stand on line near a desk where a severe-looking man had several boxes with documents.

Not arbitrarily, I invoke *Moby Dick*. Who could have told me I would one day learn English—*my* English—thanks to it? I flew across the Rio Grande with very primitive language skills, but one night, in my small bedroom at Broadway and 122nd Street, I made a commitment to myself: Amerika had opened its arms to me, having proffered a full fellowship to perform graduate studies; in return, I should turn it into *my* America, I would attempt to perfect my English as much as I could and become a useful citizen. In my practical mind, the term "useful" carried a concrete meaning: a voice to count, to listen to. I was in my mid-twenties, more than capable of self-knowledge. After all, I had taught myself to appreciate Jewishness anew in Ciudad de México, and in Israel I forced myself to read Tchernichowsky and Bialik in the original. Why couldn't I vastly improve my skills in the tongue of Shakespeare, make myself literally fluent in it, as fluent, as Joseph Conrad would say, "as an unimpeded river"?

Those were nights of verbal definition—lonely nights, enraptured by the music of words. To make ends meet, aside from my duties as a correspondent for Mexican newspapers and my studies, I also worked at the translation agency of Columbia University. Once or twice a week, the agency would send me a set of legal documents or a short story or would ask me to meet such-and-such a person to teach him or her an hour's worth of Spanish. These efforts were an invaluable exercise to me; indeed, I'm still amazed today at my fearlessness, for the requests were always to render a text into English, in which I was weak, and hardly ever the other way around. But it was in *Moby Dick* that I found my true teacher. The method was simple yet dogmatic: with my atrocious pronunciation, I would read a single paragraph, sometimes even a single line, at low speed: "Kol mi Ismael. Som yiars agou—never maind jau long precaiseli—jabin litel or no moni in mai purz, and nottin parhkular tu interes mi on shour, ai tout ai bud seil abaut a litel and si de guatery part of de gorld." With a pad in hand, I would make a list of all the words I had failed to understand, without looking for a definition in my pocket-size *Oxford English Dictionary*, which my father had given to me as a present; I would then put the book aside, turn the light off, and repeat the list in order. At this time came the best part of all: I would try to imagine what these words meant; I would then turn the light on again, look in the dictionary for the right response, smiling at how off target I had been, and finish by going over the list again, this time repeating to myself what each word really meant. The following night, I would read the segment again and repeat the list from memory. Obviously, this was a nightmarish approach; it taught me much but eliminated all possible pleasure from the act of reading itself.

English is almost mathematical. Its rules manifest themselves in an iron fashion. This is in sharp contrast to Spanish, of course, whose Romance roots make it a free-flowing, imprecise language, with long and uncooperative words. As a language, it is somewhat undeserving of the literature it has created. This might explain why I enjoy rereading *One Hundred Years of Solitude* far more in English than in the original, as well as *Don Quixote*. For me, mastering English was, as I convinced myself, a ticket to salvation. Spanish, in spite of being the third-most-important language on the globe, after Chinese and English, is peripheral. It is a language that flourishes in the outskirts of culture, more reactive than active.

The immediate results of my reading methods were less than gratifying. The response I got to the dispatches I sent

to the newspapers *Excélsior* and *La Jornada* was univocal: I
was writing in Spanish, editors would claim, but thinking in
English; my grammar was bizarre, polluted, unconvincing.
They often sent the wired articles back with endless nasty
comments. This tension achieved its climax when, in a trip
to Mexico, I stopped by the offices of *Unomásuno*, one of the
newspapers I occasionally wrote for, and Humberto Batis, a
ruffian of a veteran, told me to stop writing altogether. "Your
future, my friend, might as well be in business!" he said. But
the road to fully formed polyglotism was filled with mines, I
knew, and my response was not to return to Mexico but to
become an American writer of sorts. Could I ever? This
seemed an evanescent dream, of course; so many writers
were totally in control of the English language, who was I to
push myself into the crowd and become one of them? No, I
could never become an American writer; as a Jew in a long
chain of generations, I was a wandering soul, inhabiting
other people's tongues. I could, indeed, make myself comfortable in English, but I could not dispel the sense of inhabiting a rented house, of borrowing another person's suit.

A sense of inferiority also lived within me. Actually, it
still does. It is aggravated by the very ambivalent attitude the
United States has toward multilingualism. Polyglotism, in
spite of the general perception, is a rather common phenomenon in the world—not simply the sign of an immigrant, but a means of being a world citizen. As it happens,
there are some three to four thousand languages on the
globe, and only about 150 countries. Most countries are
home to more than one language: Belgians, for instance,
speak French and Dutch; Luxembourgians use three
tongues—French, German, and Luxembourgian; citizens of
Switzerland speak Swiss German, French, Italian, and Ro-

mansh; India has about two hundred classified languages; Russia, around 122; on the island of New Guinea, about seven hundred. But in America, multilingualism is an immigrant's attribute, in spite of the polyglotism in the past, when the British pilgrims arrived in the seventeenth century. In fact, it has been estimated that between five hundred and a thousand native languages coexisted before English became the dominant and domineering force. Little trace of them is left. English became so overwhelmingly powerful, so omnipresent, that multilingualism was reduced to a newcomer's trademark; for what is an immigrant if not a verbal traveler?

Curiously, in the United States, to be a member of the upper class and a polyglot is a ticket to success. But multilingualism among the poor is unacceptable and, thus, immediately condemned. One has only to walk the streets of New York to be made conscious of this double standard: Spanish is spoken by tourists on Fifth Avenue, but Colombian and Dominican children in Washington Heights are told that English must come first. Still, I crossed the Rio Grande at a moment of thorough re-evaluation of linguistic patterns. If, in the 1940s and 1950s, Spanish was invalidated without the slightest remorse, bilingual education, its seeds planted by the exiled Cuban community in Florida—first in Dade County, then in Miami—and spread to other Hispanics and non-English-language immigrant groups such as Koreans and Creole-speaking newcomers from the Caribbean basin, had, willy-nilly, somewhat legitimized Spanish. So much so that, when I arrived, it was, by most accounts, the nation's unofficial second language. In spite of their poor quality, TV and radio channels in Spanish, and newspapers in Los Angeles, New York, and Miami, enjoyed tremendous influence. And I, hoping to retain my two tongues, was active in them, often contributing to the opinion pages of *El Nuevo Herald* and *La Opinión*, and having a weekly column in *El Diario/La Prensa*, while simultaneously filing pieces in the *Miami Herald* and the *Washington Post*. My education and skin color—and my Jewishness, too, I'm convinced—also made me a regular guest on TV news programs. Once, as the Berlin Wall was crumbling down, my wife, watching the news at 10 P.M. in Univisión in our Upper West Side apartment, caught an interview with me in which I was asked for my reaction to the Russian leader Mikhail Gorbachev. Underneath, a subtitle read: "Ilan Stavans, Soviet Specialist."

My feelings toward bilingual education were nothing but ambiguously complex, though, and sometimes put me at odds with community leaders and hard-core activists. My predisposition to injustice made me sensitive to the plight of Latinos, and generated a strong curiosity about their popular culture. But I didn't fall back on my years as a student activist. "Blood and skin do not think," Ralph Ellison wrote once, and I agreed wholeheartedly. I believed Spanish needed to, and eventually would, be retained, but not at the expense of English. After all, what makes America a single unity, what stresses the *unum* against the *pluribus*, what highlights the "c" instead of the "k," is a common vehicle of communication, an equalizing language. Through sheer mathematics, in the late twentieth century Latinos were called to play a major national role at all levels, but they would suffer dramatically if their assimilation were to be completed the way previous minorities had achieved it, through the acquisition of English-language skills.

The interest in polyglotism and bilingual education hit a sensitive chord in me. In Mexico I had been—I could not escape being—a Jew, whereas in New York I was a Mexican, although a peculiar one, no doubt. In the supermarket once, while I was standing on line at the checkout counter, a pair of Puerto Rican girls made a nasty comment *en español*. To their amazement, I replied in Spanish.

"*¿Pero de dónde es Ud?*"

"Ciudad de México, of course. Don't I look the part?"

"You don't—you're teasing us," one said, astonished at my verbal fluency. "You learned Spanish in school, didn't you? You aren't one of ours. It is impossible."

Imposible. They said goodbye with respect, unconvinced yet giving me the benefit of the doubt. I laughed at the exchange, but for days kept on thinking about it. Since the arrival of the conquistadors and surely even before, society in the Americas has been structured by class. And class is often defined by degrees of foreignness. Thus, as a white-skinned Hispanic, I was automatically awarded a higher status, and among the Latino community in New York, that status— again, attached to my Jewishness—opened doors to me. I often wrote autobiographical notes about my vicissitudes as a "non-Mexican Mexican," always emphasizing the fact that Hispanics north of the Rio Grande were not only a minority but an extremity of Latin America in the United States. General Simón Bolívar, in the mid-nineteenth-century, dreamed of an all-encompassing republic that would embrace most of the Southern Hemisphere and perhaps even extend itself beyond. His romantic dream came to nothing at the time, but, magically, at the end of the twentieth century it suddenly became a reality inside *El coloso del Norte*, the neighbor up north. Not along the lines Bolívar envisioned, of course, but the conglomerate of backgrounds was still the same, with Spanish as an essential part of it. Only a part, though: English, and American popular culture, were the other fundamental ingredients, and it was preposterous to ignore these ingredients, or to keep battling them as merciless enemies, a strategy many Chicano activists of the civil-rights era endorsed. In my view, Latinos needed to recognize, and reconcile, their forking self, part Hispanic, part American. Ancestry ought not to become a political agenda.

In English, *en español*—my double life made me far more aware of my polyglotic past. It also magnified my interest in the impact of multilingualism at the personal level. I avidly read Jerzy Kosinski, Guillermo Cabrera Infante, and Joseph Brodsky, and I returned to the Nabokov of my youth. The prose of the latter struck me as sublime, especially his collection *Less Than One*. (I have never been a serious reader of poetry.) Brodsky taught at Mount Holyoke College, not far from New York. I met him at a café in Greenwich Village, and we talked at length about translation and a life in two languages. "There is nothing disloyal about carrying on with several lovers," he said, "especially when the duality is honest and open." I told him I was struck by Henry James's comments on languages and women. If the first, the native tongue, James once claimed, is the maternal one, what is the second? And the third and fourth? Is it proper to talk of paternal tongues? Or should we talk of a stepmother's tongue? James opted for the mistress tongue, suggesting that one's liaison to a mother is essentially different from the one we keep with a lover. Brodsky dismissed this proto-psychoanalytic view. "In Russian and English, in English and Russian—I am alive in both." And he was, in a happy balance. Language is more than a lover. When I got home, I opened Joseph Conrad's *A Personal Record* and reread the magnificent passage in the "Author's Note" to the reprint edition:

The fact of my not writing in my native language has been of course commented on frequently in reviews and notices of my various works and in the more extended critical articles. I suppose that was unavoidable; and indeed these comments were of the most flattering kind to one's vanity. But in that matter I have no vanity that could be flattered. I could not have it. . . . The impression of my having exercised a choice between the two languages, French and English, both foreign to me, has got abroad somehow. . . . The truth of the matter is that my faculty to write in English is as natural as any other aptitude with which I might have been born. I have a strange and overpowering feeling that it had always been an inherited part of myself. English was for me neither a matter of choice nor adoption. The merest idea of choice has never entered my head. And as to adoption—well, yes, there was adoption; but it was I who was adopted by the genius of the language, which directly I came out of the stammering stage made me its own so completely that its very idioms I truly believe had a direct action on my temperament and fashioned my still plastic character. It was a very intimate action and for that very reason it is too mysterious to explain. The task would be as impossible as trying to explain love at first sight. There was something in this conjunction of exulting, almost physical recognition, the same sort of emotional surrender and the same pride of possession, all united in the wonder of great discovery; but there was on it none of the shadow of dreadful doubt that falls on the very flame of our perishable passions. One knew very well that this was forever. A matter of discovery and not of inheritance.

Discovery, not choice. As time went by, I began to see myself not as a speaker of Yiddish, Hebrew, Spanish, and English, but as their conduit. For instance, it became easier for me to think of myself as having been born into Yiddish and Spanish and then having been lured away by English. It was the only way I could explain the singular feeling of having found my true self the moment I spoke Shakespeare's tongue. True, I frequently felt uncomfortable when listening to my own voice, my appalling accent, on the radio or an answering machine. But my reaction was far stronger when, self-conscious as I was, I would hear myself talk on the phone long-distance to my parents or sister. Oh, that horrible melodiousness of Spanish. I couldn't stand it!

I ENROLLED AT the Jewish Theological Seminary. My objective: a graduate degree in Jewish philosophy. In Ciudad de México I had embarked on the self-taught study of my Jewish sources. But I wanted a more methodical approach, less open-ended. The institution had an outstanding intellectual tradition—Abraham Joshua Heschel, Louis Greenberg, Norman Podhoretz, even Michael Lerner had all passed through it—and its library was incalculably rich. I would pass sleepless nights reading Leo Strauss's meditations on Maimonides and Spinoza, T. Carmi's English translations of medieval Hebrew poetry, Gershom Scholem's study of the false messiah Shabbetai Tzevi, Henry Wolfson's interpretation of Hasdai Crescas, and, of course, Franz Rosenzweig's *The Star of Redemption*. An Israeli friend advised me to take a course on Kabbalah with Moseh Idel, and another on Yiddish literature with David Roskies. I had not read Sholem Aleichem's *Tevye the Milkman* in the original since high school, and the opportunity to dwell on it again, but with mature, critical eyes, encouraged me to return to the language of *der heim*. The days when Bobbe Bola had talked to me about the book returned to my mind. Soon he, Tevye—in its Spanish pronunciation, Tebie—became my icon. It isn't difficult for me to explain why. In the novel's last chapters, suitably called "Tevye Leaves for the Land of Israel" and "*Lekh-Lekho*," the Biblical "Get Thee Out," the protagonist moves to the Promised Land to escape bad luck and pogroms only to return to Russia the same shlimazl he always was. He doesn't "ascend" to holy Israel, nor does he emigrate to America; instead, he remains a wanderer. Therein his magnetic appeal: a true diaspora Jew. Tevye's final monologue takes place during a train ride, much like the many short stories, the so-called "railroad stories of a commercial traveler," that Aleichem wrote in the early decades of the twentieth century. One of the final sentences is still in my mind: "Today, Pan Sholem Aleichem, we met on the train but tomorrow may find us in Yehupetz, and next in Odessa, or in Warsaw, or maybe even in America . . . unless, that is, the almighty looks down on us and says, 'Guess what, children! I've decided to send you my Messiah!'" Neither a Zionist nor an American immigrant, Tevye was simply a homeless soul. And is it possible that he, too, is *rascuache*? Yes and no. He is a *mensh*; or better, he is the ultimate *mensh*: funny, faithful to G–d, but childish about what religion is all about, humble yet impolite, honest, obnoxious, goodhearted to the point of foolishness, a confused man in a confused world.

At the seminary, I was also introduced to Mendele Mokher Sforim's complete oeuvre and reintroduced to Isaac Leib Peretz and the brothers Singer. These readings encouraged me to explore the impact Yiddish literature as a whole had in the Jewish-American imagination, which brought me to authors like Delmore Schwartz, Saul Bellow, Isaac Rosenfeld, and Bernard Malamud. In all, the two years I spent at the seminary were some of the most exciting in my life, for they allowed me to explore my own Jewishness from an intellectual viewpoint. During the day I attended classes, in the afternoon I filed my dispatches to Mexican newspapers, and at night I improved my English and, money permitting, went to the movies. When possible, I attended lectures by Bashevis Singer, Harold Bloom—I recall one in which he spoke rambunctiously on Kafka, Scholem, and Walter Benjamin—and Irving Howe.

Howe became a compass. Or is it a map? I read everything I found of his—memoirs, anthologies, studies on William Faulkner and on the novel as a political genre, his marvelous introduction to Israel Joshua Singer's *The Brothers Ashkenazi*, his studies on socialism, and, most crucial, his award-winning sociological study, *World of Our Fathers*, widely considered his masterpiece, which chronicled the life of first- and second-generation Jews in America from around 1870 to 1950. A considerable amount of my energy was spent reflecting on his role as a public intellectual, using his odyssey as a canvas against which I projected myself. In my eyes, Howe was an erudite, vociferous phoenix, invariably daring in his political dissent, a left-wing plebeian critic with a passion to confront and antagonize the reactionary and conservative voices of his time. But I also recognized, and studied, his shortcomings. He was not, I realized, an original thinker. Nor was he the possessor of a distilled, crystalline style like that of Edmund Wilson, Howe's predecessor, to whom I was introduced by Howe in *Selected Writings: 1950–*

1990, and whose stature today is far higher than Howe's in my intellectual firmament. (I have first editions of each and every book Wilson ever published.) Howe's work is the product of a rough-and-tumble observer of a turbulent era whose Jewishness was not a limitation but a stepping-stone to a wider world-view. The constellation of so-called New York Jews (Schwartz, Philip Rahv, Clement Greenberg, Alfred Kazin, Lionel and Diana Trilling, Sidney Hook, Daniel Bell) enchanted me, but somehow Howe's oeuvre stood closest to my heart—to my *Hispanic* heart.

Jewishness as a stepping-stone. The Hispanic world, I concluded, had its share of public intellectuals (Octavio Paz, Julio Cortázar, Eduardo Galeano), but none were Jewish. What was *my* role as a Latino intellectual in America? Could I ever become a New York Jew, too? I arrived in New York when Howe (né Irving Horenstein) was at the apex of his career. His reputation as *the* literary critic of Jewish literature was unparalleled. I knew that he, along with Bellow, had been instrumental in launching the career of Bashevis Singer, the only Yiddish author ever to win the Nobel Prize in Literature, thus achieving global recognition for a language that, as a lexicographer once put it, "never had an army behind it." Howe had studied at CCNY, the cradle of young radical intellectuals in the 1940s and 1950s, and had been connected with *Partisan Review*, a journal founded in 1937 that epitomized, more than any other, the bloody battle in which culture and politics meet. *Partisan Review* was also the forum where Howe and his peers first got to know one another, as were *The Nation, The New Republic, The New York Review of Books*, and, of course, *Dissent*, an influential left-wing quarterly that Howe cofounded and edited and which was initially sponsored by the Independent Social

League. In 1986, the same year I received my master's from the Jewish Theological Seminary, Howe retired from CUNY after a teaching career at Hunter College and the Graduate Center that lasted twenty-three years. Shortly after, he was awarded a MacArthur Fellowship, just around the time he published his anthology *The Penguin Book of Modern Yiddish Verse*, coedited with Ruth R. Wisse and Khone Shmeruk.

I first discovered him in Spanish (how else does one read the canon and its promulgators from the so-called Third World?), through his essays on ideology and culture in Octavio Paz's monthly *Vuelta*, which, incidentally, also featured the work of another so-called New York intellectual, Daniel Bell, quite prominently. For years this publication was the channel through which the Latin American intelligentsia got acquainted with European and American thinkers of the caliber of Milan Kundera, Hans Magnus Enzensberger, and Brodsky, and Howe was in this crowd. But I didn't get to know him solely as a political commentator. Around 1980, a friend of mine, returning from Manhattan, brought me a copy of *World of Our Fathers*. I was fascinated as I realized what a certain distance from one's own Jewishness can bring. Here was an essayist who could write with erudition and without obfuscation about a wide range of topics, a true *hombre de letras*, one in my mind much closer in spirit to Latin America's literary tradition than so many other so-called American thinkers that reached me in translation, like Alvin Toffler and Desmond Morris.

I read *World of Our Fathers* with enormous difficulty, for my English was less than serviceable, but I still managed to admire its breadth and vision, hoping some day to embark on a similar enterprise pertaining to the Jews in the Spanish-language Americas. What I most envied, what I felt lacking in my Mexican-Jewish education, was that he had sprung from a culturally solid Jewish environment and had sparkled his way into secular circles. I had come to believe, mistaken though I was, that Howe's family was one where books were appreciated, even adored, a family so literate and politically aware that the written word was considered both a beacon and a weapon. The Jews I grew up with were far fewer in number than those living in the East Bronx of Howe's childhood. I could count on a single hand the Jewish artists and intellectuals who had emerged in Ciudad de México a generation before mine, and none of them inspired my admiration, if only because they were afraid to speak up, suspecting that any criticism of Mexican-Jewish life would inevitably give room to anti-Semitism.

In childhood, Yiddish was Howe's prime language of communication. To succeed as an intellectual and teacher, he switched to English, as did everyone his age; but he paid tribute to Yiddish by serving, in his role as critic and editor, as a window through which second-generation Jews like himself could appreciate the beauties of Yiddish literature. One of my favorite Howe books is *A Treasury of Yiddish Stories*, which he coedited with Eliezer Greenberg in 1954, an outstanding anthology reprinted numerous times that includes some of the most beloved Yiddish writers, in semi-chronological order. I found a worn-out copy of a first edition at the Strand bookstore one day. My teachers at the seminary should have introduced me to it, but Howe apparently didn't sit well with the new generation of academic Yiddishists, for whom he was too subjective an editor, with too big an ideological bone to chew, and who failed to supply the proper academic apparatus to their research subjects.

But my all-time favorite is *Selected Writings*, an extraordinary collection of essays and memoirs that range from the Holocaust and Isaac Babel to George Orwell and black literature. It was Howe at his best—especially Howe the Jewish commentator—and a volume that clearly complements his anthology of Yiddish stories: edgy, lucid, methodical, a substantial number of the pieces in it simply masterful. I studied them as I've studied Cynthia Ozick's essays, which are almost of equal caliber; or those by George Steiner, another erudite voice though far more pretentious. I return to it almost as often as books by Borges and Paz—and, later on, by Edmund Wilson.

Often I thought of sending him a personal letter, asking him to spare some time for a cup of coffee with me. For some reason, I procrastinated until it was too late, for Howe died seven years after his retirement. To this day I regret not having a tête-à-tête with him. All the obituaries described him as "the last New York Jewish intellectual." "Last" is too strong a word. Did the expression mean that the public intellectual no longer has a valid place in society? I wondered. Or did it imply that, in the age of the information superhighway, to debate ideas in public, to evaluate art and politics is a thing of the past? Surely Howe's career coincided with a rapid transformation—some would call it "decline"—of intellectual life in America and the world at large. Between 1941, when at the age of twenty-one he became managing editor of the Workers Party weekly *Labor Action*, until his last published essay in *The New Republic*, the landscape has changed. But has it been erased altogether? Howe's generation had a wide impact on social conscience because it had chronicled, without melodrama, the dramatic urbanization of Eastern European Jews. By the time of Howe's death, though, American Jews had almost totally lost their ethnicity. When the fever of multiculturalism took hold in the early 1980s (and Howe wrote about it in *The New Republic*), younger Jews, especially on campus, attempted to re-ethnicize Jewishness, to turn themselves again into a minority. This younger generation felt little connection to Howe and his peers. It wanted to do what Howe had done without: to return, through nostalgia, to the boundaries of the shtetl; it wanted to revitalize Yiddish and its world.

It is in this context that Howe's legacy became emblematic to me. It didn't take me long in America to see that, as a whole, the middle and upper-middle classes are far better off than their parents ever were. But a mercantile existential philosophy was ubiquitous when I settled in Manhattan, one based on an insatiable need for leisure. In response, a new brand of white American public intellectual has emerged: sarcastic, uninterested in finding ways to improve society, with a corrosive sense of humor, irreverent toward history and ideology, disdainful of anything remotely like a succès d'estime.

Through Howe I sought to understand my own place in America's intellectual culture and my links to Mexico and the rest of the Hispanic world. After I graduated from the Jewish Theological Seminary, it became obvious that, to stay in the U.S., I needed to further my academic career. Universities offered the leisure of a sustained intellectual life; on the other hand, academics were aloof, lacking a connection to the outside world. I wanted the opportunity to read and write, but I didn't want to isolate myself in an ivory tower. Howe was a colossus: even while teaching, he remained active in the public sphere; and he used literature as a mirror of modern angst. I enrolled in a doctorate program in Spanish literature at Columbia University. But the pedagogical approach I encountered was outright anachronistic: it applauded masters like Cervantes, Lope de Vega, and Góngora without establishing connections between their time and ours; and the teachers' views of Latin America and the Caribbean were of a wasteland where only exorcism and magic dared to emerge. The bridge between the public and the academic spheres was fragile at best. At one point, a professor of mine, the Chilean scholar Félix Martínez-Bonatti, whose politics were in sharp contrast with those of most of his peers, complained that I contributed too frequently to dailies and monthlies. "Not serious publications," he told me. A scholar, he added, rejects deadlines. "His only deadline is the grave." I remember being often struck by the fact that outside the school, in Harlem and Washington Heights, the flux of Puerto Ricans, Colombians, and Dominicans was endless, but not a single course I encountered addressed their concerns. Bridge-building, obviously, was not a priority. From coast to coast, Spanish departments had become a refuge for leftist activists from south of the Rio Grande— Chile, Argentina, Uruguay—running away from military dictatorships. They were ready to calm down in exchange for tenure. Their attitude toward American culture, and especially toward lower-class Latinos, was biased: the U.S. was a voracious beast with little regard for history, its own or others'. And the *jíbaros* and *campesinos* in their midst? Well, they were gorillas. Or, less disapprovingly, *analfabetas*, illiterate, intellectually unsophisticated people who deserved no attention. Years ago, while still in Ciudad de México, I had rejected Marxism as a redemptive ideology, but even a fool could see the contradictions in their predicament: for these self-proclaimed "champions of the oppressed," the ideological battlefield was south of the border, far away, whereas America—though not Amerika—was a mere bread-giver.

The elitism was not exclusive to academics. In the national press, the coverage of Hispanic issues was dismal. And no major publishing house in New York would publish a novel by, say, a Cuban American. The reason stated was always the same: there was an absolute lack of audience for it. Things changed dramatically at the time I received my doctorate in 1990. The year before, Oscar Hijuelos, the Cuban-American novelist, published *The Mambo King's Play Songs of Love*, about the plight—sexual, emotional, financial—of a pair of musical siblings. Its release, by the mainstream publishing house Farrar, Straus & Giroux, felt like a liberation. Suddenly, it was clear that the intersection where English and Spanish, where the Caribbean and the United States meet, had been legitimized. Almost overnight a torrent of fictional accounts by Dominican Americans and Chicanos (Julia Alvarez, Sandra Cisneros, et al.) were embraced by a larger readership. To me in particular, this explosion felt like a vindication of the hybrid self. Most of these authors were a bit older than I, but their language felt closer to mine than anything I came across in American or south-of-the-border letters. It also partially justified my intellectual endeavor. I realized that my role, inspired by Howe, was to meditate, in critical terms, on the role played by literature, and culture in general, in society. The problem, though, was that, with the exception of *The Nation*—which one day would become the place where I could voice my opinions as a critic—none of the so-called intellectual magazines (*Commentary*, *The New*

Republic, Partisan Review) had the slightest interest in Hispanic civilization. They were all Eurocentric, with an understanding of Europe that often excluded Spain and Portugal,
too. (Jose Saramago, the Portuguese Nobel Prize laureate,
indirectly delivers an astonishing metaphor in *The Stone
Raft*, imagining what would happen if, miraculously, the
Iberian Peninsula literally seceded from the rest of the con-
tinent. No one misses it.)

LOVE — IS IT a form of utopia?

My Jewish-Mexican education, so plagued by melodrama, had taught me—foolishly, of course—to look at the
redeeming nature of love with suspicion. After my bumpy
sojourn in Spain with Hoddie, I was a consummate skeptic:
Love? A Renaissance invention, really. Petrarch ought to be
thanked for it—the brave knight, dreaming of his Dulcinea,
travels the world looking to prove the strength of his passion. Instinct is altogether something else, I would tell myself. Sexual urge, insatiable, ought to come first; but it
shouldn't be allowed to eclipse the powers of the mind. One
day, while working on a temporary job at the library of the
Jewish Theological Seminary, I met a Jewish woman also on
staff: Alison Sparks, born in St. Louis but raised in Hartford,
Connecticut—the route of Mark Twain—and a New Yorker
ever since she enrolled at Barnard College. Solitude was inspiring, and I was not especially looking for companionship,
so at first the relationship was just a passing friendship.

Love finds its path in mysterious ways, though. With
Alison I had endless conversations—about Leibniz, about
Dorothy L. Sayers's rendition of Dante's *Divine Comedy*,

about the Holocaust and Primo Levi. (Since early on, I was mesmerized by her pronunciation, especially of words containing the sounds "ea" and "oa": "soap," "pear." She makes the short vowels shorter and sweeter.) We first met at a dinner party and soon after found ourselves in a college auditorium watching Werner Herzog's film *Woyzeck*. Herzog led to Woody Allen, at which point love took over.

Yes, my love for Alison has the rhythm of films such as *Hannah and Her Sisters* and *The Purple Rose of Cairo:* Manhattan with a Gershwin tune, perhaps in black and white, with the kind of humor Groucho Marx would have been proud of. . . . We spent memorable afternoons walking around Central Park, sitting in darkness at the Planetarium, on the banks of the Hudson River eating tuna sandwiches bought at Mama Joy's.

Once, on a Sunday afternoon, in the declining years of the Cold War, she and I were together picnicking in Riverside Park when there was a sudden explosion in the sky.

"The atomic bomb," she said.

Alison looked at me, scared. A burst of fire ignited in midair, then descended to the ground. Was the world coming to an end? Would we be the only two survivors?

And then: a kiss.

(Next day, I read the news in the paper and she heard it on the radio: a pair of small airplanes had collided in New Jersey.)

Alison had studied anthropology and went, via the Fulbright Foundation, to Egypt while I was in Israel. (A private joke is that we crossed paths climbing Mount Sinai but fate wanted us to wait for a livelier place.) Her sensitivity to cultural clashes is the result of a passion for language—she is a speech-and-language pathologist—and parents involved in theater and politics.

After a few years, our romance was no longer confined to Manhattan: its stage was the whole of New England, from Martha's Vineyard to Amherst. The result was my discovery of Hawthorne, Whitman, Poe, and Emerson as authors with whom I felt a close empathy. It was through them—and thanks to them—that I came to realize their country, Nueva Inglaterra, was where I felt most comfortable. Or is it the emphasis on the intellectual and spiritual as redeeming factors? Is it possible that I should have been born in the region but mistakenly ended up elsewhere?

In the late 1980s, I married Alison in Hastings-on-Hudson. Around that time I began to write for *The Nation* and Madrid's *Diario 16*, in English and Spanish respectively, which prompted me to return to the literature of Latin America in general, and Mexico in particular, and to begin speaking out on issues of language and culture. And then, in 1991, my son, Joshua, was born. His birth was an act of egotism, for no other single incident ties me more closely to New England than his arrival: I was, I realized, finally at home in Manhattan and the geography that surrounds it. Never, not in a thousand years, could I be made to leave.

HENRY JAMES ONCE coined the phrase "the figure in the carpet" for the patterns that run through a person's life. What does my odyssey mean? Why do I no longer feel torn between loyalties, between languages, between selves?

I hear the voice again. I'm on line, and an INS agent calls my name: Ilan Stavchansky. I smile; she does, too.

"Mexican?" she asks.

"I'm about to give up the vice," I reply.

I'm about to hand her my Mexican passport in exchange for the U.S. one she holds in her hand.

"Don't bother," she says. "You may keep it. What use is it to me?"

"But don't I have to give up my Mexican citizenship?"

"Well . . ." She implies that it is up to me. Or, rather, that the agreement is between me and the Mexican government.

Up to me. I smile again, caress the passport she has just given me, and move away.

I think again: Up to me? What sort of agreement should I strike with Mexico? Have I ever struck one? And does Mexico really care?

Twenty minutes later, together with the other two thousand congregants, I stand up proudly to recite the pledge of alliance to the flag of the United States and to sing the national anthem:

> *O say, can you see, by the dawn's early light,*
> *What so proudly we hail'd at the twilight's last*
> *gleaming? . . .*

I look around: people are crying. This is a highlight in their life, I tell myself. Is it also one in mine?

I drive home, where Alison and Joshua receive me with open arms. A nice meal is waiting on the table. I show them my two passports. "I didn't have to give anything up," I say. "So I'm now officially binational and bicultural. An *Amerikanisher bokher* . . ." And I add, with irony: "Perhaps, true to form, I will have several more passports by century's end."

"No Jewish passport, though," she replies.

In my absence they've brought out some things for me, which lie wrapped on the living-room sofa. I open them. One is pure kitsch: a handsome T-shirt with a huge flag of the United States.

"Cheers to the new addition to ugly America," Alison says, parodying a Texas politico.

I unwrap the second present: a deluxe edition of *Moby Dick*.

{ 6 }

The Lettered Man

Remembrance is the secret to redemption.
Forgetfulness leads to exile.

—YAD VASHEM

*G*RACIAS . . ." I SMILE as I thank the waiter, a slim, tall black man, for the glass of orange juice he just brought me. He hears me speak Spanish and tries a few words. "*Dee naide*—is that how you say it?"

I smile.

"*De nada*," I say.

"Sorry," he adds. "I know my pronunciation is terrible. . . ."

It is a sunny winter morning in San Francisco and I'm having breakfast with my friend Richard Rodríguez, whose 1982 volume, *Hunger of Memory*, the un-self-righteous coming-of-age chronicle of a mestizo Mexican American marked by Catholicism and—even though the topic is not overt in the volume—homosexuality, I have read many times.

The conversation ranges until we reach the topic of autobiography. I tell him I have just finished mine. Richard is curious. He perceives a sense of relief but also of anguish. Last time I spoke to him, a couple of months ago, I did not tell him about my endeavor. So he asks me more.

"I want it to be about the languages I bestow upon myself—or, rather, the languages that chose me—and how they define or deform who I am." I mention briefly the chapter sequence and talk at length about my father and brother and how their own distinct views of the universe shaped mine dramatically. "It focuses on items whose significance gives meaning to my own journey: a meticulously typed personal diary, a set of car keys, a pistol stowed way, a childhood photograph hanging on a staircase, a dated passport. . . . These items constitute a kind of almanac, a registry of reminiscences."

I take a breath, then continue. "My book is not really a memoir in the traditional sense, but a series of snapshots that, I hope, add up to a cinematic picture, not of me but of my mind. A disjointed picture, the way life really is—incongruous. In retrospect, life appears to be full of meaning. But only in retrospect, since the meaning is not usually understood as events unfold, because the sole guiding force shaping our existence is chance. Nothing more, nothing less than Darwinian accidents make us the people that we are. I see my odyssey through the prism of natural selection: variations occur without purpose. How many paths have been rejected for me to end up seated across from you today?"

I recite a couple of stanzas from a favorite poem by Thomas Hardy:

"When I took forth at dawning, pool,
   Field, flock, and lonely tree,
   All seemed to gaze at me
   Like chastened children sitting silent in a school;

Upon them stirs in lippings mere
   (As if once clear in call,
   But now scarce breathed at all)—
   'We wonder, ever wonder, why we find us here!'"

Richard says he is anxious to read the memoir and asks: "What does the switch from one language to another really entail? You've gone from Yiddish and Spanish to Hebrew and finally English. . . ."

"A language is a set of spectacles through which the universe is seen afresh: Yiddish is warm, delectable, onomatopoeic; Spanish is romantic, perhaps a bit loose; Hebrew is rough, guttural; English is precise, almost mathematical—the tongue I prefer today, the one I feel happiest in. . . . No, perhaps spectacles are the wrong metaphor." I take another breath. "I should try to explain what it's like to switch languages by invoking the many personalities of an actor, each nurtured by different obsessions. The person remains the same, but the persona—in Greek, 'mask carrier'—varies. Changing languages is like imposing another role on oneself, like being someone else temporarily. My English-language persona is the one that superimposes itself on all previous others. In it are the seeds of Yiddish and Hebrew, but mostly Spanish." I invoke the Yiddish translation of Shakespeare's *King Lear*, which, in its title page, read *"fartunkeld und farveserd"*—translated and improved. I follow this reasoning with a confession. "But is the person really the same? Is it accurate to compare myself to an actor, whose personality remains the same from play to play? You know, sometimes I have the feeling I'm not one but two, three, four people. Is there an *original* person? An essence? I'm not altogether sure, for without language I am nobody. Language makes us able to fit into a context. And what is there to be found in the interstices between contexts? Not silence, Richard—oh, no. Something far less compelling: pure kitsch."

I sigh.

I tell him about the occasion, a few years ago, when I attended the three hundredth performance of *Cantando bajo la lluvia*, a Mexican theater version of *Singin' in the Rain*, with my father in the cast. And as I convey my recollection, I can hear and see the character played in the movie by Donald O'Connor, sing "Make 'Em Laugh," the famous number in which he dances on top of a sofa and along a wall, while making everyone chuckle. Except that in my father's play the song is in translation.

> *Haz reir, haz reir,*
> *porque a todos les gusta reir.*
> *Papá me dijo, sé un actor,*
> *si es de comedia, mejor.*

> *Vas a ser popular,*
> *en las carpas serás estelar.*
> *Yo sé que hacer Shakespeare es de mucho cach,*
> *y los críticos te aplauden, pero y la papa ¿qué?*
> *En cambio, con un chiste tu los haces puré.*
> *¡Haz reir, haz reir, haz reir!*

I also recall the duo, sung by the actors playing O'Connor's character and the one Gene Kelly did in the movie, immersed in a free-for-all elocution exercise: "Moses supposes his noses are roses, but Moses supposes erroneously...." The problem, of course, is that "Moisés" in Spanish is almost impossible to rhyme, so it becomes "Rosa":

Rosa no pasa la taza de arroces,
mas pasat la taza de arroz al ras.
Si rasa la taza de arroz que pasa Rosa,
no pasa la taza de rasa de más.

"Can you believe it, Richard? The quintessential American musical—*en español*? To say it was dreadful hardly conveys the complexity of the performance, for what I saw was a collision of cultures which, struggling to find a perfect balance, results in an exaggeration, a caricature, an artifact more baroque that its creators ever intended. *Rascuache*, I think, is the perfect word to describe it. You might claim that the original, *Singin' in the Rain*, is already hokey, but that hokeyness is multiplied a zillion times when the material travels to another culture. Like the musical in Ciudad de México, I often find myself becoming pure kitsch—a caricature of myself. 'Kitsch,' the critic Clement Greenberg used to say, 'is vicarious experience and faked sensations.' I've sometimes talked about a life on the hyphen, as a neither/nor, a life in the in-between, but it is precisely that in-betweenness that makes me so uneasy."

"Neither/nor. Or, better, either/or," Richard comments. "In Hebrew, *or* means 'light,' doesn't it?"

I tell him about a dream I had a few nights before that

made me think of Shakespeare's *The Tempest*. In it I saw myself roaming without a precise objective in a library of ancient Hebrew volumes. As I climbed a wooden ladder to reach a volume of the Babylonian Talmud and extended my right hand to touch it, I realized its letters had been magically sucked into the air. I could see them take off from the spine into the air and buzz around my head like flies, until a few landed on the skin of my face, arms, and fingers. I wasn't sure what to feel, but I knew I wasn't scared. Did it hurt? Not at all. On the contrary, the feeling of them on my epidermis was rather pleasant. "Oh, they're out of order, and thus no meaning will emerge from them," I told myself. I stepped down from the ladder and tried in vain to decipher some sequence on me. "It will be my fault if the meaning is lost." I looked to see if the librarian was around but couldn't find him. Then I realized I had totally forgotten how to speak Hebrew. It was at this point—clearly disappointed—that I woke up.

"The Lettered Man," Richard announces.

I tell Richard what Bobbe Bela used to say to me when I was little: "You have a prodigious memory." Her words echo in my mind. In school I had an easy time remembering numbers, the world's capitals, different national currencies, historical personages from England, France, Italy. I had no touble memorizing the oversentimental poems of Adolfo Bécquer, and to this day I have no trouble reciting the one that has a kiss as its protagonist: *"Érase un beso enamorado, de una mano de nieve...."* Did all Mexican schoolchildren memorize it? I also remember learning stanzas from Ya'acov Glatshteyn, Chaim Nakhman Bialik, Rubén Darío; and I recited without any mistakes Sor Juana Inés de la Cruz's philosophical satire *"Hombres necios que acusáis / a la mujer sin razón / sin ver que sois la ocasión / de lo mismo que culpáis...,"* all sixty-eight lines. I can recollect scenes, encounters, dialogue, no matter how long ago they have occurred, and can retell a story told to me months before, even a year, in great detail; but I have trouble remembering the clothes people wore yesterday, the food I ate the day before, the names of friends and teachers I heard only this morning.

Soon the conversation moves to Mary Antin's autobiography, *The Promised Land*, published in 1912, about the journey of an Eastern European Jewish girl to America. A few days later, at home, I took it from my shelf and was mesmerized by its opening paragraph: "I was born, I have lived, and I have been made over. Is it not time to write my life's story? I am just as much out of the way as if I were dead, for I am absolutely other than the person whose story I have to tell. Physical continuity with my earlier self is no disadvantage. I could speak in the third person and not feel that I was masquerading. I can analyze my subject, I can reveal everything: for *she*, and not *I*, is my real heroine. My life I have still to live; her life ended when mine began." What impresses me is the split Antin establishes between her previous self (the *she* of her past) and the present one (the *I*). Can I create a similar split? Not really, for I sense that miscegenation has taken place: my Mexican self is not altogether gone, nor is my American self so prevalent as to erase everything else. In between the two stands my Jewishness, moderating the tension, becoming an arbitrator—and perhaps a censor.

Silence. I say: "Richard, the book I wrote is a chimera. My life has gone into it. Since I began to draft the first chapter, I hoped that it would justify me to myself. But I am consumed by its inevitable imperfections. What is it that drives people to write memoirs? How to explain the need to turn ourselves into fictional characters?"

"A fictional autobiography?"

"Aren't they all? Better to say: a dreamed autobiography. For, even though it strives for objective truth, it is, like all memoirs, an exercise in self-deception."

Richard recalls an interview conducted by Rudyard Kipling with Mark Twain in 1889. In it Twain recounts an experiment. He tells of a friend of his who was painfully given to speak the truth on all occasions, a man who wouldn't dream of telling a lie. Twain asked him to write his autobiography for his own and his friends' amusement. He did it. The manuscript, Twain says, would have made an octavo volume, but, as honest as he was, in every detail of his life he turned out to be a formidable liar. He just couldn't help himself.

Suddenly, I feel as if a bright mirror is in the middle of the table between us. Richard is me and I am Richard. I can hear myself uttering Richard's sentences, one by one. . . .

I have been visited by this eerie, inexplicable sensation before, and it almost always happens with artists—particularly writers: I see them as alter egos. I first felt this sort of empathy when I encountered the works of Pinhas Kahanovitch, aka Der Nister, a Yiddish-language Russian symbolist killed by Stalin in one of his purges, as if his soul had somehow taken over mine. And I experienced a similar sensation when I met Felipe Alfau, an émigré Spaniard in New York, an anti-Semite and the author of *Locos: A Comedy of Gestures*. He was in a home for the elderly in Queens when a mutual friend introduced us. "Had I been born in Guernica before the First World War," I remember thinking, "I would have been him."

I prefer not tell Richard about the mirror. Instead, I

mention a phone call I received that morning. It was my father, from Ciudad de México. He told me that Bobbe Bela's senility has become more severe. At barely eighty-five, she fails to recognize her own children, let alone their offspring. Her mind has become obsessive, circuitous. No pills, no mnemonic exercises are of any help. What afflicts her is simply the inevitable decay of the self and its central command, the human memory. She repeats herself ad infinitum.

Another silence. "Her memory is empty," I say, and then add: "My father says that, despite all the people in my immediate family around her, Bobbe Bela, in her obsession, feels intimately linked to me, the one who is farthest from her physically. Every single morning she asks for me. My name she remembers perfectly: 'Ilan, Ilan . . . When will he visit me?' she often asks, even in Yiddish. 'When? The journey by train and boat is long, too long.'

"My father says she is convinced I am a Pole. 'Warsaw, I want to hear about Warsaw from him,' she says. About her own parents—Tate Mame—about the racetracks, about the old store on Minka Street. . . ."

I am still thinking about döppelgangers. What if, on a trip south of the Rio Grande, I came across the Ilan Stavans who never left Ciudad de México? In "The Jolly Corner," Henry James makes his protagonist, Spencer Brydon, return to his New York home after an absence of thirty-three years. The house might be empty, but Brydon is convinced it is inhabited by his other self, the man he himself would have been had he stayed in America rather than live in Europe. I close my eyes and see myself wandering around the tortuous downtown streets of my past, not far from Calle Tacuba, looking for my own Brydon. I enter a *callejón*, a dead-end road, and find myself in a *vecindario*, a poor neighborhood much like the ones depicted by Buñuel in his mid-career films. At a distance I see a man wandering around, just like me though slightly taller and also heavier, dressed in an elegant gray suit, white shirt, multicolored tie, and shiny shoes. His well-formed thick beard makes him look like an executive. He sees me, too, and studies my looks. We begin to talk. In what language? It doesn't matter, for we begin to chat amicably: he is single, has a six-year-old daughter from a failed marriage, a one-year-old boy from an affair with a popular soap-opera actress, an expensive apartment in Colonia Polanco, a Sunday TV show on national politics, a high-profile job as an editor at *Reforma*, the fashionable metropolitan newspaper.

"*¿Y tú?*"

I tell him about me. He is uninterested.

"*¡Te fuistes, cabrón!*" He complains that I left without ever looking back. He says that Mexico has changed dramatically since I left, and so has everyone there. "*El México de tu memoria es mentira.*" The country you cherish in your memory is not a lie. And so are you. . . . Beware, *compadre*!

Before I have time to reply, he walks away.

Ayyy . . .

The encounter is not altogether implausible, I tell myself, especially in light of a bizarre incident that occurred to me in 1992. I had been browsing through the Manhattan White Pages when, suddenly, I came across Bobbe Bela's name. There it was, slightly misspelled by adding an "l" to her first name: "Bella Stavchansky." My astonishment was beyond belief. By then, Bobbe Bela was already too old to travel. In fact, she had not left her apartment, my father told me, more than five or six times in the last semester. What was she doing listed in the New York directory? I checked in a previous edition but the name was absent: obviously, she— whoever the *she* was—had settled in the city not long ago. I phoned and got an answering machine with a voice message in a heavy Russian accent. An hour later, Bella Stavchansky returned my call.

She was a recent immigrant from Moscow, working for an international bank, married and with a child, but seeking a divorce. Her husband's name: Anatoly Stavchansky.

"Surely, a lost cousin," I said. How many Stavchanskys are there in the world? While growing up, I was convinced I was a member of an exclusive club. The same conviction was shared by the whole family. Zeyde Srulek was long dead, but Bobbe Bela knew of no relatives left behind in the Ukraine.

The Ukraine, not Russia . . . Anyway, shouldn't my father know immediately about Bella and Anatoly?

Anatoly, Bella told me, planned to travel to New York within a month. She promised to pass along word of my phone call.

"Hih veell telephown yu."

And he did. We decided to meet in the Hungarian Pastry Shop, at Amsterdam and 110th Street. I gave him directions.

His physical appearance shocked me tremendously, but little else about him left a strong impression. Anatoly obviously resembled my father: he was short and round, wore sportsclothes, and dyed his hair dark. His divorce was imminent, he said. Bella had taken a job in Amerika. He and their child were left behind. But the couple were on friendly terms, and he was eager to find a way to emigrate. Did I know of a job, any job, he could find? Could I put him in contact with an honest lawyer?

Anatoly also knew nothing about a Mexican family connection. Khashchevate, in the Ukraine—did it ring a bell? I asked. No, not really, but he had heard of Stawczany (in transliteration, Stavchany), a town southwest of Lwów. *Staw* means "pond" in Polish, so "Stavchansky" might well be "a pond dweller." Had *I* ever heard of Stavchany? The truth is, he wasn't interested in finding lost links in his family genealogy. More urgent needs were on his mind.

The same night, I reached my father long-distance. He, too, seemed far less interested than I.

So I opened the White Pages again. This time the name Bella Stavchansky was not listed.

THE WAITER BRINGS the bill and Richard pays it.

"*Gracias.*"

Again: "*Dee naide.*"

Richard looks at the clock with an expression of anguish. "My mother is ill," he says. He is about to go and see her. I say goodbye, and he gets into a taxi.

After the breakfast, I stay another day in San Francisco and then travel to Houston, where I'm switching planes on my way home. I miss my connection and find myself stranded in the international airport. Houston was the place in the 1970s where Mexican Jews traveled on shopping sprees, and it has the unpleasant taste of excess in my mouth, with its huge, anonymous shopping malls, its dull highways, its rough, illiterate, oil-rich bourgeoisie. My parents used to have close friends, the Podgaetz family, who owned a small apartment on the outskirts of the city. Ishai Podgaetz, a tall, round, intelligent man in his late forties, had contracted a form of Hodgkin's disease. The best, most advanced treatment for it at the time was found in Houston, and so he would stay long months there, visiting the nearby hospital on a daily basis. But when he and his family were not around, my parents would borrow the apartment and use it as a base for day trips to parks and recreation areas in Texas, and to outlets and discount stores. In their Mexican eyes, all American items, no matter what quality, were treasures: bubble gum, Levi's, hair spray, bikinis, dishwasher soap, Walkmans. . . .

The banal memories of Houston from my teens are with me as I sit in a waiting area, distressed at how long I have to wait for my connecting flight to New York—three to four hours. I buy the *New York Times* and some refreshments and settle down to read in a nondescript room, failing to accept my exhaustion and lack of concentration. As usual in these circumstances, time goes by unusually slowly. I give up soon, put the paper aside, and let myself be hypnotized by the nervous procession of people on the corridors, going from one terminal to another, trying to find their gate. My eyes settle on a strange woman—gray-haired, wearing polyester pants, a cotton T-shirt with a pink teddy-bear design on it, cheap white tennis shoes, and a black imitation-leather purse—a middle-class woman just a few feet away from me. She sits stoically, staring at the empty horizon outside a nearby window, clutching her purse. "Isn't she the incarnation of Hemingway's 'ugly American'?" I ask myself. She looks frequently at her left wrist, where her watch should be but isn't. She is puzzled, and so am I. Did she have a watch at some point but lost it? Did someone steal it from her?

Probably she is scheduled to meet somebody, I tell myself as I imagine her son-in-law—a young man who resembles a rough rider, with a cowboy hat, worn jeans, plaid shirt, and pointed brown boots. Or is she waiting for her blonde daughter? But no one comes, and the woman just waits, as I do.

There is something bizarre, almost abnormal about her behavior. Her immobility, for one thing. She holds herself in a composed manner that seems artificial. Is she asleep with her eyes open? I stand up and wander around for a bit, looking for a toilet, browsing in a duty-free shop, then circle the waiting area to look at the woman's face. No makeup. Her skin is as white as snow. Wrinkles near her eyes, on her chin, neck, near her ears. Late fifties, I estimate her age to be, perhaps sixty, but surely not older. Her nails have been manicured recently, painted red. On her left hand, her third finger, she has the mark of a wedding ring, but not the ring itself.

The pale woman does not notice me. In fact, she doesn't notice anyone. She is not a part of the world. Her demeanor makes her look more like a lifeless object. Her sight seems lost, uncommitted, absent, except for the minute or two when, at regular intervals, she opens the purse and looks desperately for something. Her passport? It is doubtful. She doesn't look like the type of American who goes abroad. If she is waiting for a plane, it will probably take her elsewhere in the state. Fort Worth, perhaps? Or San Antonio, where some sort of football event is scheduled for later this week? What is she looking for inside her purse? Her wallet? A telephone number? A lottery ticket? Every seven minutes or so, she opens it up, looks worried, concludes the item she is searching for is not there, and proceeds to close the bag and return to her statuesque position.

Next to her seat is a colored umbrella, but she never looks at it.

An automaton, I say to myself, a robot: a woman without a self. I am sure nobody else has noticed her except me. I sit back down in the seat I had occupied before and get ready to study her movements more attentively. The same routine. Should I talk to her? She might need help. . . . I stand up, approach her, and ask in English: "Is everything OK?" She looks at me, first frightened, then suspicious, and quickly says, "Yup, yup." Disingenuously, I try Spanish, then French, but her response remains unchanged: "Yup, yup, yup," followed by a gracious smile and a resumption of her pose. No complete word comes out of her mouth. I decide not to bother her anymore, and return, yet again, to my nearby seat. She remains immobile for a few more minutes, and then, once more, looks apprehensively into her purse.

Nothing found. Perhaps nothing lost, either.

Half an hour goes by, if not more. By now I am frankly worried. The woman seems lost, disoriented, her repetitive behavior a sign of exhaustion. I ask an airline employee about my departure time and am told a mechanical problem has delayed the flight again. I take another walk, wander to the other end of the terminal, make some phone calls, and am ready to return to my seat when I notice that a couple of men are standing next to *my* lady. Mine? I thought she was lost, I thought she belonged to no one. I thought no one else had noticed her since I first spotted her bizarre behavior an hour or so ago. But I am wrong, of course, and happily so, for she needs help and I have been too passive, too irresponsible to provide it.

By their demeanor I realize the two men are policemen

dressed like civilians. One of them shows her his ID. The other interrogates her. But she isn't talking, not a word. Only "yup"s and more "yup"s and gracious smiles. That's as much as they get from her. I come closer and hear the policemen ask: Do you know where you are? Who are you waiting for? Where is your watch? In response, she looks at her wrist, then searches in her purse, only to close it again and smile. "Yup . . . Yup . . ." Nothing more specific.

After a few minutes, she allows an officer to look inside her purse. He takes out a pack of Kleenex, a roll of Life Savers, a comb, and a set of keys.

The other policeman continues to talk while I observe. Then one of the men comes over to me.

"Good afternoon, sir," he says.

"Hello."

He shows me an ID. "Police Officer McMuffin."

"Pleased to meet you," I respond.

"Sorry to disturb you, sir. Have you been in this area for long?"

"Yes, on and off." I tell him about the woman's repetitive behavior. He then says: "She apparently doesn't know who she is or what she is waiting for."

"No ID?"

"None. So I thought perhaps you had seen someone with her, a relative, a friend. . . ."

"Unfortunately, I'm afraid I haven't," I reply.

The conversation ends, and so does the whole encounter. It takes less than five minutes for the paramedics to arrive at the scene, interrogate the woman again, and then take her away. I am in my seat for another half-hour, reflecting on what I've just witnessed. I have been a mere bystander. The woman, obviously, has lost her memory: when asked, she cannot remember her address, telephone number, even her own name; she doesn't know what has brought her to Houston and whether she lives in the city; she doesn't know how and why she arrived at the airport. . . . Has someone taken advantage of her, stealing her wallet, credit cards, wedding ring? Has she ever carried photographs of those she loves in her purse? What did she do yesterday? And the day before yesterday? And last year? Had she really been *somebody* at one point?

Have I?

Memory: Is there a more fragile human faculty? Without it, what are we? It is the only record we have of who we were and what we want to become. Take it away and only a spiritless machine is left, free of conviction, free of purpose.

I suddenly realize that the woman has left her colored umbrella behind. It is lying next to the chair where she sat, untouched, disowned.

I pick it up and begin to run toward the hallway where the paramedics and policemen took her, but I'm unable to find anyone.

I am uncertain what to do. Shall I throw it away? Better take it with me home.

Hine-ni . . .

FOR THE BEST IN PAPERBACKS, LOOK FOR THE

In every corner of the world, on every subject under the sun, Penguin represents quality and variety—the very best in publishing today.

For complete information about books available from Penguin—including Puffins, Penguin Classics, and Compass—and how to order them, write to us at the appropriate address below. Please note that for copyright reasons the selection of books varies from country to country.

In the United Kingdom: Please write to *Dept. EP, Penguin Books Ltd, Bath Road, Harmondsworth, West Drayton, Middlesex UB7 0DA.*

In the United States: Please write to *Penguin Putnam Inc., P.O. Box 12289 Dept. B, Newark, New Jersey 07101-5289* or call 1-800-788-6262.

In Canada: Please write to *Penguin Books Canada Ltd, 10 Alcorn Avenue, Suite 300, Toronto, Ontario M4V 3B2.*

In Australia: Please write to *Penguin Books Australia Ltd, P.O. Box 257, Ringwood, Victoria 3134.*

In New Zealand: Please write to *Penguin Books (NZ) Ltd, Private Bag 102902, North Shore Mail Centre, Auckland 10.*

In India: Please write to *Penguin Books India Pvt Ltd, 11 Panchsheel Shopping Centre, Panchsheel Park, New Delhi 110 017.*

In the Netherlands: Please write to *Penguin Books Netherlands bv, Postbus 3507, NL-1001 AH Amsterdam.*

In Germany: Please write to *Penguin Books Deutschland GmbH, Metzlerstrasse 26, 60594 Frankfurt am Main.*

In Spain: Please write to *Penguin Books S. A., Bravo Murillo 19, 1° B, 28015 Madrid.*

In Italy: Please write to *Penguin Italia s.r.l., Via Benedetto Croce 2, 20094 Corsico, Milano.*

In France: Please write to *Penguin France, Le Carré Wilson, 62 rue Benjamin Baillaud, 31500 Toulouse.*

In Japan: Please write to *Penguin Books Japan Ltd, Kaneko Building, 2-3-25 Koraku, Bunkyo-Ku, Tokyo 112.*

In South Africa: Please write to *Penguin Books South Africa (Pty) Ltd, Private Bag X14, Parkview, 2122 Johannesburg.*

P.O. 0003340680